Women workers and society

International perspectives

Foreword by Helvi Sipilä

International Labour Office   Geneva

ISBN 92-2-101483-5 (paperback)
ISBN 92-2-101489-4 (hardback)

First published 1976

Printed by La Concorde, Lausanne, Switzerland

Foreword

INEQUALITIES between men and women are likely to arise in many fields, of which employment is one of increasing importance.

At a time when almost half of all women of working age (representing more than one-third of the employed population of the world) are in the labour force, discrimination against women—wherever and whenever it exists—has serious repercussions. It does not affect women alone, but has a negative influence, direct or indirect, on children and other members of the family as well, and through them on society as a whole.

From its earliest days the International Labour Organisation has paid special attention to the situation of working women, particularly in their capacity as mothers and prospective mothers. It has also worked in close co-operation with the United Nations and its Commission on the Status of Women since its inception. Various international instruments, Declarations and Conventions bear witness of these joint activities.

It was therefore no wonder that the International Labour Organisation became an active partner in the implementation of the programme of International Women's Year, 1975, proclaimed by the United Nations General Assembly. This national, regional and global programme mobilised governments, intergovernmental and non-governmental organisations, institutions, mass media and individuals, men and women, to review the present situation of women all over the world. Comparisons were made between men and women and also between women in different countries and in different groups within countries.

The Year and the World Conference held in Mexico City offered all organisations in the United Nations system an opportunity to evaluate their past achievements and to make plans for the future. In this respect the International Labour Organisation made an outstanding contribution by placing the question of equality of opportunity and treatment for women workers on the agenda of the 60th Session of the International Labour Conference for general discussion on the basis of a report prepared by the International Labour Office.[1]

---

[1] ILO: *Equality of opportunity and treatment for women workers*, Report VIII, International Labour Conference, 60th Session, Geneva, 1975.

As a result of this discussion the Conference adopted a Declaration on Equality of Opportunity and Treatment for Women Workers and a plan of action with a view to promoting these aims which, together with the Declaration and Plan of Action for the Implementation of the Objectives of International Women's Year adopted at the World Conference in Mexico City, offer guidelines for national, regional and world action.

The decisions and recommendations of these Conferences should now be translated into concrete action without delay by States, organisations of the United Nations system and intergovernmental and non-governmental organisations. To that end the XXXth General Assembly of the United Nations proclaimed the period 1976-85 the Decade for Women: Equality, Development and Peace, to be devoted to effective and sustained national, regional and international action, with short-, medium- and long-term targets and taking into account minimum objectives recommended for achievement by 1980.

As a first step towards the achievement of these aims it is important that the recommendations adopted and the various materials gathered during International Women's Year should be made widely known to all—including women, who are most directly concerned and who should be fully integrated in the process of implementation, beginning with planning and decision-making.

In this respect this new ILO publication[1] is highly appreciated and deserves the widest possible distribution.

Helvi Sipilä,
United Nations Assistant Secretary-General
for Social Development and Humanitarian Affairs.

---

[1] Most of the studies collected have first appeared as articles in the *International Labour Review* (Geneva, ILO), during 1975.

Contents

Women at a Standstill: the Need for Radical Change

Elizabeth REID [1]

THE economic, social and political problems facing women are becoming increasingly better documented. Disparities in work opportunities, income, educational opportunities, political representation, health care, legal treatment, training opportunities and so on exist, with local variations, in every country of the world. The gap between policy, legislation and practice, between good intentions, rhetoric and reality is felt by all women.

Given our knowledge of these inequalities, of these differences of treatment and expectation, why are the solutions not obvious and why has so little real progress been achieved? The reason appears to lie in a failure to distinguish between symptoms and causes, in the choice of ineffectual means of achieving unclearly perceived ends and in an under-estimation of the rigidity of the established structure of society.

Reforms without progress

The present fight to better the conditions of women has been going on for at least the last 150 years, and throughout this period it has been bedevilled by piecemeal reforms—small concessions granted under economic pressure or for political gain—which have inevitably failed.

A pertinent example arises in connection with the granting of extended leave for child-rearing. Given that women still remain the child-rearers, moves of this nature have been designed to allow them time out of the workplace for the socially desired end of looking after a child and without prejudice to their employment. Yet if the aim was really to ensure that women were not placed at a disadvantage, that their position in the paid workforce and in their careers was not prejudiced by raising children and that their skills, qualifications and expertise were not lost by society, then the introduction of child-rearing leave would have been accompanied by the provision of extensive child care facilities and by measures to ensure much greater flexibility in working life.

---

[1] Personal adviser to the Prime Minister of Australia.

1

The fact that this has not been done has reinforced a wide range of prejudices about women's occupational irresponsibility, especially where there are provisions for the woman to re-enter the workforce in the same or a similar position after an extended period of absence. For even if women are sincere in their intention to return to their employment, it will be just these other factors—lack of child care facilities, of part-time employment, of workplace flexibility—which will prevent them from doing so. Employers will justly feel cheated having held their jobs open; other employees will justly feel cheated out of an earlier opportunity for promotion and permanent employment. Employers, trade unionists and fellow employees will all feel justified in saying that women are not really serious about work.

Last century when the women's movement began making demands in the political arena, one of these was the demand for equal pay, equal employment opportunity and equal status. After a long, hard and bitter fight the principle of equal pay for equal work, and in some countries the principle of equal pay for work of equal value, has been accepted and is slowly being implemented.

However, it is now beginning to be realised that equal pay alone will not achieve the justice which was implicit in the original demand, and hence there is a new demand—for equal job opportunities, training opportunities and promotion opportunities. Such equality of opportunity is necessary, for the force of social convention frequently restricts women in their choice of training or employment, either by reserving some jobs for men only or, indirectly, by denying women access to the necessary educational and training facilities. As a consequence women, particularly the semi-skilled or the unskilled, can be kept concentrated in jobs for which rates of pay are lower, and the principle of equal pay for work of equal value can be effectively bypassed.

If a more searching analysis had been undertaken from the start into the causes of differential wages, perhaps the emphasis would have been not on equal pay but rather on equal job opportunities. For if women had been as free to enter and progress in all areas of the labour market as men have been, then in the absence of other constraints on that market the forces within it would themselves have pulled towards equal pay for work of equal value.

It is the realisation of the inadequacy of the demand for equal pay even for work of equal value that has led to this second demand, namely for equal job, promotion and training opportunities. Is this demand then the correct response to our original problem? If it were met would we then have a more equitable situation? The brief answer to this is, I think, no—for many reasons.

The first is that it does not follow automatically from the availability of training schemes or of unrestricted job opportunities that women will be able to take advantage of them. For there is a whole range of quite firmly entrenched beliefs amongst the women themselves about their own capacities and proper places as well as on the part of their mostly male employers which, unless changed, will inevitably hold women back. These beliefs are based on oft-repeated generalisations about the limitations of women, and employers are notoriously reluctant, even in the face of well-documented evidence, to give up these beliefs.

The second reason why this demand is insufficient is that it is still very widely true that entering the workforce means that a woman now has two jobs: her old job of cook, charlady, child-minder, shopper and servant, as well as her new one. Work in the home, that is, domestic labour, is both time-consuming and demanding, but it is rarely acknowledged to be productive labour. With the increasing rate of participation of women in the workforce, society finds itself in the awkward position of being dependent on women's work in two places at once—at home and in the paid workforce.

The third reason why this demand does not go far enough is that the existing career pattern is based on the expectation of unbroken continuity of service from recruitment until retirement, and most women do not fulfil that expectation. The most common reason for not fulfilling it is child-bearing. The time when a woman is most likely to leave the workforce to give birth which almost inevitably means remaining out of the workforce at least for some time to raise the child, is the time when top management is looking at the younger staff to pick out those who will follow in their footsteps. And even if the woman would like to return to the workforce at any stage after the birth of her child, this desire is often frustrated by the non-availability of permanent part-time work, of suitable child-care facilities and of flexibility in work arrangements.

However, the most important determinant of career/work patterns is not the availability of child care facilities, of retraining schemes or of unrestricted job opportunities. All these, along with a recognition that women are often underemployed and must be able to upgrade and update their skills, are necessary. But the basic determinant occurs undoubtedly in youth. It is the range of possibilities, expectations and limitations about the future instilled in children at school that decide the scope of their later aspirations and determine the pattern of their future employment. The need for extensive and early vocational counselling as part of a non-sexist education should thus be recognised.

More fundamentally the question must be raised as to what the claim for equal opportunities amounts to. For the concept of equal opportunities seems to be visualised in terms of a race to get to the top, the ambitious pursuit of wealth and prestige. It is one thing to speak of fitting opportunities to talents so that everyone can realise her or his capacities for a full and enjoyable life; it is another thing to demand equal opportunities to compete for prizes of status and wealth. The latter merely reinforces the values of our society: the former implies acceptance

3

of differences as they actually exist and the adaptation of social norms affecting work and career to the needs of personal fulfilment without differentiation on sex lines.

As well as being bedevilled by piecemeal reform, the struggle has been hampered by blinkered reforms: reforms which set out to solve a problem only as it relates to women, rather than to all those affected by it. Protective legislation is an example. Although in the short term this legislation may have benefited women workers, in the long term it has often worked to their disadvantage by creating artificial and unnecessary barriers to their employment in certain occupations. These in turn have helped to ensure the continuing existence of low-paid, low-status jobs, which inevitably become women's jobs.

This is not to argue that various categories of workers should not be protected, but it *is* to argue that workers should not fall in or out of these categories just because of their sex: *all* workers should be protected against conditions which are injurious to their mental or physical well-being.

Another example is the introduction of a benefit for mothers supporting a family. A significant number and often a majority of those living in poverty conditions in our society are in this situation and there is no doubt that a Welfare State should extend protection to these people. However, to pay such benefits only to supporting mothers rather than to single-parent families in general is to open the way to demands for a different and even financially greater benefit to be paid to supporting fathers, based for example on the argument that though a woman's place is in the home, a father's place isn't.

These few examples illustrate the falsity of the claim that any reform is better than none, that the final goal, no matter what it is, is nothing, and that the impetus of change is everything.

Many problems can be tackled in more than one way and hence one must have a means of deciding between different possible reforms. In most cases this choice will be impossible unless the reformer has a very clear idea of the sort of society which she or he is trying to bring about.

It should be clear from the above that true equality will be brought about only by an almost complete restructuring of our society in such a way as to safeguard the essential dignity of women, men and children. To achieve this aim all solutions must be rejected which, though in the short term they may ameliorate an existing inequality, in the long term reinforce the present social prejudices, beliefs, attitudes and expectations about women.

Means and ends

In the face of ever more voluble demands for at least legal equality a variety of strategies have been adopted.

Party and government policies are increasingly incorporating the slogan of equality between men and women. This is normally interpreted as a demand that women be given the same opportunities as men and leads ironically to an increasing acceptance not only of the role of men but more importantly of the existing structure of economic life.

Thus rather than leading to a breakdown of the organisation of work following rigidly defined patterns in rigidly defined workplaces or to a breakdown of the notion of work as hardship, the acceptance of this aim has often led to a strengthening of the status quo. Emphasis is given, for example, to the employment of women in traditionally male jobs, to cost-benefit analyses of child care, to ensuring that girls are encouraged to study physics, mathematics and other technical subjects or to the attainment of a shorter working day to the exclusion of other kinds of flexibility in the organisation of work. In this way the role and responsibilities at present assumed by men are extended to all instead of being tailored to the needs of each member of society.

When a government accepts the need for action to ensure that justice and fairness extend to women there remains the choice between legislation and persuasion. The drawbacks to legislation lie mainly in the difficulty of interpretation and enforcement, in the impossibility of applying it to many kinds of discrimination and in the difficulty in any particular case of proving discrimination conclusively. Furthermore, such legislation gives rise to a litigious mentality and employers, rather than observing the spirit of it (or trying to), often direct their ingenuity and their pockets to finding loopholes and let-outs. On the other hand, persuasion, particularly if it is backed up by bribes in the form of subsidies, deductions, protection and other benefits, is often much more effective. Employers not only agree to accept the terms and conditions but often find to their surprise that, far from being outrageously expensive, they are often to their own benefit.

When governments decide none the less to implement a policy of legal equality, two types of machinery can be established: one to ensure equality of employment opportunities amongst their own employees, and the other to do the same for the other sectors.

The establishment of such machinery for government employees is an admission that existing procedures, practices and policies are inadequate. It poses an unwelcome dilemma: if the machinery is staffed by career officers, they may well be unprepared to take strong and effective measures that would prejudice their own careers; on the other hand, a good working knowledge of the institution is necessary to carry out the job adequately and hence it is often unsatisfactory to bring in outsiders to do it.

Government procedures to ensure equality of workforce opportunities in the private sector have proved an administrator's nightmare as tales of individual discrimination, discrimination by firms and discrimination in whole industries have flooded in. More importantly, machinery of this sort channels the anger of women into structures that are controlled by the decision makers and so lessens the pressure for more radical change that might otherwise have been felt.

There are also various dilatory or diversionary tactics that can be employed to absorb or redirect pressures for change—seeking expert advice, calling for community participation, establishing commissions or committees of inquiry, insisting upon statistical evidence, even losing files—all are well-known and well-tried ways of responding to women's demands. The spaces which are marked as child care centres, family planning centres and women's refuges on the plans for new towns, suburbs, shopping or factory complexes but are never built upon are good indicators of real intentions.

However, the most detrimental aspect of these strategies for change is that they encourage the belief that when properly implemented they will solve all problems. This is not to say that women should not be given equality before the law but rather that, even if this were achieved, everything else would still remain to be done.

It should be clear by now that (as in the case of reforms) the choice of strategies to adopt will depend upon the aims to be achieved. Of course it does not follow that if the final aim is socialism (capitalism, non-sexism, . . .) this is sufficient to make a reform truly socialist etc.: some strategies work towards a particular final aim, some against it and some are neutral to it. But the choice can be clear only if the final aim is clear.

The power game

But whatever the final goal and whatever the chosen strategy, reforms conceded and contained within a social structure in which women wield little or no power have been of limited value to women.

As women have come to realise this limitation, they have become more serious in pressing their demand for representation in all parts of the decision-making process and the power structure, and their concomitant demand that questions of special concern to women be given effective consideration.

These demands, which have led in recent history to the formation of various lobbies and pressure groups, are bringing women more and more into contact with the many institutions in which power resides and thus with the power game. The rules and limits of this game have been evolved within essentially male institutions until they have become fixed, sacred and invested with tradition and importance. It is a game in which until now almost all the players have been men. It is a game which is, of course, inextricably concerned with the gaining and use of power. It is a game which is solidly based on the old-boy network, on contacts established with other men at school, at university, on the job, in the pub or in the course of playing the game itself.

Women who engage in this game will suddenly find themselves faced with the intricacies and frustrations of sub-games such as the " play it cool " game. There is a certain type of behaviour required for successful participation which excludes overt passion, commitment, concern and sensitivity—in other words, those very attributes which are the marks of people fighting against decades, if not centuries, of being at best ignored and at worst actively discriminated against in every way.

Then there is the " terms of reference " game, perhaps best illustrated by the put-down comment, " yes, dear, that is all very interesting but it is outside the terms of reference of this group ". There is no reason why the existing limits and categories should be accepted by people who have been forced to intervene precisely because those hitherto responsible have shown an inadequate understanding of the issues involved.

Next, there is the " standing orders " game: presumably standing orders were originally formulated to facilitate proper discussion, but over time they have too often become the tools of the tyrannical chairman concerned that issues of passion should not interrupt the smooth running of his meeting.

As well as the " Rome wasn't built in a day " game there is another " play it cool " game, the aim of both being inaction through procrastination: " You're right, but you won't get anywhere if you do it that way " or " Sure, but now's not the time to move " or " We agree with you, but . . . ".

Then there is the power game in which the issues ostensibly being discussed are merely a front for the interplay of power, a means for gaining power and using it. The skills required for successfully playing this game are the traditionally masculine traits: ambition, competition, aggression, self-confidence, decisiveness, pragmatism, objectivity and the ruthless competitive pursuit of planned goals.

And now, since women have entered the arena, there are new games. There is, for example, the "sex-object" game. The more pleasing the woman is to the eyes of the beholder, the more likely she is to be listened to. Linked to this is the inability of those playing the game to perceive women as people. The women coming into the power game presume that they will be communicating on a person-to-person basis. However, many men seem unable to overcome years of bad habits and may even go so far as to play yet another game which could be called the " put-down " game. A mild version of this involves the use of expressions such as " ladies ", " girls ", " members of the fair sex ", phrases like " well, ladies, now what do *you* think? ", as well as backhanded compliments like " she does a good job—for a woman " or " she thinks like a man " or, said with surprise, " she's quite intelligent/articulate ", as a not-so-subtle means of downgrading the opinions of women. A more frustrating version of this could be called the " invisible woman " syndrome. This often happens in meetings and discussions where a woman puts forward a well-argued case which at the time is ignored, but if later repeated by one of the men present seems to gain so much more significance.

Having decided, despite all this, to enter the power game rather than to opt out completely, women will then be faced with the dilemma of either accepting its rules, strategies and limits or of attempting to change them. But no continuing benefits and changes will ever come about until we change the very structure of this game, not just its rules and so on, but more importantly the roles that the game itself forces on participants.

The demands of the women's movement

To the four demands concisely formulated at the British National Women's Conference in 1970—equal pay, equal education and opportunity, 24-hour nurseries, and free contraception and abortion on demand—many others have been added. They fall into two general categories: those amounting to a demand for equity, and those designed to meet pressing needs.

Equal pay, child care, maternity leave, equal educational, training, employment and promotion opportunities, and legal equality are not in themselves revolutionary demands. They are not political acts which will lead inevitably to the restructuring of our society: they will merely help women gain a bigger slice of the existing economic resources. In fact if granted in a piecemeal way, they could form an essential part of long-term planning to maximise profit and to maximise control over the means of production and its output, without necessarily changing the distribution of wealth or control over the means of production in any essential way favourable to women. Indeed it would be naive not to believe that sophisticated cost-benefit analyses—sophisticated in so far as non-economic factors are taken into account—have already been carried out. An indicator of this is the increasing concern about wastage of human resources and increasing emphasis on the need for maximum utilisation of the potential of women.

The present economic growth rates of most countries can only be maintained or increased by encouraging more married women to join the workforce—the entry rates of men and single women have a limited capacity for expansion. Equal pay, equal job, training and promotion opportunities, child care facilities, etc., will bring an increasing number of married women into the workforce but will not in themselves result in any significant changes in the structure and patterns of working life.

Demands for women's refuges, health centres, abortion on request, contraceptive counselling, rape counselling centres, and so on, arise out of a desire to lessen the distress and suffering of many women. These demands must be recognised and the necessary facilities provided. But there is nothing revolutionary about them; although they will require financial outlay, they will neither strengthen nor threaten the existing economic system. However, satisfying them can often lead governments, politicians and social reformers to believe that the problems giving rise to them have thereby been solved, whereas the remedial measures taken are too often in the nature of first-aid which leaves the root of the trouble—the stresses faced by women and their changing perceptions and expectations—untouched.

Changes of this sort are essential to creating a more humane world for all women to live in. To the extent that none of them actually threatens the structure of society it is surprising, at least to a rationalist, that there is so much emotional resistance to them. Pressure to secure these changes must continue despite the knowledge that, even if they are implemented—separately or simultaneously, well or badly—they will not in the long term have any fundamental effect on the status of women. This is the lesson that the past and the present teach us.

A social revolution

Discrimination arises not so much out of discriminatory legislation and practices as out of the psychological and cultural climate of societies. It arises out of social attitudes, out of society's prejudices, myths and beliefs. Because of this, most men and some women remain ignorant of its extent, and because of this and since it is in the interests of many different sectors of society that the status quo be preserved, it is very difficult to combat it by direct means, by reforms. However, in a few rare instances legislation and other practical measures may help modify not only behaviour but even deeply held prejudices and beliefs, as well as lessening the difficulties experienced by women both in and out of the workforce and the destructiveness and oppression of their surroundings.

In other words, the demands for change are necessary and should be pursued but before they can prove really effective and have long-term benefits there must be a vast social change, a revolution. For most women—at present—revolution is a luxury; they are too deeply trapped in a life that destroys their confidence in their own ability, lessens their self-respect, deforms their self-image and denies them financial and other independence. Certain basic preconditions will have to be met before they are in a potentially revolutionary situation. This is why the equity demands must also be implemented. That is why revolutionary change is for the time being possible only for the well-educated, the self-confident and the financially independent.

The revolution that women require will not be quick, brief, glorious or dramatic: it will involve much hard work and offer few immediate rewards. As compared with a political revolution it will require much less of that form of activity which becomes an end in itself: demonstrating, brandishing banners or whatever.

Its strategies will be bewilderingly vast and slow, and to many of the old-school revolutionaries they will be unacceptable. It *is* nevertheless a revolution for it will require a thoroughly radical consciousness and a sensitivity to the vital issues and a will to make a revolution. The nearest models for this kind of revolution would be the Copernican or the Industrial Revolutions.

Giving women and men a wider range of choices, more freedom, fewer limitations on the patterns of their lives will create as well as solve problems. The attack on existing social, political and moral consciousness must be accompanied by the development of alternative institutional forms which reflect and support these changes.

Notions such as that of the breadwinner and the homemaker, the values of ambition, prestige, status and incessant promotion, the dichotomy between public and private, between work and home, between the personal and the political, must be challenged. Both men and women must be made aware of our habitual patterns of prejudice which we often do not see as prejudice but whose existence manifests itself in our behaviour and in our language. ("All the world and his wife were there.")

The social inequalities, the hidden and usually unarticulated assumptions about women's abilities, capacities, life patterns, needs, skills and desires must be attacked, for these affect women not only in their employment but in the whole range of their opportunities in life. If necessary we must take to the streets armed with facts and statistics and aggression, for our patterns of prejudice are often so deeply rooted as to remain unrecognised unless dramatically confronted. (*Of course* we'll be accused of being unladylike: such an accusation is merely another means of trying to divert us from the barricades.)

Only in these ways will the attitudes which keep women where they are now be changed.

Some Suggestions
for the Advancement
of Working Women

Eliane VOGEL [1]

An outcast majority

TO TALK about the need for a policy to integrate women more fully in society generally and in employment in particular strikes nobody as odd, yet almost everywhere there are slightly more women than men. They present the only example of a majority relegated to the fringe of society, where they are kept firmly in place by the concerted and highly effective mechanisms of a male-dominated system.

The problems arising from the legal, social, economic and political status of women in contemporary Western society are interdependent and cannot be arbitrarily separated. Characteristic of this status is a fundamental ambiguity between theoretical equality of rights and effective discrimination in their application.

The anatomy of oppression

All those who have gone into the matter in any detail agree that the following are the factors chiefly responsible for discrimination against women:

(1) *Socio-cultural attitudes and prejudices*. These are inculcated chiefly by education and upbringing and help to perpetuate a value-system which, though based on assumptions that have been overtaken by events both historically and sociologically, continues to justify the sex-typing of roles across the whole range of human activities. The constant propagation of this value-system leads people to conform with the stereotype proposed for each sex. This way of thinking is the product of " socialisation ", i.e. the sum of the various kinds of conditioning which

---

[1] Professor at the Faculty of Law, Université libre de Bruxelles, and Research Director at the Institut de sociologie.

11

transform the child into a social being with the motivations needed to make him or her assume the roles expected or required by society.[1]

(2) *The double exploitation of women in the family, the basic unit of society.* This takes the form of unremunerated, socially unrecognised domestic labour, and constraints on the capacity of women to transfer property. Thus the wife becomes a mere childbearer subject to the authority of her husband, who in addition exploits her supposedly non-productive labour.

There is nothing gratuitous about this charge. It is borne out and exemplified by the fact that economists and statisticians deliberately omit the value of women's unremunerated work from national accounts statistics, and refuse to count women doing domestic work in their own homes as part of the active population, even though it has been estimated that the " invisible " work of housewives in fact represents some 25-40 per cent of GNP.[2] There seems no doubt that if housewives were included in the labour force and the value of their unpaid work were added to the total cost of services (which with the cost of goods constitutes GNP), the repercussions would be felt in various fields of social policy: certain forms of social security would be extended to them, so would access to adult vocational training programmes presently restricted to the " working " population, and greater investment would be made in some types of social facilities.

(3) *The exclusion of women from productive work as full and equal partners.* This refers to the various ways in which women workers—whose labour is vitally needed by the economy—are exploited: the existence of industries employing an excessively high proportion of females, certain types of work reserved for women, the limited range of skills and jobs available. In all the industrialised countries of Europe and North America the pattern of female employment is much the same. The designation of certain jobs as women's work is justified and perpetuated by inadequate or non-existent vocational training and leads to low wages, bad working conditions, inferior status and lack of promotion prospects, unemployment and, finally, to a refusal to adopt a social policy covering society as a whole, even though nothing short of such a policy can hope to bring workers into the labour force by virtue of their aptitudes and qualifications rather than their sex, and with equal opportunities for all. The situation in which working women find themselves stems from the supposedly " natural " division of jobs along sex lines and is exploited to the full by industrialised capitalist society.

---

[1] See the select bibliography at the end of this article.

[2] In 1958 Colin Clark calculated that the value of unpaid domestic services in industrialised societies represented 44 per cent of the national product. In the United States in 1964 the value of housewives' activities was estimated at about 24 per cent of GNP.

(4) *The exclusion of women from political and social life.* This is justified by their biological and domestic " functions " and by their legal or culturally induced " incapacity " for exercising power or discharging responsibilities, which is also held to be " natural ".

The deliberately oversimplified picture painted above indicates the main processes by which women are kept in bondage and also, by the same token, those by which they can be emancipated. To put it another way, before we can improve their condition we shall have to reform society radically by changing the respective roles played by men and women, in the family, in productive and non-productive work, in the management of the economy and public affairs, and above all in people's minds.

For it must not be forgotten that, if the institutional and historical roots of sexual discrimination are to be destroyed, it will first be necessary to end the conditioning to sexual roles passed on from generation to generation. Nowadays we can see that these stereotypes are harmful to society and its development; not only do they stultify the lives of individuals, and of women in particular, but they deprive political life and the economy of an immense reserve of human resources and qualities. The sex-typing of roles in industrial society can no longer be justified by reference to the alleged immutability of human nature.

The demographic revolution

A new kind of society is being born. The old moulds are being broken by a demographic revolution which is going to transform all our social relationships. Society at large and the family—its basic unit—are being influenced by three new factors:

(i) the increased average life expectancy of human beings, which has doubled in less than a hundred years;

(ii) the equally spectacular reduction in infant mortality; and

(iii) family planning and lower birth rates.

There is nothing natural about these three phenomena; they are the direct result of scientific and medical progress and new ways of life.

While this new demographic dimension obviously concerns the whole of humanity, it has certain particular consequences for the feminine half of it. The reduction of infant mortality and the advent of family planning are freeing women from age-old slavery: no longer do their entire lives need to be devoted to ensuring the survival of the species. The limitation of the birth rate to an average of 2.3 children per family considerably reduces the amount of time a woman needs to spend on her maternal functions. Births are already being concentrated within a restricted period; in general, women stop having babies at about 30. Thus even if mothers give themselves up entirely to looking after their pre-school children, the compulsory education system will take them off their hands for the greater part of the time and release them for other work at around 35. Moreover, since women appear to have a considerably greater life expectancy than men, at this age they still have half or more of their lives in front of them.

Social and cultural attitudes in this field nevertheless continue to be fashioned according to the demographic criteria of pre-industrial society, although it is obvious enough that sexuality, reproduction and the rearing of children—three traditional elements of woman's role—are not intrinsically related to one another in the modern family. It is no longer possible to consider reproduction as a constant atemporal phenomenon, biological rather than historical.[1]

Thus it seems quite absurd to exclude women from economic, political and social life and confine them to roles based on a sexual division of work which itself stems from the biological, procreative function of each sex. To do so can only serve to increase the crushing burden imposed by the economically inactive population on the active. If the legal and social situation of elderly women in many countries is examined, for example, the danger of basing social security programmes on obsolete concepts becomes apparent. It is simply no longer acceptable that the security of so many aged persons should depend on the presence or employment status of a husband. Widows and separated or divorced women are becoming more and more numerous in post-industrial society, and it is high time that the basic principles of the social welfare system were thoroughly re-examined. Woman is no longer to be thought of as a rib taken from Adam's side, as a kind of appendage to her husband, but as an adult human being in her own right, with political, economic and social rights and obligations.

Lack of space compels us to deal very summarily with certain aspects of women's alienation. In any case there is such a rich and abundant literature on the subject that we shall confine ourselves to discussing only the main features as they affect the position of women at work.

The patriarchal structure of women's employment

It is of course impossible to effect changes in the field of labour as though it were a microcosm, as though the organisation of the economy and working conditions could be isolated from the rest of society. There can be no question of separating the mode of production from social structures, functions and roles. Hence the existence at the workplace of patriarchal structures which are oppressive to women employees. Even in the factory or office women are not considered the equals of men. Not only are their working conditions and wages inferior, but they are once again confronted by the system which allots them certain " appro-

---

[1] See Juliet Mitchell: *Woman's estate* (Harmondsworth, Penguin Books, 1971), p. 107.

priate " roles, occupations and careers. Surveys carried out in the six original member countries of the EEC in 1971 [1] showed that the women interviewed nearly always worked alongside other women.

This sex-based division of labour, generally accompanied by physical segregation at the place of work, does not correspond to any technical division; but it does produce a massive proletarianisation of women. As the author's investigations have shown, conditions of this kind help to keep women's wages at a low level, since rates of remuneration increase as soon as tasks and functions begin to be performed by workers of both sexes.

The patriarchal organisation of women's work reproduces the segregation that characterised ancient or pre-industrial societies for eight or nine hours every day. The woman worker must moreover bear the double burden of a full working day in addition to her domestic tasks.

How can equality be achieved?

All these closely connected factors must be taken into account in formulating a policy to bring about equality of opportunity and treatment for women workers and for women in general. This will certainly be no easy matter, since it is the system of values itself—with which women as well as men are imbued—that makes the continuation of women's economic, political and social inferiority acceptable to the majority. Any policy which is seriously intended to eliminate discrimination in employment and achieve equality of opportunity and treatment will have to operate simultaneously against the four discriminatory processes briefly described in the introduction. The following objectives must be attained:

(1) *Reform of the system of values.* This must be carried out essentially among the agents of socialisation, i.e. the family, school, cultural environment, mass media, etc.

(2) Application of *dynamic vocational training and employment policies.* This implies

— the restructuring of the vocational training and guidance system for girls;

— the creation of new jobs for women, taking due account of structural and regional disparities, perhaps by introducing quotas, and granting them access to recurrent education institutions.

(3) The adoption of *legislation and regulations* which would secure the application by enterprises and the incorporation in individual con-

---

[1] See E. Vogel-Polsky: *Les conditions de travail des femmes salariées dans six pays de la CEE* (Paris and The Hague, Mouton, in press).

tracts and collective agreements of measures to ensure equality of treatment in respect of working conditions, the elimination of wage discrimination, the introduction of new methods of job evaluation and an equitable status for male and female workers with regard to social security and fiscal arrangements.

(4) *Effective family welfare programmes.* In particular, these would include:

— the provision of facilities such as crèches; cultural, educational and leisure services for children, adolescents and old people; day hospitals for workers' dependants in need of treatment; production of labour-saving household devices at reasonable prices; and low-cost housing complete with domestic services, etc.

— practical recognition by society of the time women spend looking after their young children and of the unpaid work they do in the home. By this we mean that the State should take into account the essential role of the housewife in looking after the breadwinner's material needs, restoring his energies, educating and caring for the children, etc. There should also be reform of the fiscal legislation and social security programmes for women outside the labour force and reform of the legal status of married women (covering such matters as nationality, parental authority, equality between the sexes as regards inherited and other property, etc.).

Drawing up the practical details of this vast programme and adapting it to the legal systems of the various industrialised countries of Europe are tasks that would have to be entrusted to teams of experts in the relevant fields. Obviously, space is lacking to go into the whole matter here. On the other hand, it is possible to examine certain specific problems and to draw practical conclusions from some recent successful experiments which may serve to inspire legislative reforms in the matter of equality of opportunity both before and during employment. We need to transform our institutions from conservative bastions of the established social order into agents of change.

A propaganda counterblast

To return to the first point, it should be the aim of government social policy to bring about a profound change of attitudes regarding the role of women in employment. This would be a considerable but by no means impossible task. It has already been begun in a number of countries which could be widely imitated.

In the United Kingdom, for example, the Department of Employment began in 1974 to publish a series of booklets under the general title

Women and work.[1] The four that have so far appeared discuss with great scientific rigour various problems encountered by women at work and in everyday life. The texts are clear, precise and easy to understand. They are invaluable propaganda tools which could have an enormous effect on people's attitudes if only their publication were accompanied by a large-scale publicity drive. In particular, the booklet entitled *Sex differences and society* deserves to be made compulsory reading in secondary schools and to be widely promoted on television.

In Sweden efforts to promote equality of opportunity and treatment go back many years. More recently a labour shortage, particularly acute in the case of skilled labour, has induced the Government to mount a campaign to bring more women into industry in jobs appropriate to their training and skills. In particular, it is encouraging them to be more ambitious in their job aspirations and choice of training.

The accent is on education, legislation being considered less effective in practice. As regards more particularly the barriers hindering the promotion of women to the highest and best-paid posts, special efforts are being made in the schools in an attempt to stop pupils choosing their careers in accordance with sexual stereotypes. All classes are mixed, regardless of whether the subject is science, sewing or metalwork. Pre-school education is not neglected; it too is aimed at eliminating all distinctions between boys and girls. Steps have been taken to recruit more male teachers for kindergartens and also for teachers' training colleges turning out kindergarten personnel, but so far with limited effect.

It should be mentioned that children's books have also come in for close attention. Those which depicted men and women in sex-typed roles have been weeded out, and the accent is now on showing them engaged in all sorts of occupations traditionally reserved to the other sex.

In this far-reaching educational drive the Government has the backing of the trade unions, the Swedish Women's Labour Market Committee (which includes representatives of both the Swedish Employers' Confederation and the trade unions), the Advisory Council on Equality between Men and Women (set up at the end of 1972 within the Prime Minister's office), and of female pressure groups.

It will be seen that in Sweden no pains have been spared in promoting the role of women in economic life. And yet, in spite of this coherent, comprehensive social strategy, in spite of fairly wide agreement among the most influential institutions, particularly the Government, the employers and the trade unions, it cannot yet be said that the position of Swedish women is entirely satisfactory. There remain important disparities with regard to education, training and economic status which serve to per-

---

[1] Department of Employment, Manpower Papers, No. 9: *A statistical survey*; No. 10: *Sex differences and society*, by J. S. King; No. 11: *A review*; No. 12: *Overseas practice* (London, HM Stationery Office, 1974).

petuate the traditional allocation of certain jobs to women. It is still rare to find women in positions of responsibility, whether in the private or in the public sector. This is a reminder that social policies and educational reforms take a long time to have practical effect.

Social policy and working women

The rise in the female labour force participation rate is due to the fact that more wives and mothers are going out to work.[1] The trend is most noticeable among those in their early childbearing years, who are remaining in the labour force, and among the middle-aged with adolescent or grown-up children, who are returning to it after an interruption. In the industrialised countries generally, however, the unfavourable situation as regards vocational training and access to employment constitutes a grave handicap to women seeking careers. Not only does it tend to preserve job segregation, wage differentials between men and women and bad working conditions, but it causes notable disparities in unemployment rates. Similarly, women have relatively little job mobility or opportunity for further vocational training because they have the extra burden of homes and children to look after.

When governments decide on a social policy with respect to working women they usually begin by adopting the principle of equal pay for equal work or work of equal value. However, it has to be admitted that even in countries where there are laws providing for penal sanctions in case of sex-based wage discrimination it is very difficult and sometimes impossible to apply them in practice. There is not so much " equal " work or work of comparable value about: less than a third of the jobs available to women come into this category. As to jobs which are reserved for them —" women's work "—employers can go on paying low wages without risk.

VOCATIONAL TRAINING AND GUIDANCE

It follows that efforts should be made to remove the objective *causes* of this occupational apartheid, i.e. the disadvantages and handicaps suffered by women in their preparation for and access to employment. In this section we shall consider what certain countries have done to reform their systems of vocational training and guidance, both for youngsters and for adults, and try to analyse the results achieved and the difficulties encountered.

Many governments have already abolished all legal obstacles to the enrolment of girls and women in any branch of technical and vocational education, but a UNESCO report emphasises that girls continue to opt for " women's " occupations, for courses which relate to running a home,

---

[1] See ILO: *Equality of opportunity and treatment for women workers*, Report VIII, International Labour Conference, 60th Session, Geneva, 1975, pp. 13-15.

or for short, specialised types of training rather than long, fundamental ones.

Various ways of changing these attitudes have been proposed, for example:

— employing more women teachers in boys' schools or for subjects mainly taken by boys;

— modifying the basic education syllabus so as to cover a broader variety of subjects and allow subsequent access to the full range of vocational and technical training;

— making vocational education more flexible by introducing training by stages or modular training;

— reorienting vocational training and basic education to take account of the further training and retraining courses now being made available throughout the adult's working life [1];

— adopting systems of paid educational leave whereby workers are entitled to a certain amount of time off on full pay to follow training courses;

— instituting courses for vocational training and guidance staff with a view to changing their attitude with regard to suitable choices of occupation, and thereby helping to eliminate segregation in this field.

It should be emphasised that these various forms of action, embodied in a single over-all policy, must be applied in decentralised fashion in the regions, towns and municipal offices responsible for placement and education. Individuals should not be expected to approach the governmental monster and its octopus-like administration; on the contrary, this whole training and guidance effort should be supported by a very light, flexible administrative structure directed by small teams with a thorough understanding of the industrial background and the needs of the economy.

A highly successful experiment is being carried out in Denmark. This consists of two-week " pre-training " courses organised by local employment offices either on their own initiative or at the request of an enterprise, a trade union or a women's group. The courses deal with general employment problems and inform participants about the availability of vocational guidance and training and the position with regard to job prospects. The lecturers are experts in legal or economic matters, but women workers are also called in to report on their life and experiences at work. Participants visit factories and other workplaces, spending two days a week at an enterprise. They are not paid for attending the course, but travel costs are reimbursed and crèches are arranged for their children.

---

[1] In many countries, including France and the Federal Republic of Germany, financial incentives are offered to adult workers taking vocational training courses. In Denmark women workers attending such courses receive 80 per cent of the basic wage for the trade they have chosen, regardless of the husband's income.

Local employment offices regularly advertise the dates of such courses in the press, together with an indication of the probable job prospects. Television films show the new employment possibilities open to women, and these are followed by discussions and interviews with working women who explain their needs, their desire for independence or their wish to supplement the family income, the problems they have encountered and the solutions they have found. Aware that by their work they are contributing to the national economy, they also describe how it enriches their family relationships.

In Austria public information campaigns about the availability of vocational training and guidance take the very simple form of brochures and folders distributed in all public places frequented by women (e.g. town halls, schools, railway stations, tram and bus stops), radio and TV flashes, mobile information centres covering the whole country and visits to factories.

THE RETURN TO WORK

An aspect of recurrent training to which special attention must be given is the return of women to the employment market after a period of absence for family reasons (marriage, childbirth and caring for small children). This is a problem specific to the female working population. Men generally face only two potential interruptions in their careers— military service and unemployment. The first of these concerns only the youngest workers and in any case, wherever it exists, there is a legislative safety-net guaranteeing the serviceman's right to return to the same employer together with all the advantages of seniority he has acquired. Not only this, but periods of military service are counted as work for purposes of social security. As for unemployment, it can hit workers of either sex but tends to be worst among the categories where women are in a majority. For years unemployment insurance schemes have sought to introduce guaranteed income arrangements, facilities for further training and retraining, and placement services that can find the unemployed jobs suited both to their qualifications and to the needs of the economy.

In a word, the normal male career is characterised by continuity. Society does its best to ensure that adult males find employment. Where women are concerned social attitudes remain ambivalent and in many countries—the socialist countries are an exception—the public authorities and society in general accept discontinuity in the female career as natural and inevitable. However, the famous three-phase cycle is no longer quite so pronounced in the more highly industrialised countries. The steady growth of the female working population is due to the increased labour force participation of wives and mothers. We have already mentioned the mainly demographic changes which account for this new phenomenon, and it would seem a matter of urgency to modify the organisation of economic and social life in such a way as to allow for it. Henceforward the human resource potential of half the adult population must be taken into account. To go on considering economic activity on the part of women as a choice, an option which they are free to take up or not, is a grave error that could substantially increase the burden borne by the active population. On the contrary, it must be anticipated that women stopping work for family reasons will increasingly attempt to re-enter the labour force later and that the time spent away from work will become progressively shorter.

An equitable social policy in this field should aim at prevention rather than cure. The various institutional solutions that have been adopted in certain countries take effect too late, i.e. at the end of the interruption of employment when the consequences of domestic " withdrawal " and the prolonged absence from the workplace have left their mark on women contemplating a return to work. In fact the period of economic inactivity should be used precisely to prepare women for a smooth re-entry to the labour force. This calls for a whole range of measures both in the field of social security and as regards vocational training and instruction in domestic science.

It is well known that women outside the labour force spend much more time on housework than women with the same family responsibilities who go out to work; indeed, they make extra work for themselves. Thus the first step must be to teach school and pre-school children how to rationalise the household chores. Radio and television can be used to convey the same ideas to adults. Next, housewives and mothers must be encouraged to use the time thus saved to follow training courses by correspondence, via the mass media, or by other means.

If the potential of the national education system were exploited to the full, many women could improve their qualifications. For example, large numbers of women work in the tertiary sector, but at very low levels of skill and responsibility. The period when they are off work could be used to broaden their occupational skills: a typist could learn one or more foreign languages, a book-keeper could learn accountancy, stock control, commercial correspondence, and so on.

Women should not remain totally isolated from the outside world during the career break. Various connections can be kept up or established, for example refresher courses or temporary replacements. These contacts will lessen the psychological, material and professional problems that may occur when the time comes to return to work. Moreover, they encourage husbands and children to accept a fairer share of the domestic tasks and to have greater respect for the woman's work.

Care should also be taken to provide financial and psychological incentives such as the assimilation of the period spent off work to periods of employment for purposes of social security entitlement (old-age, sickness and invalidity insurance), the award of study grants and scholarships irrespective of the husband's situation, and, finally, access to all

recurrent education and training hitherto reserved to the working
~~on~~.

OCCUPATIONAL SEGREGATION AND WAGE EQUALITY

Even in countries where, as in Scandinavia and the socialist States,
an effort has been made for many years to integrate women into the
economy with greater equality of opportunity and treatment, occupational segregation still exists, and when women do move into formerly
male strongholds the trades concerned promptly lose economic and
social prestige. Moreover, it appears that even in traditionally female
fields such as teaching it is men who hold the key posts, the administrative
positions and are given preference in selection and promotion.[1] The dis-
quieting phenomenon of self-propagating segregation should also be
noted.

At best, equality is achieved at the bottom of the occupational
ladder; promotion, especially to the top posts, remains extremely dis-
proportionate. Social policy aiming to remedy these deficiencies is generally based on such measures as the following:

— elimination of unjustified obstacles to women's employment;
— guaranteed equality of access to all jobs and sectors on the basis of
aptitude, qualification and experience without reference to sex or
marital status;
— upgrading " women's " jobs by the application of objective methods
of evaluating comparable work, the revision of occupational classifications and the improvement of career prospects;
— arrangements to ensure equal opportunities for promotion on the
basis of qualification, merit and experience;
— the introduction of more flexible working hours enabling workers of
both sexes to fulfil their family responsibilities;
— guarantees against dismissal on grounds of maternity and provision
of maternity leave on full pay at the expense of the State rather than
of the employer.

These measures certainly deserve credit, but usually they are ineffec-
tive. Although the causes of discrimination are known and legislation and
regulations have been introduced to deal with it, the real difficulty lies
in supervising and enforcing the application of the relevant provisions.

WOMEN'S ROLE IN ENFORCEMENT

It is obvious that the various anti-discriminatory measures mentioned above need to be applied in the spirit in which they were conceived.
Only too often, however, important conditions of work are negotiated,
job classification systems are drawn up, individual jobs are evaluated,

---

[1] ILO, op. cit., p. 39.

and the supervision of labour legislation and regulations is exercised entirely by men sitting in governmental, joint or tripartite bodies from which women are practically excluded.

A basic first step must therefore be to insist on ad hoc representation of women workers in all bodies concerned with the application of anti-discriminatory legislation, since the struggle against discrimination cannot be carried on by men alone. It is true that in recent decades " women workers' committees " or " councils for equality " have been set up in most Western European countries.[1] These mainly consist of women or of experts on women's questions, but are purely consultative. By contrast, the direct representation of women workers on the decision-making bodies affecting them remains absolutely insignificant, a state of affairs which needs to be stressed.

It should be possible for the application of anti-discriminatory measures to be effectively ensured right from the outset, in advance rather than retrospectively. For example, women workers should be compulsorily represented on all committees carrying out new job evaluations or classifications, in administrative services responsible for placement, vocational guidance and retraining, on economic planning bodies drawing up employment creation policies, and in the joint labour-management machinery for negotiating and concluding collective agreements. In all these fields there is a need for special vigilance by persons with direct experience of the difficulties encountered by female personnel.

Clearly the existing situation must also be kept under continuous scrutiny. Where women constitute a certain percentage of the workforce in an enterprise the workers' representative bodies should include a given quota of them. These bodies should ensure that equitable regulations regarding wages, promotion, working conditions and fringe benefits are observed.

As regards official services, the labour inspectorate needs to recruit a large number of women officials who are thoroughly conversant with the remuneration and employment conditions of male and female workers. Flexible procedures, adapted to national conditions, need to be established so that complaints can be lodged—even anonymously—in cases where the principles of equality of treatment and pay are infringed. Finally, legal proceedings should be backed up by the imposition of heavy penal, administrative and civil sanctions. The conviction of enterprises or trade unions for discriminatory practices should receive plenty of publicity.

Workers with family responsibilities

Apart from the right to maternity protection, it is the recognition of maternity as a valuable social function that seems most urgently

---

[1] Bodies of this sort also exist in Australia, Canada, the United States, etc. See ILO, op. cit., pp. 72-76.

required. The increasing proportion of married women in the female labour force is highlighting the insufficiency of existing facilities for the care of children and other dependants.

The distribution of responsibility between the family and the community is as yet ill-defined. Too few countries have done any short-, medium- and long-term global planning to meet the enormous needs which exist in this field. It is at this stage that the value of the " invisible " domestic work of housewives should be included in the calculation of GNP, whether or not they form part of the active population. It is here too that a thorough overhaul of social security systems is needed in order to eliminate differential and prejudicial treatment of women, whether in the labour force or at home.[1] Child care services for the benefit of working parents need to be considerably expanded to meet the demand in most Western European countries; so far only the Eastern European ones have set up a full-scale network of crèches and similar institutions. Paid leave enabling one of the parents to stay at home and look after a sick child should be envisaged, together with assistance to workers with sick or elderly dependants.

It is essential that studies on the " costing " of children should be carried out, and that the principles to be applied in crèches etc. with regard to costs, standards and staff training should be defined with flexibility and imagination. The financial burden of bringing up children should be largely shouldered by the community, whether by means of direct income transfers or by tax relief.

Families where there is only one parent have special problems which should not be neglected in drawing up social policy.

Finally, there needs to be an intensive public education campaign in favour of rationalising household tasks and distributing them more fairly among the various family members. In this field practically nothing has been achieved as yet.

* * *

The foregoing is an attempt to suggest some of the ways in which social policy could be used to promote equality between the sexes. Policy, however, is nothing without people. In the last resort it is they who must create the material conditions for the economic, social and political liberation of women.

SELECT BIBLIOGRAPHY

Department of Employment, United Kingdom: *Women and work*, Manpower Papers, No. 9: *A statistical survey*; No. 10: *Sex differences and society*, by J. S. King; No. 11: *A review*; No. 12: *Overseas practice* (London, HM Stationery Office, 1974).

---

[1] See ILO, op. cit., pp. 53-57.

... *Etre exploitées*, by an Italian research team (Paris, Edition des femmes, 1974).

Figes, Eva: *Patriarchal attitudes : women in society* (London, Faber and Faber, 1970).

Greer, Germaine: *The female eunuch* (London, MacGibbon and Kee, 1970).

Huber, Joan: *Changing women in a changing society* (Chicago, University Press, 1973).

ILO: *Equality of opportunity and treatment for women workers*, Report VIII, International Labour Conference, 60th Session, Geneva, 1975.

Komarovsky, Mirra: " Functional analysis of sex roles ", in *American Sociological Review* (Menasha (Wisconsin)), Aug. 1950, pp. 508-516.

Lainé, Pascal: *La femme et ses images* (Paris, Stock, 1974).

Lenski, Gerhard E.: *Power and privilege*. A theory of social stratification (New York, McGraw-Hill, 1966).

Lipman-Blumen, Jean: " How ideology shapes women's lives ", in *Scientific American* (New York), Vol. 226, No. 1, pp. 34-42.

Mead, George Herbert: *Mind, self and society from the standpoint of a social behaviorist* (Chicago, University Press, 1934).

Millet, Kate: *Sexual politics* (Garden City (New York), Doubleday, 1970).

Mitchell, Juliet: *Woman's estate* (Harmondsworth, Penguin Books, 1971).

Organisation for Economic Co-operation and Development, Manpower and Social Affairs Directorate: *The role of women in the economy* (Paris, 1973; doc. MS/S/73.3).

Rowbotham, Sheila: *Woman's consciousness, man's world* (Harmondsworth, Penguin Books, 1973).

Vogel-Polsky, E.: *Les conditions de travail des femmes salariées dans six pays de la CEE* (Paris and The Hague, Mouton, in press).

Socialisation of children

Bandura, A., and Walters, R. H.: *Social learning and personality development* (New York, Holt, Rinehart and Winston, 1963).

Fauls, L., and Smith, W. D.: " Sex-role learning of five-year-olds ", in *Journal of Genetic Psychology* (Provincetown (Massachusetts)), 1956, Vol. 89, pp. 105-117.

Goodenough, E. W.: " Interest in persons as an aspect of sex difference in the early years ", in *Genetic Psychology Monographs* (Worcester (Massachusetts)), 1957, Vol. 55, pp. 287-323.

Lynn, D. B.: " The process of learning parental and sex-role identification ", in *Journal of Marriage and the Family* (Los Angeles), Vol. 28, pp. 466-470.

Mischel, W.: " A social learning view of sex differences in behavior ", in E. E. Maccoby (ed.): *The development of sex differences* (Stanford (California), University Press, 1966).

Active population, gross national product and the unremunerated services of housewives

Clark, Colin: " The economics of house-work ", in *Bulletin of the Oxford University Institute of Statistics*, May 1958, pp. 205-211.

Hacker, Helen Mayer: " Women as a minority group ", in *Social Forces* (Baltimore), Oct. 1951, pp. 60-69.

Heller, Celia (ed.): *Structured social inequality* (New York, Macmillan; London, Collier-Macmillan, 1969).

Marshall, Alfred: *Principles of economics*, 8th edition (London, Macmillan, 1920).

Shamseddine, Ahmed Hussein: " The value of housewives' activities in the United States ", in *Economics and Business Bulletin* (Philadelphia), summer 1968.

The Division of Labour and Sexual Inequality: the Role of Education [1]

Elzéa AVENTURIN [2]

OUR CIVILISATION is facing a crisis. Psychologists, sociologists, philosophers, economists, technicians and observers of all kinds are agreed that never before has mankind been in such a plight—escalating violence, social unrest, conflict between nations, challenging of institutions, demands on all sides for the right to work, to justice, to freedom, world-wide dissemination of information by the mass media.... It is within the framework of this general reappraisal that the problem of the place of women in society is posed.

We have reached a turning-point, and the total liberation of women is one aspect of a trend in which all the exploited peoples, all the oppressed minorities are rising up in revolt, this being one of the *critical* periods contrasted by sociologists with the *organic* periods, when hitherto accepted values are overthrown and rejected. Access by women to the spheres of decision making is accordingly bound up with access by peoples to their own government, with the ability of societies to realise their full potentialities, with a fairer economic and political balance between nations in the interests of greater justice.

It follows that, even if we refer solely to the emancipation of women and the role education can play in it, this problem is inseparable from all the others. If the United Nations proclaimed 1975 to be International Women's Year, it was because it is in respect to women that the violence and the injustice are the most flagrant and the most irrational.

[1] This text is based on a paper presented to the symposium organised by the International Institute for Labour Studies in Geneva from 17 to 19 November 1975, on "Women and Decision Making: A Social Policy Priority"; it is reproduced here by kind permission of the IILS. In the pages which follow—even though I believe many of the observations made to be valid within a wider context—I shall be referring above all to the situation in the developing countries, and more particularly in those of the continent I know best: Africa. Certain remarks concerning industrialised countries are intended to refer to market-economy States.

[2] Assistant Professor at Dakar University.

Admittedly, over the past two centuries women have been slowly gaining ground in their societies, mainly in the industrialised countries. Rights have been won, spheres hitherto reserved for men are now open to women. They have acquired the right to vote.

Woman—man's last colony

As the twentieth century draws to a close, woman remains the last colony, the last serf, the last minor in many respects. The influence of tradition, culture and social patterns is so strong that notwithstanding the progress of science, technology and law, there are social, economic and psychological obstacles that still prevent her from liberating herself entirely and perpetuate inequality in every sphere. The most important of these obstacles is the division of labour, which persists in defiance of laws, declarations of principle and even a few spectacular exceptions.

History has shown that many revolutions succeed thanks to the support of groups who in the end derive no benefit from them; this was the case with the revolution of the *bourgeoisie* in the eighteenth century, launched with the backing of the common people in the name of humanity. In staking their claims today, women are likewise participating in a great movement for the renovation of society; but, if they do not watch out, if they are not alive to their opportunities and their rights, if they do not make every possible effort, together with men of good will, to take advantage of these opportunities and ensure the exercise of these rights, they may well find themselves no better off than they were before. The powers that be know how to win back the support of all the groups (young people, women), and turn to their own ends all forms of protest (art, political action, sexual freedom).

Men, when they are oppressed (colonised countries, disinherited or unrecognised minorities), fight for their liberation against another people, another group, another class, but it is symptomatic that they maintain within their movement the traditional division of labour which hallows inequality between the sexes. Sometimes, in the thick of battle, they do grant women equality, the power to take decisions. For instance, Franz Fanon [1] has described the political role played by women in the Algerian revolution. But once the struggle is over, the same old myths usually rise up again. In reality, the more a group is oppressed, the more its womenfolk are enslaved, as if it were a form of assuagement.

There is no denying it: women are still the victims of inequality. Methods may vary from one society to another; the reasons for their enslavement, the form of division of labour, may differ from one continent to another; but one feature remains constant: the inferior status

---

[1] *L'An V de la révolution algérienne* (Paris, Maspéro, 1968).

of women, if not in the home (though that is considered to be of minor importance), at any rate from the economic, social, political and cultural standpoint. They are never recognised to have rights equal to those of men.

They are cherished, pampered, protected, venerated, proclaimed to be saints (in their role as mothers), exploited (as domestic objects, sex objects, or shock troops in revolutionary movements), viewed with suspicion (as temptresses, sinners or over-possessive), but rarely esteemed for their true worth, recognised as such. When compelled by circumstances to accord such recognition, men view the woman concerned as an exception, an anomaly, a freak in fact—a man's mind in a woman's body. The comments made by men are telling in this respect.

The effects of conditioning

These attitudes may not always be voiced clearly, but men (and women themselves) are so strongly influenced by stereotypes that women see themselves through a distorting glass firmly established by their education and their entire cultural environment. In consequence, even though education and culture alone cannot alter a woman's destiny, they have a capital role to play if the ancient myth of inequality is to be destroyed once and for all.

Many arguments are put forward to justify the division of labour between the sexes, the job hierarchy and the inequality—phenomena which are at the same time causes and effects. Women have become habituated to tasks regarded as inferior because, deemed to be incapable of anything else, in many cases they have come to think of themselves as inferior. If, as Marx said, work is a self-creating act whereby man humanises and come to terms with nature, there can be no doubt that centuries of " women's work " giving little or no scope for initiative—or in which initiative, if it was important, was perceived both by them and by society as not being an essential part of the job—have served to entrench and even worsen their position of inferiority in society. Jean-Jacques Rousseau made the profound remark that " any man born a slave is born to be a slave. Slaves lose everything in their fetters—even the desire to rid themselves of them".[1]

In the case of women, many of them have finished by accepting the existence of a " woman's nature ", adapted from birth to a clearly specified series of tasks. Hence the invocation of anatomical and physiological characteristics (constitution, primordial biological function of motherhood) in order to perpetuate the division of labour between the sexes; of pseudo-scientific arguments (a woman's brain being smaller and lighter) as justification for inequality; of social and historic argu-

---

[1] Chapter II of *Le Contrat social:* " Des premières sociétés ".

ments as evidence of the small role played by women in culture (the change-over from a matriarchal to a patriarchal society is seen as a step forward). Freud, as we know, asserted that the collusion of sons against their father, to murder him literally and then symbolically represents the passage from the primitive horde to the social community, the dawn of culture. Woman has no part to play here—or rather she plays a negative role in concealing from man his castration. The change-over from a matriarchy to a patriarchy marks the institution of social order. The violence undertaken jointly by the sons constitutes the first attempt to socialise the aggressive urge and the first act of sublimation. It marks the birth of law, of morals. Moreover, according to Freud, there is no tangible sign of fatherhood; it is above all a legal status, and, as such, the pivot around which the entire culture revolves. Woman, on the other hand, is represented in *Civilisation and its discontents* as the obstacle standing in the way of culture, inasmuch as she represents life and death in life. Woman is the biological function; the genuinely social and cultural, and thence human, level can be reached only by man. Even allowing for the disagreement expressed by some of Freud's disciples and certain commentators upon his work, this is just one example to show how deeply entrenched in people's minds is the idea that woman is an inferior being. She is deficient; she suffers all her life from the lack of a phallus. As remarked by B. Groult, the novelist, if this theory has survived, it is because it is in harmony with centuries-old prejudices, and it has had a devastating effect upon women's personality.[1]

Economic and technical arguments have also been put forward, alleging that women are too physically weak to perform arduous work, or to shoulder heavy responsibilities—as though history were not a categorical denial of such assertions, as though domestic work, work in the fields or at the factory bench required less physical and moral strength than other activities. Moral reasons have been invoked for keeping women at home and out of public life.

All this is not to deny the existence of sex difference and its implications. The stages which modulate the biological life pattern (puberty, climacteric, old age) differ from one sex to the other; maternity will always be the lot of women. But these differences do not signify that women have a destiny, an " essence ", all of their own.

A new task for education : changing mental attitudes

Every thinking, honest man knows that one's biological, biographical and social background are nothing more than raw materials; that one's fate is not inexorably conditioned by one's sex; that everything depends upon the socio-economic and cultural environment in which one develops; that physical strength, in this technological paradise of the

---

[1] B. Groult: *Ainsi soit-elle* (Paris, Grasset, 1975).

twentieth century, is no longer of much importance; that conditions of life and circumstances all help to mould one's personality. Besides, it is well known what a part events (wars, revolutions, or simply widowhood or divorce) can play in enabling women to project a different image of themselves when confronted with tasks or responsibilities hitherto the preserve of men. Notwithstanding all this, the prejudices subsist. To quote the famous quip of Simone de Beauvoir, " one is not born a woman, one becomes one ", because, right from birth and throughout her forma-tive years, society forces a woman into a place, a status, a role, and it is difficult to deviate from the pattern, as from the images and values associated with it.

Already in the nineteenth century, John Stuart Mill, in *The sub-jection of women*, pointed out how decisive the influence of education was and how society had kept women in a state of enslavement, as prejudicial to men as it was to themselves. " We may safely assert " he wrote " that the knowledge which men can acquire of women, even as they have been and are, without reference to what they might be, is wretchedly imperfect and superficial, and always will be so until women themselves have told all that they have to tell."

Admittedly, in our twentieth century, the situation has improved, but the problem of according to women all the opportunities and rights that are their due has not been resolved. Scientific progress may well have given the lie to the old conceptions, but they persist; this shows that it is not simply a question of imparting fresh knowledge, but of changing mental attitudes. A whole cultural background of more or less conscious prejudices continues, unchallenged, to mould the mentality of both men and women.

To alter these attitudes, the remedy is twofold: transform society, and change the content and style of education. The two go hand in hand: only a society which condemns and rejects the traditional division of labour and which, through legal, political and social reforms and through the setting up of new structures, enables women to play their role to the full can lift the ancient curse; only a scientific and human education which debunks the taboos and prejudices can help women to stand more firmly on their own feet, to do a job in society unhampered by discrimination, without for all that renouncing their biological function of motherhood.

Socio-economic revolution and cultural demystification are the two aspects of a single revolution, and the second, if it is to succeed, must operate at several levels. Women must be educated, informed, receive vocational and political training; they must be able to discern other prospects than those—however noble—of being a wife and mother. They must realise clearly that they are capable of doing work useful to society, not only in intermediate and subordinate positions but in posts of responsibility.

It is time to reappraise the work hitherto regarded as the purview of women, both by recognising housewives as workers and by encouraging men to share household work with women. There will then be no more discrimination between the different activities, no more jobs strictly reserved for women or for men. It is, by the way, intriguing to note that a so-called woman's job increases in stature as soon as it is performed by a man. This is the case with cookery and dressmaking in the West. A woman is a mere cook, or at best a *cordon bleu*; a man is given the title of *chef*. A woman is a stitcher, a seamstress; a man is a great *couturier*. A woman who writes books is a scribbler; a man is an author, for, as B. Groult has remarked, even today, " literature written by men is Literature with a capital L ".

There can be no denying the role that in-depth education of men and women can play in destroying these images; it is all the more important in that, ideas having progressed, a gap yawns between what is legal, what is scientific and what is real, between what is prescribed by law and what is actually done—in short, between law and practice. This discrepancy may be observed in many fields. For instance, everyone condemns racialism; penalties are imposed upon those guilty of racialist behaviour, but such behaviour persists nevertheless. The social integration of minorities is urged, but innumerable barriers stand in its way; equality for all men without distinction on grounds of race or religion is one of the principles embodied in the Universal Declaration of Human Rights, but these are fine phrases carved on the façades of the temples and edifices of social progress. Equality between men and women is proclaimed, too, but rarely respected.

In principle, men and women are equal in terms of their right to equal work, equal pay. But in practice, in marriage, in the family, in working life, in regard to their right to work, to pleasure, to remuneration, inequality is the rule. Admittedly there has been progress, there are exceptions; but either this progress has benefited only a minority or a specified sector of the world of women (such as teachers—with reservations, as we shall see later), or there are just a few privileged women, who are moreover ensnared, satisfied with their own success, and have forgotten that the cause is a universal one; or else a majority does indeed benefit from a reform (such as the right to vote), but the motives behind it are often demagogic. Even where social structures are transformed to allow plenty of scope for women, the cultural and psychological barriers created by their education cause them to oppose their own liberation. This brings us back once again to the need to transform education.

As Durkheim so rightly said, every society, at a given moment in its development, has a system of education which is imposed upon individuals with a force that is generally irresistible. Children who have been brought up in accordance with ideas which are either too out of date or too progressive are out of tune with their times, and unable to live a normal life. Commenting freely upon this remark, one may say—

— That there is a continuous relationship between the educational system and the other aspects of society. Education is designed to uphold the values of society. This is proved by the fact that any man who transgresses, any woman who rebels, is looked upon as a " deviant " and rejected, or eliminated if possible.

— That the ideas underlying our present systems of education are out of date, bearing in mind the scientific, political and economic facts of the twentieth century; hence the uneasiness and dissatisfaction felt by all of us.

— That a new system of education will meet with resistance of all kinds, not only from the males in power but from the women themselves, so crushing is the burden of tradition and cultural conditioning.

If getting educated consists not only in acquiring knowledge, experience, know-how, but also in choosing one's way of life, promoting values, shouldering responsibility, being self-reliant finding one's place in society as a whole in order to play a role in it, then educating a human being means preparing him to fend for himself. Now, as far as the majority of women are concerned, one may say that they have not been educated, but trained from birth to view themselves in a particular light. This conditioning begins even before they emerge from the womb.

Admittedly, women do play several roles, but the one assigned to them by society is that of wife and mother. The others are played furtively, exceptionally, often in the face of opposition. According to the traditional division of labour, a woman is born to serve, to be submissive, to bring children into the world, to be a dutiful daughter, a good wife, a good mother. Her job, if she has one, revolves around clearly defined tasks and she has a minimal say in any decisions. If she oversteps these bounds she feels guilty, and moreover finds herself overwhelmed by her twofold or threefold task of running a home, holding down a job and engaging in politics. Ill prepared, inhibited, she not infrequently fails to stay the course, thus marking a point in favour of the old division of labour. It is a vicious circle. She can rarely realise to the full her aspirations or her potentialities, as she is torn asunder, divided against herself. It is symptomatic that such a woman, in appearance very liberated intellectually and professionally, remains trapped by the traditional image and takes initiatives only in so far as they do not clash too much with the established pattern. Parallel with this, a man is born to command, to ply a trade, to provide for the needs of his family, to preserve and increase his heritage, to defend his country, to perpetuate the family name or dynasty. Even if a woman is working on her own (widowed, divorced, single), or helping her husband to run a business, the traditional image persists.

Men—even the most clear-thinking ones—cannot escape from the stereotyped pattern. They frequently disagree, which explains many contradictory attitudes. Some champion equality, but go no further than fine theories. Others apply the principle at work, but in fact discriminate at the slightest opportunity, and in any case, sometimes quite unconsciously, in the family circle. They blithely sacrifice their wives to their careers, treat them as chattels, and bring their daughters up in the old tradition of meekness and submissiveness. There is nothing polemical about these remarks; they describe a commonplace situation.

Some thinkers have quite rightly analysed the concepts of basic personality (A. Kardiner or R. Linton), collective unconscious (Jung), unconscious structures (Lévi-Strauss), which determine to a large degree our attitudes and behaviour. These concepts apply perfectly to the problem we are dealing with here. Alongside the content of education, already heavily oriented, a whole series of values and images exert their influence upon the idea every human being has of his intelligence, his personality and his role, and exert it from birth.

Influence of the family circle and cultural values

During pregnancy, and the preparation of the layette, the plans made by the parents are significant. They usually hope for a boy. If a girl is born, there is sometimes joy, but often disappointment; if a boy is born, joy is coupled with pride. For a couple to have a succession of sons is deemed to be an honour, but a succession of daughters is looked upon as a calamity, and, throwing family planning to the winds, they will keep on having children until the indispensable son is born.

Right from earliest childhood, the educational conditioning begins: the attitudes, comments and plans of their *entourage* are different for each sex; the tasks to be performed, the games to be played are different. Girls learn to sew, wash the dishes, do the housework and play with their dolls. Boys play soldiers, act out adventures, pretend to exercise the noble professions; at most, they run a few errands, whereas little girls are protected from the outside world. Both are already learning their future role as men and women, and for models they need look no further than their own family.

At school, the discrimination continues, in the content of teaching, in the courses followed and in the career planned for them. All parents are agreed upon the need to " push " a boy, to give him a sound education and training, to expect him to show initiative at an early age so as to prepare him for his role as a man (it is only recently that girls have been allowed to go out and travel alone). Even if they do think in terms of an occupation for their daughters, they will never set their sights as high as in the case of their sons; are not their daughters in fact destined for marriage? Admittedly the picture is not quite so stark today; in the past 20 years or so many girls have been able to study, undergo training, take a job. But the level of studies, their orientation, the type of occupation and the proportion exercising it often differ from one sex to the other. Arts studies are more likely for girls; those who go in for sciences often do so with a teaching career in mind.

Economic obstacles do not suffice to explain all the differences between the sexes. Cultural obstacles are just as important. Children, parents and educators continue to cling to an image of qualities and talents regarded as specifically feminine which is still dominated by the centuries-old pattern of the division of labour. This may easily be seen when one questions female students about their aspirations and motivations, which continue to reflect the traditional values. Occasionally they may give a rational or utilitarian explanation for doing socially useful work, but more often they fall back on phrases such as " service to others ", or " sympathy ", or the moral precept of " doing one's duty ".

As concerns political life, girls generally take less interest, are less likely to hold trade union office, read fewer and less political newspapers. We shall revert later to the women's press. As for their occupational status, everyone who has analysed the problem agrees that the higher one goes in the scale of qualifications, grades and responsibility, of jobs which involve attending meetings abroad, or which offer opportunities for research, the smaller the percentage of women becomes.

The reason why, in a country like France, teaching has become more and more of a woman's profession is that it is thought less highly of, and is less well paid; and even here there is discrimination according to the level. Sixty per cent of primary and 50 per cent of secondary schoolteachers are women. The situation changes abruptly, however, at university level: 0.9 per cent in medicine and pharmacology (although the proportion of women in pharmacology has risen steadily over the past few years); and although 20 per cent of arts professors are women, women account for only 7 per cent of the National Education inspectors. A great deal could also be said about women doctors and lawyers, who rarely accede to posts involving high responsibility.

To what may this be ascribed ? To many things: to the structure of society, to motivation at school, to traditional stereotypes, to the prospects really offered right from childhood, to the negative behaviour of women themselves. Not so very long ago, women doctors or dentists had great difficulty in attracting patients, and the prejudice persists. Every aspect of culture, whether it be the precepts and knowledge imparted, the comments made or the attitudes adopted, determinedly and insidiously pins women down in a subordinate position.

The situation in the Third World

Turning to the countries of the Third World, we see that the situation is no better—far from it.

For example in Africa the problem of education is even more complex. A distinction has to be made between education of the traditional type still imparted in the countryside and that available in the large towns, which lies half-way between tradition and modernity, with all the inconsistencies and imbalances that this implies. In both cases, the division of labour is still the general rule, even if some women do have jobs outside the home and others have political responsibilities.

In the traditional society, African women are well integrated into their milieu and their education spells out for them their role as wives and mothers. Although boys and girls are brought up in the same manner until they are about 4 years old, from then on the patterns diverge. Admittedly, in this division, a woman is not looked upon as an inferior being: the mother is held sacred throughout the African culture, some women perform religious functions, and the worth is recognised of certain exceptional women who are consulted before any important decision is taken. Today 90 per cent of the population still derives a living from agriculture, and the role played by women in this sector is considerable. They thus participate in the development effort. As a rule, however, they are mainly occupied on tasks around the house and in the fields, and remain subject to the authority first of their fathers and then of their husbands.

Colonisation not only did nothing to improve the situation but it made it more complicated than ever by introducing a monetary economy and Western lifestyles, and by disrupting the traditional family unit. Women who claim to be progressive cannot manage to organise their lives harmoniously. Few of them have had adequate education and training. They live in a topsy-turvy world where long-standing prejudices are compounded by the aftermath of colonisation and the problems of underdevelopment. Men, during the colonial period, were given the rudiments of an education, and began to take outside jobs, while the majority of women, quite illiterate, continued to perform purely domestic and agricultural tasks. Even today, if we look at the independent African nations, the number of women who have completed their schooling and exercise an occupation is tiny compared with the number of men in the same position; those women who are in employment, with a few rare exceptions, have lowly jobs, are poorly paid and are still under the thumb of their husbands.

A basic education geared to marriage, schooling which begins too late and ends too soon (many girls, even today, leave school under pressure from their parents to contract a marriage deemed to be advantageous), a crushing burden of family responsibilities (birth control is a recent innovation and still meets with strong resistance), arduous working conditions in the countryside, few welfare facilities in the towns, low pay or impossibility of finding a job—these are the conditions most commonly found. To these cultural obstacles must be added psychological disturbances and financial difficulties. Although men and women have to contend with the same vicissitudes, it is women who suffer from them most, confined as they are by the division of labour to roles which give them no scope for taking decisions.

Thus, although there are differences, depending upon political and cultural structure and problems peculiar to each country, and upon the progress achieved in certain fields, all the various societies embrace a standard concept of femininity—a slippery, ambiguous concept, difficult to debunk, comprehension of which, to use the language of the logicians, is indefinite. How can one ward off the dangers and avoid the snares of love, of courtesy? How can one reconcile work in the home and outside it? Or, in Africa, tradition with modernity? The solution in all cases is the same: only education can improve the picture. The goals have to be adapted to the actual needs of each community, but the situation as a whole is identical.

In the industrialised countries, although women have not entirely freed themselves from the old taboos, most have received a minimum of education, information, vocational training; but these are still too strongly influenced by the traditional values. The problem for women is to acquire better vocational training, to secure improved conditions of work that will enable them to reconcile their family life with their working life, to accede to posts of responsibility, to take a detached view of the information fed to them, to resist the consumer society which constantly seeks to entrap them.

In the developing countries, all this is made more complex by the prevailing political and economic situation and by cultural factors which are more difficult to eradicate—inconsistencies arising from the " deculturisation " process. Prejudices die harder, the all-powerfulness of the male still too often goes unchallenged. Education is sketchy or non-existent, the literacy rate is low, and rule-of-thumb methods are used. The economy of these countries is in a state of flux, marked by the sequels of colonisation, worsening terms of trade, the lack of a balanced market and chronic unemployment.

All this renders the struggle for equality more ambiguous. Men make use, as it suits them, of tradition or modernity. On the employment market, in accordance with the traditional pattern, if there is one job for 50 applicants, it will go to a man. By the force of circumstances, even though a few women do accede to posts of responsibility (ministers, doctors, midwives), the traditional division is the rule; a woman is destined for domestic tasks, and is not always mistress of her own earnings if she does work. This disheartening but factual picture of education and its consequences does show us, on the other hand, what education should be doing today if it is to abolish inequality, present women in their true light, facilitate their integration in modern life, or, in the case of Africa, hasten their development. It should be a rehabilitation of the past and a revolution of the present, a transformation of both men and women. It should take different forms according to whether it is addressed to the old, the young, or children of both sexes.

Older people will continue, no doubt, to conform to the traditional pattern; in any case, they no longer have a very active role to play in society. Adult males need to be re-educated in order to overcome their resistance, while women should be properly informed so as to be in a position to re-establish the truth as to the achievements of women in the past, and become full members of the community. As for the younger generation, both boys and girls, the inherent contradictions are part and parcel of their daily life and all the opinion polls show that they are more enthusiastic than their elders about the new style of education that is beginning to emerge. They are at odds with their parents (conflicts between generations, revolt of daughters against forced marriages) and with society (strikes by young people for the right to work, condemnation of the educational system).

But the most efficient job can be done with the children, so as to banish once and for all the cultural vestiges of outworn concepts. From earliest childhood, parents and teachers must destroy the myth of femininity, of male and female occupations, of woman destined to be a wife and mother, and replace it by the idea that they are all children, irrespective of sex, and free and responsible beings. The criterion for making distinctions should not be sex, but aptitudes, aspirations, capacities. This presupposes a reform of our day-to-day language, which is the vehicle for a whole petrified philosophy; for there is a tendency to associate all that is capricious, foolish or disastrous with the female of the species. For instance, all the cyclones which periodically ravage the West Indies are given girls' names.

The role of the media

Of course it will also be necessary to reform the mass media. The women's press, for instance, which some have seen as a sign of progress: at last, periodicals addressed to women ! In fact, in the form they usually take, they are yet another trap. It is time for them to help women to emerge from their ghetto by talking to them about other things than cookery, their homes and their beauty. Glance at any women's magazine and all you will find will be advice on how to slim, make up, enlarge one's bust—recipes, in short, for pleasing men, and building up an image that will meet with their approval.

Never, or hardly ever, do these magazines make any demands on women's intelligence. All of them have a lonely hearts column, but rarely a page on social problems. Most have nothing to say to women about their legitimate aspirations, their vocational training, the economy (apart from its domestic connotations), or major international problems. Away with these photo-strip love stories—a veritable scourge which is at present sweeping over Africa. Not only do they adopt the wrong psychological approach in nurturing the dream of a prince charming who will come to save the girl from her unhappy lot, but they develop an unprecedented intellectual sloth. The headmistress of the girls' high school in Dakar felt compelled to protest against these publications a few months ago. This lenitive press is perhaps even more dangerous in our countries than elsewhere. An end must be put to the situation where there is a superficial, misleading women's press on the one hand, and a serious men's press on the other; what we need in their place are journals that speak to all of us about the problems of women, of the nation and of the world.

The cinema and advertising could benefit from a similar purge. If a man sweats, it is a sign of virility, of hard work—unless it is to be inferred that only women suffer from this unpleasant experience since, if we are to believe the deodorant advertisements, a woman will lose her fiancé, her friends and her job if she is not spick and span, asepticised and perfumed. A plump, mature or ageing woman is no longer a woman, since she is not appetising; a corpulent man, on the other hand, may be seen from afar to have achieved professional or political success; he has " made it ", and he can help himself to any young thing that takes his fancy.

I have no objection to advertisements showing us the ecstasy of a mother, or the happiness of a fiancée or a young wife, as publicity for a maternity dress or a bridal headdress; but, for heaven's sake, let them show us also the serious and serene faces of women at work; let them show us the elegant and competent secretary, but also the woman building-foreman, driver, doctor, working side by side with men; let them show us shimmering national costumes, but also peasant women, and people at work in the fields of Casamance. Let television, which draws our attention to the gadgets and the thousand-and-one technological marvels which facilitate the domestic chores, show us, after a day's work at the office, at the factory, in the fields, a man and a woman commenting upon a newspaper together, or preparing a meal in the kitchen while boys and girls set the table, as a change from the traditional image of the mother, exhausted by her outside job, wearing herself out doing everything possible for the comfort of the man of the house. Admittedly, the conditions of modern life are such that, in many cases, men actually do their share of household chores, but the mass media continue to propagate the image of yore.

Bearing in mind the powerful impact a picture has, it is obviously imperative to make changes in the mass media. This constant and insidious conditioning is perhaps more dangerous than that resulting from basic education, which allows time for criticism, and which nevertheless, as history and literature show, produces exceptions to the rule.

The role of the school

This does not mean that education is less biased; here, too, changes are called for. One of the first means of achieving the new-style education is, it seems to me, to generalise co-education and the practice of sports. The former is the best way of putting an end to sexual segregation, changing outlooks, banishing the over-valued image of the male, enabling the sexes to get to know each other better. The latter will enable an end to be put once and for all to the idea that practising sports deprives a woman of her femininity. Of course, there are women's sports teams, and women champions, all over the world, but they are a minority, when the goal should be sports for all.

In vocational training and guidance, equal opportunities should be given to everyone, the only criterion being, not sex or social background, but intelligence and aptitudes.

As for the subjects taught, a change of perspective is necessary. The pattern of education is constantly building up men to the detriment of women. Parents, educators and textbooks must re-establish the truth, highlight all the examples in literature, history, science and ideological movements of women who have contributed alongside men towards human progress. They must not hesitate to cite examples, and explain them. This is a stage that has to be gone through; only afterwards will it be possible to write history or literature which makes no distinction, instead of history glorifying the male, or novels for women or for men.

The problem is even more acute in the Third World, as in addition to sex discrimination we have the rejection of the traditional culture. Let African children be told, for example, about " la Grande Royale ", whom Sheik Hamidou Kane wrote about in *L'aventure ambiguë*[1], and Anne Zingha, Queen of Matamba, in Angola, in the seventeenth century, who personified the resistance to the Portuguese; let there be no hesitation in informing pupils about present-day events which show the role played by women, their achievements, their political and social activities—for instance, the appointment of a woman, Jeanne Martin Cissé, Ambassador of the Republic of Guinea to the United Nations, as Chairman of the UN Special Committee on Apartheid. These things are all too often unknown to the public at large.

* * *

---

[1] Paris, Julliard, 1962.

In the developing countries there is urgent work to be done: literacy campaigns for the rural masses, modernisation of farming methods, forming of co-operatives in which women participate alongside men [1], the teaching of child care, with the use of locally grown produce (millet, manioc flour), speedy integration of women in all sectors of the economy. Novels should stop talking about pure, frail young girls being awakened to life and love thanks to an all-conquering male, and give us instead healthy, straightforward young people, liberated from taboos, and free to choose their own partners; literature and the press should proclaim woman's right to pleasure, to do with her body as she thinks fit, to decide when she wishes to procreate.

No further credence must be given to the fallacious arguments used by employers, who condemn women to a minor role in economic life on the pretext that society has made investments on their behalf, but that, victims of their sex, they represent a loss to the general economy of the country because of their higher rate of absenteeism (indisposition, maternity leave, absence to care for a sick child). In reality the progress of contraception now enables them to regulate their pregnancies, while more numerous community services should free them in part from their domestic duties. If the law were more flexible, father and mother could absent themselves alternately when one of their children was sick.

It is almost inevitable that in the initial stages of this rehabilitation innumerable cases and forms of discrimination will have to be denounced and attention focused on everything women have achieved, if the balance is to be restored. There are so many mistakes and injustices to be put right, so many stereotypes to be refuted, such a backlog to be made up, that women everywhere must make their voices heard so that all women become aware of their rights and their potentialities. Only on this condition will real collaboration be possible, but this can only be a stepping-stone towards genuine association.

In this new-style education, one must not allow the debate to become heated. What women must do is to point out the impediments that have hampered their progress, refute the ancient myths, acquire rights, play a bigger part in the life of the community, and act without indulging in crankery, sexual militancy or sterile opposition, which is another approach to adopt to the old criteria. A woman who pursues the wrong kind of liberation, uninhibited eroticism, is still an object. Replacing the power of the male by the power of the female is merely an expression of what Bergeron called " the law of double madness ", when what really needs to be done is to strike a fresh balance by demonstrating everything that men and women stand to gain from the complete liberation of women.

---

[1] Admittedly, in this field, a number of experiments in rural animation have been carried out, but they should be generalised.

Taking the family first: in the opinion of biologists, educationists, psychologists and psychoanalists, the human animal is an incomplete being, because he is " social " and " historic ". Human children are the only young who have to be educated, and in this task father and mother have a complementary role to play. The creation of the indispensable harmonious family circle is a task for them both; what education must banish is the image of the potentate father and the submissive mother, to be replaced by a couple of free parents.

As regards marriage, education must show men that they have nothing to lose in agreeing to a fairer sharing of the household chores, the opportunity for their wives to take a job, to have a say in decisions affecting not only the family but the nation as well.

In more general terms, education must develop solidarity between human beings and calm the apprehensions felt by men. The division of labour, sexual discrimination and the pretexts invoked to justify them (loss of femininity, abandonment of women's child-rearing role if they work outside the home on an equal footing with men) are merely the expression of a reluctance to share power, of the need to dominate by crushing one's partner in order to reassure oneself as to one's own strength.

If it is true that, as Plato put it, our eye sees itself in the mirror of another eye, to despise or belittle another human being is to lower oneself to the same level. Men must therefore be made to realise, to use the words of M. A. Simet-Lutin [1], that they will still stand to gain when a women is " no longer a beast of burden, a plaything, a child-bearing machine, but a real companion—that is to say, a free and responsible person ".

---

[1] President of " Maternité consciente " (Guadeloupian family-planning association), and author of a memoir on the role and status of women in the history of the French West Indies.

Development and Mounting Famine: a Role for Women

René DUMONT [1]

W HEN PEOPLE in the prosperous nations of Europe or North America and in the various bodies responsible for administering aid—whether at national or European level, the United Nations, the World Bank or some similar institution—speak of development, up to now they have generally meant development along the lines of their own civilisation as symbolised by the private car, the jet airliner, overconsumption (e.g. of meat, fats and clothes) and waste.

This type of consumption is typical of countries which are already rich, a state they have attained partly owing to the low prices paid over the years for the raw materials and labour of the poorer or so-called underdeveloped countries. The élites which hold power in these newly independent States desire to live in the style to which many of them became accustomed, especially during their student days, in developed countries. In order to attain this high level of consumption they have been obliged to allocate an excessive proportion of the meagre national income to luxury expenditure—and, worse still, to armaments—so that not enough is left over for agriculture and the industries needed to modernise it. The famines in the Sahel, Ethiopia, India and Bangladesh bear witness to the failure of this type of development.

Thus we are going to have to change our way of thinking with regard to a good many points, and women can and should play a key role in the process. The spread of famine is due partly to the population explosion in which women, as the childbearers, play a primordial part, and partly to insufficient agricultural production, where they again have an essential though generally underestimated role. Moreover, the task of preparing meals in the home, which is such an enormous source of saving or waste, is entirely in their hands. Again, woman in her maternal role is an educator, especially during early childhood which is the crucial period for her children's whole physical and intellectual development. Finally, women, like men, have an essential political function to perform and

---

[1] Former Professor at the Institut national agronomique, University of Paris-Grignon, and author of numerous works on agricultural economics and development.

must be able to speak out against the kind of development which, as we have seen above, has proved a failure. The purpose of the present article is briefly to review these various roles.

Woman as a self-limiting agent of reproduction

The basic precondition is this: if mankind does not quickly put a stop to the unprecedented catastrophe commonly known as the population explosion, it will soon disappear. Many experts estimate that before the population of our small planet can be stabilised, towards the middle of the next century, it is likely to reach 12,000 or 14,000 million. This prospect is often accepted as quite " normal ".

In *Stratégie pour demain* [1], Mesarovic and Pestel have analysed the most dramatic situation of all, that of South Asia, which in 1973 had 1,300 million inhabitants. If the above-mentioned projection is correct, there will be 3,800 million by the year 2025. By that time, when the point of population stability will not be far off, the authors estimate that there will be an annual shortfall of 500 million tons of cereals in the region, even if a major effort is made to modernise agriculture. If this amount is not forthcoming from outside, they predict that 500 million *additional* children under 15 will die over the following 50 years.

There is no task so vitally urgent as to slow down the expansion of population *soon*. After investigating the world's agricultural potential I consider that on no account should a population figure of 7,000 or at most 8,000 million be exceeded, and if we could stop at a lower figure, so much the better. Once the peak has been attained one could even think about reducing the world population, and it seems to me that 2,000 million may one day be considered the optimum level if human life is to be sustained for any great length of time on this little planet with its limited resources.

The most obvious correlations with reduced fertility are wealth, standard of living, and, in particular, education. Educated women have far fewer children than illiterate ones. However, everybody knows that the school attendance rate is almost always lower for girls than for boys. Moreover, the cost of traditional schooling is such that in a large number of poorer countries many decades must go by before it can be extended to the entire population, by which time the population explosion may well have brought universal starvation. We are faced with a formidable race against time.

The solution is to provide all young people who have already started work, whether in the towns or in the countryside, with some functional literacy, including basic economic and political instruction, priority being given for once to girls and young women. In their own vernacular people

[1] Paris, Editions du Seuil, 1974.

can achieve literacy in a year, and at the end of the year the best students could become " literacy instructors " in their turn. In Mali such persons serve without pay. By this method the multiplying effect is very high and the cost so slight as to be within reach of the poorest countries *provided the necessary motivation is there.* The best age is between 10 and 20, because at 10 one can hardly hope any longer to obtain a traditional teaching diploma under the formal educational system (the usual " escape " route from farm labour), while after or even before the age of 20 girls are liable to be married.

It has often been said that the birth rate cannot be reduced until a certain level of prosperity has been reached, as happened in Europe. If this were so, in view of the number of countries whose production, especially agricultural production, is making little progress, there would be no hope of averting demographic disaster. However, China affords an example of a major reduction of the birth rate achieved prior to any great rise in the standard of living thanks to a high level of education and political motivation. Women must first be freed from domestic bondage so that they will be encouraged to free themselves from ignorance: each step on the road to liberation facilitates the next.

Woman as farmer and grower of food

In a good many Chinese provinces it used to be dishonourable for women to work in the fields. The poorest, who had no choice, were degraded by the mere act of doing so, and their " virtue " called into question. Women were among the most ardent supporters of the Chinese revolution, since they were fighting for a double liberation: like their husbands, from landlords, mandarins and money-lenders, but also from the unending family oppression by fathers, husbands and mothers-in-law, and even by sons in the case of widows. Before long, women were claiming the right to play their part in food production so as to contribute to the success of the revolution, and they set about organising crèches so that their children should not suffer.

By contrast, if one visits a Bengali village in Bangladesh, especially if it is a Moslem one, one finds the women still confined to the house and the farmyard. Again, only the poorest and thus most despised go to work in the fields. They are prisoners in their own homes, allowed only to thresh and husk the rice, but never, as in China, to share in the work of transplantation, harvesting or irrigation.

In the tropical forest zones of Africa the situation is reversed. The entire burden of agriculture rests on the women, while the men hunt and fish, and formerly made war. Originally, the men spent much of their time picking wild fruit, and this supplied most of the food. Cultivation was an accessory, and it was logical for the women to do it. Now that it has become the main activity this is no longer the case, but the men still

45

do no more than clear the forest. When I was studying this situation in the Congo basin in 1961, I pointed out that compulsory schooling for all girls, such as was then being projected, would cause a famine if all those educated continued to refuse to do agricultural work. I replied frankly to one young pupil (a budding bureaucrat, as he candidly told me): " If your sister goes to school, you won't have anything to eat but your fountain pen." [1]

In Upper Volta, in the overpopulated Mossi region, the young adult males have to seek work in Ghana or the Ivory Coast, so that villages are peopled chiefly with women, children and old men. Here again, women carry much of the agricultural burden. The official education system still ignores this fact and offers places in the agricultural colleges only to boys, whose main hope in going there is that they will never have to do any more manual agricultural work. If adult education following the provision of basic literacy is ever introduced, it will need to have an agricultural bias and be given to women in the first place.

However, if women are to play a larger part in agricultural production without being overburdened, their domestic tasks will have to be cut down; in other words they will have to be shared increasingly by their menfolk and children. This raises the question of food preparation. Manioc, in particular, takes a very long time to prepare; in a village on the Dayes plateau in Togo I once watched two women spend three hours pounding a *foutou* of manioc for a small family.

Woman as cook and dietitian

In Tanzania, close to the frontier with Kenya, maize remains the staple diet as in most parts of East Africa. Even in the natural state its lack of certain amino-acids such as lysine is notorious, and this deficiency is aggravated by the traditional method of preparation. After soaking in water for one or two days the grain is pounded in a wooden mortar, which eliminates the germ and bran, the parts richest in protein. Dr. Krysler has estimated the nutritional losses caused by this process as 40 per cent of the calorific value, 60 per cent of the proteins, and 80 per cent of the fats and various sorts of fat-linked vitamin A. The result is widespread xerophthalmia and blindness which could easily be avoided.

Functional literacy programmes should therefore include a certain minimum of nutritional instruction, since all over the world taboos and mistaken habits prevent people from making the most of existing resources. The proud *caboclo* of the Brazilian forest, for example, keeps practically all the meat for himself, leaving little for his wife who is usually pregnant or suckling the latest baby and thus needs it more than he does, not to mention the children who easily become rickety or anaemic.

---

[1] R. Dumont: *False start in Africa* (London, André Deutsch, 1966), p. 92.

It is not possible to provide a power-driven cultivator for every African family hoeing a couple of hectares by hand, but it would be feasible—and in fact it is already being done, though not yet on a large enough scale—to buy a small power-mill for each village of 100-200 families. In remote areas where the motor might not be a practical proposition a yoke of oxen could be provided instead, and this could also be the first step towards the wider use of animal power. Women could be relieved of their role as beasts of burden (in Africa the loads are mainly carried on the head, in Asia on the shoulders by means of a yoke) by the general introduction of hand or ox-carts. The former can be built with strengthened bicycle-type wheels like a rickshaw.

However, let us return to our cornflour. If the grain is ground whole and dry, none of the above-mentioned losses occur. Mixed with a little water (not too much, so that chewing is still necessary), salt, raw onion and pimento, the flour is practically a meal by itself. It only remains to add a third of beans or a quarter of soya before grinding; these supply the lacking amino-acids. Later, when basic literacy courses have been started, Chinese cooks could explain some of the many ways of serving soya.

In coastal areas where coconut palms grow freely people can be taught to extract the milk from fresh nuts, which has the food value of full milk for children over six months old. For very young infants, human, cow or goat milk is still preferable.

A well-fed goat can stand up to a jungle climate that is unsuitable for cattle. Every tropical household could easily keep one or two goats for milking purposes and in this way the most serious protein deficiencies could be eliminated. Alternatively, they could keep from five to ten hens: a couple of eggs per week is enough for a child, provided its diet includes some whole cereals—neither too husked nor too bleached—and leguminous vegetables.

With regard to whole cereals we have already mentioned maize. White rice is not only dearer than unpolished rice in its coloured cuticle but has a much lower nutritional value, having lost most of its vitamins. The result is a danger of beri-beri. Similarly, white bread is rapidly becoming dangerously popular in tropical countries, which is precisely where wholemeal bread should be preferred from every point of view.

Woman as mother and educator

Children are normally looked after by women at an age which, as is too often forgotten, is crucial for all subsequent physical and intellectual development. If the child's diet lacks proteins the brain suffers. If it lacks iron and folates the result is pernicious anaemia and a child without energy or resistance to disease and other external threats.

47

The mother remains the irreplaceable first educator, the first teacher, even if she has no paper qualifications. Most of them know well enough how to pass on the traditional lore in which Asia and tropical Africa are still so rich. On the lonely farms of the Brazilian *sertão*, however, where language is terribly impoverished, such traditional knowledge appears to be fast disappearing.

If all future mothers could be rendered literate and thus gain a better understanding of the invasive modern world, their role as educators would become even more important. Having broadened their own horizons, they could do much more to stimulate their children's intellectual development at an early age—without neglecting tradition.

However useful they may be, simple courses in child-rearing and nutrition are not a sufficient preparation for the multiple functions of motherhood. Until such time as mothers can really be trained to fulfil their vocation as teachers, the best course would be to combine their experience by putting all the children of a village into a crèche which small groups of mothers would take turns at looking after, thus freeing the others for agricultural work. Old people could also share in the supervision, since they are the best placed to pass on the positive aspects of tradition.

Woman as citizen

This is where the shoe pinches worst. Women are excluded from public affairs even in developed countries where they have just been " liberated ". Even where they have had the right to vote for a generation or more there are very few women members of parliament or ministers, and there are still fewer in underdeveloped countries that are still not really free. The decline in the real status of women in a number of newly independent countries augurs ill for their future.

The young Christian women in Cameroon are now refusing to be bought and sold like cattle and are claiming the right to choose their own mates. Up to now they seem to be getting only limited support from the young men, although these same young men have to pay a bride price that enables their elders to live in idleness. The women who are up in arms about this situation are primarily those who have studied. They have discarded the veil and refuse to be shut up in the home. But they still have to understand the responsibility they bear towards a whole generation of women who, unlike them, have not had access to secondary and higher education.

The sight of African and Asian capital cities with their ministries and civil services tells its own tale. Even when equally qualified, women are generally confined to subordinate posts. It is true that there are some notable exceptions in Asia and even in Africa where women hold very senior positions (and anyway the industrialised countries have little to boast about in this respect). The fact remains that I have seen very few women included in delegations to international conferences. The situation at the World Population Conference held at Bucharest in August 1974 was particularly disturbing. The vast majority of African and Latin American countries refused to consider any form of birth control, a decision taken entirely by men in a field which they must sooner or later realise is primarily a matter for women, and in which women should have the predominant voice since they bear the children.

If the yoke of neocolonialism, is to be removed, if peasants are to be freed from exploitation by a privileged urban minority and women from the slavery imposed by male-dominated societies, it will be necessary first to *organise* the two most exploited groups, namely peasants and women. By taking up arms against their own oppression they will contribute more effectively to the cause of national independence.

I know of a country which claims to have achieved its revolution by a simple coup d'état. Yet when one sees the degree of oppression to which women there are still subjected, one cannot help remembering Chairman Mao's dictum that no true revolution is possible without the liberation of women. International Women's Year is an occasion to speak out loud and clear about such facts. But fine words are not enough. As the review *PAN* rightly reminded the World Food Conference in Rome, " the starving cannot eat your speeches ". They, like the oppressed of both sexes, must now envisage taking action. It is up to them to define the form it will take and then to set it in motion.

————————

Women Workers
and the Courts

Felice MORGENSTERN[1]

I T MAY BE that the trend of judicial decisions concerning women workers and their problems in work life and society is one of the more reliable indicators of their status in these times of rapid political, economic and social change. In any event, the Court is an arena of—most often last—appeal for women who seek to overcome discrimination on the basis of sex and marital status and to obtain a more realistic recognition of their role in economic life, in the family and in society as a whole. The following summary of certain key judicial decisions of recent years may be helpful in suggesting which way the wind is blowing and whether a coherent pattern is emerging from the logic underlying the decisions.

Any analysis of case-law concerning the status and the problems of women in employment must however be made subject, at the outset, to a number of qualifications.

First, reference to a Court of law is only one of a number of means for achieving the protection of workers—and usually a supplementary one. The extent to which recourse is had to the Courts differs greatly according to national traditions; moreover, in some countries, cases relating to employment are largely dealt with by relatively informal instances, whereas in others large numbers of such cases will reach the highest instances, and are thus more likely to appear in published law reports. There are also national divergencies in the type of question that is susceptible of judicial settlement; thus the Courts may in some countries be seized of allegations of discrimination on the basis of considerations of public policy, or general constitutional principles, whereas in others judicial action is possible only on the basis of specific legal provisions.

Second, reference to a Court of law is usually a matter for voluntary decision by the person concerned; it may be costly; and it may place the worker in a position of " opposition " to the employer. This means that

---

[1] International Labour Office.

relevant case law is more likely to be found where the workers themselves have the means to undertake an action, or have the support of unions with such means; where the employment situation is such that the worker is not afraid of antagonising the employer; or where there are procedures—such as actions at the instance of a public agency—which make these problems irrelevant.

Third, there are limits to what Courts are able to do. There may be national differences in the degree to which they can interpret the law as established by legislation, precedents, etc. In some countries Courts may have the power to set aside the provisions of legislation, as well as of collective agreements or of individual contracts, on the ground that they conflict with constitutional principles. Generally speaking, however, it is not for the Courts to change the law even if they find it unsatisfactory.

Despite these various limitations on the use, and usefulness, of legal action, the published law reports of different countries show an upsurge in recent years in decisions concerning the problems of women in employment. Reference is made here not to decisions on questions relating to all workers alike, which may be given on particular claims put forward by women, though even such cases reflect the greater consciousness of the women themselves—and of their unions—of their place in economic life.[1] In this note, it is proposed to analyse only decisions with a specific bearing on the status of women. These decisions fall into two main categories: those bearing on problems of equality of opportunity and treatment; and those relating to the protection of the functions of women in the family.

Equality of opportunity and treatment

Access to employment, assignment, advancement and security of tenure

A very substantial number of cases have dealt with the question whether particular restrictions on women's employment opportunities by virtue of their sex, their marital status or their family responsibilities are permissible. That question has been posed, according to national practice, on the basis of legislation designed to ensure equality of opportunity, on the basis of general constitutional equal rights provisions or by reference to public policy. Courts have usually considered the only possible justification for such restrictions to lie in the demonstrated incapacity of women as a class, as opposed to individuals, to perform the

[1] That the number of claims put forward by women remains significantly smaller than that put forward by men is suggested by an analysis, in the United Kingdom, of applications alleging unfair dismissal in 1972 and 1973; the analysis found men to be " heavily over-represented in the total " (*Department of Employment Gazette* (London), July 1974, p. 617).

requirements of jobs closed to them; in the overwhelming majority of cases, the demonstration of such incapacity could not be made.

Some strange occupations were banned to women altogether until the intervention of the Courts. Thus in England and in Chile they were unable to hold licences to train racehorses; no reason was found why they should be excluded from this occupation.[1] One problem to be overcome in this connection was that access to the occupation was controlled by professional associations which claimed the right, like a social club, to decide at their discretion whom to admit; this discretion was held not to be so absolute that it could interfere arbitrarily with someone's right to work. In Venezuela a decision of the Supreme Court was required to set aside, as unconstitutional, a provision of the Commercial Code making women ineligible to be receivers in bankruptcy.[2]

In other cases a plausible argument was made that the generally lighter physique of women necessarily limited their access to jobs requiring a certain degree of physical strength. Particularly in the United States the Courts have not held this argument valid in respect of women as a category. Thus in a number of decisions, federal district Courts or Courts of appeals have set aside restrictions on access to jobs involving the lifting of weights which did not take into account individual qualifications and considerations.[3] Similarly, in a recent decision, the California Court of Appeal held that rigid height and weight requirements for entry into the police discriminated against women as a class and that what mattered was that an individual applicant meet tests of strength, agility and endurance.[4]

By far the largest number of Court cases, the world over, have related to so-called " celibacy clauses " in works rules or contracts of employment—clauses according to which married women are not eligible for employment or retention in employment (in some variants women already in employment on marriage were permitted to stay until the birth of their first child). After a hesitant start—in 1961 Courts of first instance in France and in India upheld such clauses largely out of respect for contractual arrangements duly accepted—clauses of this type have generally been regarded by the Courts as unenforceable. In France[5], in

---

[1] England, Court of Appeal, 22 February 1966. *The Times* (London), 23 Feb. 1966, Law Report. Chile, Dirección del Trabajo, 12 May 1971. *Revista Técnica del Trabajo y Previsión Social* (Santiago), June 1971, p. 33.

[2] Supreme Court, 4 March 1965. *Revista del Ministerio de Justicia*, Apr.-Dec. 1965, pp. 362-365.

[3] For instance, two decisions dating from 1969 are reported respectively in *Labor Relations Reference Manual* (Washington), Vol. 70, pp. 28-43, and in *Fair Employment Practice Cases* (Washington), Vol. 2, p. 121.

[4] California Court of Appeal, 15 March 1974. *Fair Employment Practice Cases* (Washington), Vol. 7, p. 1091.

[5] Court of Appeal of Paris, 30 April 1963. *Recueil Dalloz* (Paris), 1963, Jurisprudence, pp. 428-430. The case was taken further, but without success.

1963, the Court of Appeal of Paris held that a celibacy clause applied to air hostesses was invalid, it not having been demonstrated that marriage affected the satisfactory performance of the functions. In India the Supreme Court in 1964 refuted in detail arguments made in favour of a celibacy clause in the pharmaceutical industry [1]: there was nothing to show that married women were more likely to be absent; they were not less efficient; the only problem was maternity leave—but the undertaking in question in the test case had expressly denied that it was trying to avoid that burden. In Japan the District Court of Tokyo in 1966 held a dismissal in pursuance of a celibacy clause in a cement company to be invalid: again, it found that there was no proof of general deterioration of efficiency after marriage, and held that individual cases of such deterioration could be dealt with by other means.[2] A labour Court of Córdoba, in Argentina, in 1967 awarded damages for dismissal in pursuance of such a clause.[3] In the United States a federal district Court held in 1967 that a celibacy clause applied to air hostesses did not constitute discrimination on the ground of sex [4]; four years later a federal Court of appeals held that it did—since married men were eligible for employment—and considered that celibacy was not an inherent requirement for the satisfactory performance of the duties of stewardesses.[5] Also in 1971 the Supreme Court of the United States called in question an employer's policy not to accept applications from women with pre-school-age children, on the ground that the evidence presented failed to show that the policy related to a bona fide occupational qualification reasonably necessary to the normal operation of the business.[6] In Italy the question arose differently: legislation was adopted which prohibited the termination of the employment of women on marriage or within one year thereafter, and the Constitutional Court was asked, in 1969, whether this was a justified limitation on the employer's freedom to carry on his business; it held that it was.[7] Conversely, in Belgium, the Full Bench of

---

[1] Supreme Court, 3 November 1964. *Factories Journal Reports* (Madras), Vol. XXVIII, pp. 233-237.

[2] Tokyo District Court, 20 December 1966. *Rôdô Hôrei Tsûshin* (Tokyo), 28 Jan. 1967. The District Court of Osaka took a similar view, on 11 December 1971, as regards a shipbuilding company.

[3] Labour Court of Córdoba, 26 April 1967. *Derecho del Trabajo* (Buenos Aires), Oct. 1967, pp. 573-578.

[4] District Court, Eastern District of Louisiana, 19 October 1967. *Monthly Labor Review* (Washington), Jan. 1968, p. 64.

[5] Court of Appeals, Seventh Circuit, 16 June 1971. *Fair Employment Practice Cases* (Washington), Vol. 77, p. 621. The Court held that marriage did not affect an individual woman's ability to create a climate of comfort and safety for passengers, and took the view that alleged passenger preference for single girls, and alleged complaints from husbands about their wives' working hours were not valid reasons for the clause.

[6] Supreme Court, 25 January 1971. Ibid., Vol. 3, p. 40.

[7] Constitutional Court, 5 March 1969. *Notiziario di Giurisprudenza del Lavoro* (Rome), Mar.-Apr. 1969, p. 52.

the Court of Cassation in 1969 upheld a celibacy clause by reference to the contractual freedom of the parties [1], and this was followed two months later by legislation making such clauses null and void. Finally, in Israel, a regional labour Court in 1973 declared invalid provisions under which the employment of air hostesses terminated on marriage or on the birth of their first child.

There have been few decisions which have related to restrictions on possibilities of advancement. The reasons for this are not self-evident, particularly as, for instance in the United States, there have been a number of decisions on such restrictions which concerned differences of race; it may be that in such cases the discrimination was easier to demonstrate. One decision in the field concerned, again, the air hostesses of the Israel national airline. The National Labour Court in 1973 held void provisions in the applicable collective agreement which established separate lists of advancement priorities for men and women and which restricted the highest grade to men. As regards the former it held that separate lines of advancement by their very nature negated equality of opportunity; as regards the latter it took the view that the burden of proof that women could not meet the requirements of the highest grade was on those who had established the rule, and that that burden had not been discharged.

Equal pay

In the field of remuneration, Courts have mainly addressed themselves to the practical implications of the principle of equal pay for equal work, laid down in constitutional or other legislative provisions. There are substantial differences between countries, particularly as to the questions submitted to the Courts.

In Argentina, for instance, a series of decisions were concerned with the question whether the principle of equal pay related to the legal rate for the job or to the remuneration actually paid by the employer. Consistently it was held that it related to the former. The conclusion was explained most clearly in a decision of the Supreme Court, of 26 August 1966 [2]: the purpose of the principle of equal pay was to ensure a just remuneration for work, without arbitrary discrimination on grounds of sex, race, etc.; that purpose was met by the determination of rates by collective bargaining; there was nothing to prevent the employer who complied with the rates so set from paying additional amounts to any person who, because of his greater suitability, devotion or output, merited such payments. A later decision [3] of the Supreme Court of the

---

[1] Court of Cassation, 16 September 1969. *Journal des tribunaux du travail* (Brussels), 30 Apr. 1970, pp. 19-22.

[2] *Derecho del Trabajo* (Buenos Aires), Sep. 1966, pp. 448-451.

[3] Dated 2 July 1968. Ibid., Sep. 1968, pp. 475-477.

Province of Buenos Aires showed that the decision to pay additional amounts could apply to a category of persons; it was there held that the principle of equal pay was not violated by the payment of amounts, additional to those required by the applicable collective agreement, to recompense the better quality of men's work, and that it was for the employer, without need for judicial review, to decide whether circumstances justified such additional payment.

In Italy the question which has come repeatedly before the Courts has been whether in fixing wages, for instance by collective agreement, different rates for men and women could be justified by reference to presumed differences in output. The Courts have held that output is a question pertinent to piece rates but not to time rates and have concluded that differences in time rates for men and women can be justified only by differences in the requirements of the jobs assigned to them.[1]

In North America it is precisely to alleged differences in requirements of the jobs that Courts have addressed themselves. Rejecting the arguments presented before them, the Courts have held that legislative requirements of " equal skill, effort and responsibility " do not imply identity of tasks. For instance, the Ontario Court of Appeal on 16 April 1970 overruled a lower Court which had found differences in pay between female nurses' aides and male orderlies in a home for the aged to be justified by the different skills and efforts required of the orderlies in lifting stretchers and transporting patients; it found that the work of the two groups was patently of the same nature or kind.[2]

Finally, decisions concerned with the implications for male wage rates of the equal pay principle are of some interest. In Italy the Court of Cassation on 30 August 1960 rejected the argument of an employer that a provision of a collective agreement giving men exceptionally assigned to a job mainly exercised by women a higher rate of pay was unlawful and that the men's pay had to be reduced to the women's level; it held that the equal pay principle was designed to lead to the betterment of women's conditions and not to the deterioration of men's and the benefit of the employer, and that the only possible recourse against the discriminating provision was by the women concerned.[3] Conversely, a United States Court of appeals held, on 24 June 1970, that, where a minimum wage was statutorily fixed for women, men employed by the same employer in the same establishment for the same work were entitled to the benefit of that minimum.[4]

---

[1] Two recent decisions of the Court of Cassation on the subject date from 18 April 1969 (*Rivista di Diritto del Lavoro* (Milan), July-Dec. 1970, p. 7) and from 17 March 1970 (ibid., Oct.-Dec. 1971, p. 511).

[2] *Canadian Labour Law Reports* (Don Mills (Ontario)), 27 May 1970, p. 14269.

[3] *Rivista di Diritto del Lavoro* (Milan), Jan.-June 1961.

[4] *Wages and Hours Cases* (Washington), Vol. 77, p. 130.

Retirement age

Another area in which the legitimacy of different treatment of men and women workers has been tested in the Courts of some countries is that of retirement age. In a number of cases the Courts have disapproved provision for different retirement ages; however, the case-law leaves open, in various degrees, the possibility that such differences may in certain circumstances be objectively justified.

In the United States the Courts have addressed themselves primarily to the question whether differences in retirement provisions, whether resulting in compulsory early retirement for women [1] or in reduced pension benefits for men opting to retire at an age at which women are entitled to retire [2], fell within the 1964 Civil Rights Act, i.e. the basic legislation requiring equality of treatment. They have held that such differences are prohibited by the Act. The question whether differences may in certain circumstances be justified does not appear to have been explored.

In Japan the Courts have examined the question of possible justification; in two recent cases [3] they have not found such justification to exist. In the one case, the differential was conspicuously large: men retired at 55 and women at 30; the Court did not find any special circumstances which could justify such a difference. In the other, the retirement ages were 55 and 50 respectively. One of the arguments made was that the physical strength of women declined earlier; it was not accepted since the job in question did not require physical strength. In both cases it was also argued that a wage system based on seniority made it desirable not to retain in employment for too long an essentially unskilled female labour force; in both cases the Courts pointed out that the same argument applied to unskilled men in the undertakings concerned. It should be noted that both decisions are from Courts of first instance; in the second case a higher Court had initially refused a request for interim measures of protection on the ground that the difference in retirement age was not, prima facie, discriminatory.

The Italian Courts have gone furthest in accepting that in certain circumstances differences in retirement ages may be defensible. Following a decision of the Court of Cassation, in 1968, that there was no objective reason for different retirement ages in the collective agreement applicable to the Rome milk marketing co-operative [4], the Constitutional Court was seized, in 1969, of the question whether differences in retirement age

---

[1] Court of Appeals, Seventh Circuit, 7 July 1971. *Fair Employment Practice Cases* (Washington), Vol. 3, p. 795.

[2] Court of Appeals, Third Circuit, 8 March 1973. Ibid., Vol. 5, p. 709.

[3] Nagoya District Court, 2 April 1972. *Hanrei Jihô*, 21 Oct. 1972; Tokyo District Court, 23 March 1973. *Rôdô Shiryô Sokuhô*, 1 May 1973.

[4] *Rivista Giuridica del Lavoro e della Previdenza Sociale* (Rome), Nov.-Dec. 1968, p. 679.

were, as a matter of principle, consistent with constitutional equal rights provisions. It held that they were: the constitutional provisions did not prevent account being taken of reasonable and objective differences of physiology, resistance to tiring work, etc.; it might also be appropriate to permit women workers after a certain age to devote themselves exclusively to their household tasks.[1] That decision was followed by a further decision of the Court of Cassation, of 12 September 1970, upholding a provision in a collective agreement fixing different retirement ages, on the ground that sex in that context implied an objectively different aptitude for work.[2]

Social security

It is in the field of social security, however, that Courts have taken account most readily of the existence of social patterns and situations which, in their view, could justify different treatment of men and women. The question has arisen both as regards certain benefits due to the worker himself and as regards the entitlements of members of the family by virtue of the worker's insurance.

As regards the former, a series of decisions in Belgium were concerned with the question whether a legislative provision fixing flat-rate unemployment benefits at different rates for men and women was compatible with a constitutional equal rights provision. Some labour Courts of first and second instance held that the provision in question was contrary to the Constitution. However, the Court of Cassation, on 24 January 1973, came to the contrary conclusion.[3] It held that unemployment benefit was designed to compensate at least in part the involuntary loss of employment, that in view of this the amount of the benefit took account of earning levels, and that the fact that in most sectors of the employment market women's average earnings were less than those of male workers constituted an objective criterion which justified a difference in benefit.

As regards the latter, a distinction must be made between entitlements of children and entitlements of the spouse.

In respect of the entitlements of children, Courts have maintained that there is no reason to make any differentiation between rights derived from the father's and from the mother's employment. The Supreme Court of Spain, on 9 June 1962, pointed out that in modern times it was common for the mother to contribute with her earnings to the maintenance and education of the children, and that unequal treatment, in

---

[1] *International Labour Review*, Feb. 1970, p. 163.

[2] *Notiziario di Giurisprudenza del Lavoro* (Rome), May-June 1971, p. 105.

[3] *Journal des tribunaux du travail* (Brussels), 15 Mar. 1973, pp. 71-72. Prior to this judgement the law was modified to provide for a benefit directly related to previous earnings, as well as taking account of family responsibilities.

social security, of the death of father and mother would mean that in the case of the father's death the family income was maintained, whereas in the case of the mother's there was an uncompensated loss.[1] Similarly, the Constitutional Court of the Federal Republic of Germany, on 24 July 1963, held that a law under which the death of the father automatically gave rise to pensions for children, and the death of the mother only in cases in which she had had the primary responsibility for their support, was contrary to constitutional equal rights provisions: as regards children, the need to replace the support provided by either parent was the same; the aim of insurance was not to replace primary support only, but to maintain a certain pre-existing standard of living.[2]

On the other hand, as regards the entitlements of the spouse, the Courts have considered that the differences in the typical economic effects of loss of support, as between husband and wife, justified a different treatment in social security. Thus the Constitutional Court of the Federal Republic of Germany, in the same decision as that cited in the preceding paragraph, held that a law giving pensions automatically to widows, but to widowers only if the wife had had the primary responsibility for the support of the family, was not contrary to constitutional equal rights provisions: typically, the support of the husband outweighed that of the wife and could not be made good in case of his death, whereas part of the contribution of the wife was often offset by a diminution of need.[3] The Italian Constitutional Court, on 29 December 1972, came to the same conclusion on an analogous question: it was a social fact that a wife was more likely to be dependent on her husband than the converse; it was accordingly reasonable to make a widower's pension contingent on evidence that the wife was the breadwinner.[4]

Protection of the functions of women in the family

Maternity protection

Generally, the role of the Courts in the field of maternity protection has been rather different from the one they have fulfilled in the field of equality of opportunity and treatment: they have usually been called upon, not to test basic principles, but to apply fairly detailed legislation to particular situations. It is a less spectacular role, but nevertheless one

---

[1] *Revista de Derecho Privado* (Madrid), Oct. 1962.

[2] *Die Sozialgerichtsbarkeit* (Wiesbaden), Special edition, 21 Sep. 1963, pp. 1-11.

[3] At the same time, in a decision of 31 March 1971, the Constitutional Court held, in a case concerning restitution of contributions, that inequality of treatment could not go so far as to deprive the widower of rights where it was demonstrated that the wife had been the breadwinner.

[4] *Rivista di Diritto del Lavoro* (Milan), 1973, Nos. 2-3, pp. 44 ff. In Belgium a labour Court of appeals on 4 January 1974 upheld different treatment of husband and wife for purposes of medical care, by reference only to the fact that this was consistent with the general pattern of family law (*Journal des tribunaux du travail* (Brussels), 30 Sep. 1974, p. 219).

which, case by case, builds up an important body of law designed to afford the appropriate protection to the different interests involved.

The largest number of cases relates to the circumstances in which dismissal of a pregnant worker may be permissible. What is the relevance of the nature of her contract? On 12 October 1960 the Full Bench of the Federal Labour Court of the Federal Republic of Germany held that a contract for a fixed period which was objectively justified by the nature of the work terminated on its expiry date even if the worker was pregnant.[1] On the other hand, the Belgian Court of Cassation held on 21 February 1973 that the statutory prohibition of the termination of the employment of a pregnant worker, except for reasons shown to be unrelated to the pregnancy, applied during a probationary period despite the fact that such a period was required to be short.[2] What is the relevance of the employer's knowledge of the pregnancy? On 28 December 1962 the Supreme Court of Israel held that a procedural requirement for authorisation by the Ministry of Labour was absolute, but that the grant of authorisation—which could be retroactive—would be influenced by the fact that the employer did not know of the pregnancy and hence did not dismiss because of it.[3] In Argentina the National Labour Appeals Court on 17 December 1971 arrived at the same substantive conclusion: a dismissal in ignorance of the employee's pregnancy was, by definition, not " by reason of the pregnancy ", and hence was not prohibited.[4] What economic circumstances permit the dismissal of a pregnant worker, or analogous action? In case of closure of the undertaking, a pregnant woman is no more protected than other workers.[5] A lockout may be applied to a woman on maternity leave, but she must be reinstated as soon as the labour dispute is over.[6] In case of reduction of staff for economic reasons, a pregnant woman could be included amongst those dismissed even though some workers doing the same work are retained and the woman concerned is capable of performing other work; otherwise a woman who is able to work in the coming months would be deprived of her employment for the benefit of one who would not be able so to work.[7]

Another question which has given rise to Court actions is that of the financial entitlements of women who are unable, because of pregnancy,

---

[1] *Arbeitsrechtliche Praxis*, No. 16 to BGB (Civil Code), Art. 20.

[2] *Journal des tribunaux du travail* (Brussels), 30 Sep. 1973, p. 213.

[3] *Jerusalem Post*, 13 Feb. 1963, Law Report.

[4] *Derecho Laboral* (Buenos Aires), 1 June 1972, pp. 362-363.

[5] See, for example, a decision of the Argentinian National Labour Appeals Court of 21 November 1972. *Derecho del Trabajo* (Buenos Aires), June 1973.

[6] Federal Republic of Germany, Federal Labour Court, 25 January 1963. *Westdeutsche Arbeitsrechtsprechung* (Bad Homburg), 15 June 1963, pp. 97-98.

[7] Belgium, Labour Court of Appeals, Brussels, 29 June 1973. *Journal des tribunaux du travail* (Brussels), 15 Oct. 1973, p. 232.

to continue to do their previous work. A series of recent judgements of the Federal Labour Court of the Federal Republic of Germany has dealt with the application, in practice, of legislation requiring the employer to make good any loss of earnings resulting from a prohibition related to pregnancy. In a case decided on 17 July 1970 a woman had been reassigned, as required, from piece-work to time-work, with the maintenance, in principle, of the average earnings achieved while on piece-work; however, the employer withheld part of these earnings on the ground that the decline in her productivity was much greater than was warranted by her condition. The Court ordered the payment of the sum withheld; it considered that, while an employer was entitled to compensation for a breach of the worker's contractual obligation, such breach had to be proved.[1] In a case decided on 9 September 1971 a barmaid was unable to continue her previous work because of a prohibition of nightwork during pregnancy; the employer argued that she should have sought alternative work and refused to continue to pay her average earnings. The woman was awarded her average earnings for the entire period in question; it was for the employer to offer alternative suitable work to the worker, who could not be expected to face the strain of job-seeking and who was not likely, because of her condition, to be accepted elsewhere.[2] On the other hand, in a third case decided on 7 August 1970 the Court held that the employer was not liable to continue to pay wages. The worker concerned in that case could have continued to work normally but for the fact that she was unable, on medical advice, to travel from home to work; the Court held that such travel was influenced not only by work obligations but also by private factors, such as choice of accommodation, and that an obligation relating to it could not be placed on the employer.[3]

There have also been some decisions on the implications of the faculty given to working mothers in some countries to take leave up to the first birthday of a child. A regional Court in Czechoslovakia held on 16 June 1966 that a claim to maintenance on the husband arose which had to be taken into account in fixing his other financial commitments; other claimants on his resources could not argue that she could maintain herself if necessary by returning to work earlier. A regional Court in the German Democratic Republic held on 5 January 1968 that a worker was entitled, at the end of the period of leave, to continued employment by her former employer, on the agreed terms; the permanent appointment, in the meantime, of her replacement did not justify the termination of the employment of a working mother returning from leave.[4]

---

[1] *Arbeitsrecht in Stichworten* (Bad Homburg), Jan. 1971, p. 5.

[2] Ibid., Jan. 1972, pp. 6-7.

[3] Ibid., Jan. 1971, pp. 6-7.

[4] *Arbeit und Arbeitsrecht* (Berlin), 1 Sep. 1968, pp. 492-493.

One question of principle has been tested in a number of recent decisions of United States Courts, culminating in a decision of the Supreme Court on 21 January 1974, namely whether an employer may oblige a pregnant woman to take unpaid maternity leave from a relatively early stage of the pregnancy. The cases in question all related to school board regulations requiring women teachers to go on leave as from the end of the fourth or fifth month of pregnancy. One argument made in support of the regulations—that of the need for continuity in the classroom—was shown by the Supreme Court to be defeated as often as served by a rigid rule. With respect to the other argument—that the presence of a physically capable teacher had to be assured—the Court held that the rules swept unnecessarily widely; the administrative convenience of avoiding case-by-case determinations of the pregnant teacher's ability to continue at her job did not warrant the interference with the woman's freedom in matters of marriage and family.[1]

Facilities for exercise of family responsibilities

It is apparently only in the past few years that Courts in various countries have been faced with issues reflecting the need of many women workers for certain facilities in relation to the exercise of their family responsibilities. The decisions in question are isolated ones and do not, as yet, reflect any pattern, national or international. They deserve mention, however, as an element in judicial awareness of women workers' problems.

In Australia, in March 1971, a Senior Conciliation Commissioner of New South Wales was faced with an employers' request for the introduction of part-time employment, opposed by the union concerned. In deciding to accept the request, and to obviate the union's objections by certain safeguards such as a loaded salary rate, the Commissioner emphasised the social desirability of giving women who wished or needed to work the opportunity of employment which satisfactorily fitted in with their family responsibilities.[2] In December of the same year, in France, the Court of Cassation was seized of the question whether an employer who had transferred the place of the undertaking had to pay damages for breach of contract to a woman employee who claimed that she could not work at the new site because, unlike the old site, it was too far from her home to make it possible for her to go there at lunch-time. The Court held that, if the fact that the original place of employment was near the home had been an essential condition of the employment contract for the

---

[1] *Fair Employment Practice Cases* (Washington), Vol. 6, p. 1253.

[2] *Industrial Information Bulletin* (Canberra, Department of Labour and National Service), Mar. 1971, pp. 712-714.

woman, the unilateral change constituted a breach of contract.[1] In England, in December 1973, the Court of Appeal had to consider the situation of two women clerks who had been dismissed after many years of employment because they were unable, by reason of their family responsibilities, to accept a change from a five-day office week to a six-day shift system. The claim made by the women for redundancy pay failed because there was not, in fact, a redundancy situation; however, the Court expressly left open the possibility that a change in hours which was unfair to a particular employee might give rise to a claim for unfair dismissal.[2] Finally, in Japan, the Tokyo District Court had to consider, in March 1973, the validity of the argument—of a male worker who had lost his employment because he refused transfer to another city—that his wife was also working and could not change her workplace. The Court referred to other cases in which couples were obliged to live separately for occupational or educational reasons, and considered that that would have been the solution if both husband and wife wished to retain their employment.[3]

* * *

It is difficult to draw any general conclusion from decisions on so wide a range of subjects. Individual decisions may seem disappointing. Certain patterns may be controversial. This is inevitable at a time when new concepts of the role of women are coming into being and society is only in the process of adjusting thereto.

The upsurge of legal decisions relating to women workers and their claims is part and parcel of the mounting pressure in many countries and in many circles for more equitable treatment of women in work life and in society as a whole and for more effective enforcement of existing legal and other provisions aimed at promoting equality of opportunity for them, removing discriminatory or anomalous treatment and safeguarding the right to maternity protection. Legal decisions constitute an increasingly important part of the total structure and machinery for the elimination of all forms of discrimination against women. The new judicial awareness of women workers' rights and problems and the pattern emerging from the decisions represent an encouraging element in the over-all situation but it remains to be seen whether the impetus achieved can be maintained in the years ahead.

---

[1] *Recueil Dalloz-Sirey* (Paris), 1972, Jurisprudence, p. 177.

[2] *The Times* (London), 28 Dec. 1973, Law Report.

[3] *Rôdô Shiryô Sokuhô*, 15 May 1973.

Social Security and Women: a Partisan View [1]

Sylva M. GELBER

AS THE TWENTIETH CENTURY enters its last quarter, social security programmes, which evolved from the poor laws of an earlier age into the comprehensive systems encompassing social assistance, social insurance and health care that we know today, appear to be remarkably rigid in the face of rapid social change. They are slow to adjust to the new role of women, particularly in urban industrial society, which the social revolution sparked by scientific and technological advances has brought in its wake. In particular, their insensitivity to the individual human rights of women, which was relatively inconspicuous in the less socially conscious world of the past, is today becoming obvious.

During the last three decades there has emerged an almost universal recognition of the rights of people to be treated in law and in practice as individuals, regardless of such factors as race, nationality or religion. That people's colour, religion or nationality should not be allowed to affect their obligations or rights is today a commonplace. International declarations and the constitutions of many countries specifically incorporate the principles of non-discrimination on these grounds as well as that of sex. Yet social security systems, the vast majority of which have been considerably developed since the Second World War, frequently fail fully to reflect this same principle, particularly as it pertains to differential treatment on grounds of sex.

The Universal Declaration of Human Rights, adopted in 1948, proclaimed that everyone has the right to social security (Article 22). But

[1] The author, who is Director of the Women's Bureau in the Canadian Department of Labour, presents in the following article a personal and—as she would readily admit—a partisan view of the position of women under social security in industrialised market economies. Eschewing a " balanced " presentation of the subject, which to her way of thinking would have had the effect of obscuring the discriminatory aspects of social security, she has preferred to denounce the inequities that result even when they represent extreme cases or arise from subjective or biased administrative interpretations contrary to the spirit of the relevant legislation.

However unrepresentative they may consider the resulting picture to be, readers may well agree with the author that an institution that leaves room for any of the forms of social hardship and injustice she describes is certainly in need of review.

on the question whether a nation might provide for different levels of social security benefits for different groups or individuals it was silent. Thus, while social security benefits were to be provided without discrimination on grounds of sex, nothing in the Declaration precluded the payment of benefits at lower rates to women.

In some of its instruments the International Labour Organisation has dealt with the question of discrimination. In those concerning social security, the prohibited grounds enumerated are nationality, race and religion. In those concerning migrant workers, sex is also included. One Convention dealing directly with the subject of discrimination prohibits discrimination on all the usual grounds including sex, but the scope of the prohibition it establishes is limited to discrimination in respect of employment and occupation. Still missing from the ILO standards is a clear, forthright declaration outlawing discrimination on grounds of sex in social security in all circumstances.

The general setting

Under most national social security programmes women are placed at a disadvantage with respect to one contingency or another and frequently with regard to several contingencies. This is due in no small part to social attitudes and moral concepts which have little or no relevance in contemporary industrial society. The first and most obvious of these stems from the almost universal acceptance of the notion that a married woman is necessarily protected by a male breadwinner upon whose shoulders rests the total financial responsibility for her well-being. This simple concept has affected not only the housewife whose unpaid domestic work is confined to the home, but also the housewife who works without pay in a family undertaking, not to mention the millions of women who combine the role of housewife with that of wage earner.

The woman wage earner can find that she is denied the same social security rights as her male colleagues on the assumption that her needs are less since she is not the head of household. This assumption has affected her rights in respect of almost all conditions of work, including the right to work itself. In times of shortage of labour or national emergency she is called into the workforce; and in times of economic slack she is the first to be laid off. Regardless of her individual circumstances, society views her as a dependant.

The various branches of social security not only designate the wife as a dependant but may also distinguish categories of dependency. Thus a widow's benefits may be contingent both on her marital status and on the duration of her marriage or on her state of health. A woman may find that her rights depend on whether she has been deserted or is divorced or widowed, the benefits varying with each status. A common-law wife or an unmarried mother who is the sole support of her children may be subject to discriminatory provisions. In some instances, age may be an additional consideration.

A dependent wife may well find herself deprived of social security protection as a result of desertion, separation or divorce, just at the moment in her life when she is most urgently in need of such protection. A deserted wife with children may be deprived of health insurance coverage because her husband has absconded and has failed to keep up his contributions. A widow may receive a pension at a level well below subsistence; or even worse, as merely the former wife of a deceased pensioner, she may not be entitled to any pension at all.

The concept of woman as a dependant without independent rights is further compounded in certain areas of social security, particularly in that of social assistance, by outdated concepts of morality. Legislation frequently permits or requires the normal statutory benefits to be denied to the deserted, separated or divorced woman, or to the surviving widow, in the event that she is living with a man not her husband. Such provisions undoubtedly rest upon the assumption that a relationship of this type necessarily implies a financial relationship, thus placing her beyond the eligibility conditions of a needs test, an argument which loses its punch when applied to programmes based on insurance principles.

The fact that such a relationship is a matter of private concern not necessarily having any financial implications whatsoever is presumably not yet acceptable nationally or internationally. The ILO itself, in a number of its Conventions, specifically allows for the suspension of social insurance cash benefits payable to a widow who is living in such circumstances. Moral values, of course, change with the years, but international instruments and the law should reflect such changes.

Quite apart from moral considerations, however, the varieties of conditions of entitlement of the dependent woman are manifold. Frequently, these result from little more than a haphazard development of individual laws and regulations; even more frequently, they are based on unsubstantiated assumptions relating to women as a class. Today, these incongruities are more apparent than at any other time, owing to the changing status of women in contemporary society.

The extent of the social revolution, which has affected the status of women in the industrial world, is reflected in vital statistics and relevant employment data. Birth rates, divorce rates, life expectancy and the rate of participation of women in the labour force all tell a simple story: radical change.

It is common knowledge that the birth rate in industrialised countries has dropped dramatically since the advent of new and reliable methods of birth control. These have brought greater freedom to both men and women, but particularly to the child-bearing parent.

At the other end of the spectrum, greater longevity has been accompanied by a growing gap between the life expectancies of men and women. In societies where it is customary for women to marry men some years older than themselves, their considerably greater longevity ultimately results in a growing population of widows, making all the more urgent a revision of social insurance systems that provide so inadequately for the surviving spouse.

But the indicator which perhaps may prove to be most significant from the point of view of wage-related social security is the divorce rate, indicating as it does a substantial increase in the break-up of marriages. For the inadequacy of present social security systems, as they affect women, becomes particularly obvious when a dependent wife suddenly becomes a deserted wife or a separated wife, not to mention a second or even a third widow of a deceased worker.

The factors so clearly reflected in these vital statistics have had a particularly convulsive effect on the life of women. If, in the past, a woman was fully occupied for the greater part of her married life with the traditional task of looking after her home and family, today, with a greatly increased life expectancy, with only some two children to care for and with a host of labour-saving devices to help her, additional hours and years have been made available to her, opening up opportunities for self-development and social activity never before within her reach. At the same time, greater expectations, coupled with the effects of inflation, have placed particularly heavy economic pressures on the family.

It would appear that these economic pressures too have considerably affected the role of women in the family in the industrialised world, for, in the majority of countries, the participation of married women in the labour force in the last decade has reached unprecedented levels. Although some women may have sought gainful employment outside the home for reasons of self-fulfilment, the vast majority have done so for the same reason that their menfolk go to work: to earn a decent living.

In addition, there is now the vast army of women who are themselves wholly responsible for their own maintenance and, all too frequently, for the support of dependants as well. These include those who have been deserted, who are separated, who are widowed, as well as the increasing number of women who are divorced. If unmarried single women are added, then it is clear that the majority of women in contemporary industrial society can no longer be assumed to be economically dependent in any sense of the word.

It may well be argued that, under social insurance programmes, women wage earners are entitled to and in fact receive benefits, since such programmes view each eligible wage earner as an independent contributor. But the amount of social insurance to which a contributor is entitled is commonly calculated on the basis of the level of contributions or earnings and the number of years for which contributions are paid. And the hard fact is that working women are employed at the lowest level of pay and only within limited categories of occupations. They are frequently denied access to the training which would upgrade their earnings, and subjected to practices which prevent them from obtaining positions of skill and responsibility. These denials of opportunity flow from the customs and traditions of generations which did not envisage women playing a substantial role away from hearth and home.

Although married women have now found it necessary to enter the workforce, the maintenance of the home for the most part is still viewed as their sole responsibility, thus placing upon them the double burden of workers in the market-place and in the home. It is for this reason that the pattern of employment of women differs from that of men.

Part-time work in industrialised countries is almost invariably women's work. The woman with a family has found part-time employment to be something of a compromise, enabling her to carry on her two jobs at one time. But the woman who works part time is a woman whose social insurance entitlement is diminished, restricted or totally nonexistent.

Another feature of women's employment, also stemming from their dual role, which can sorely affect their social insurance entitlement is the phased work career. It is not unusual in industrialised countries for a woman to leave the workforce for a number of years while her children are young. Admittedly this practice is undergoing considerable change as more public facilities are being provided for the care of pre-school children, but few countries are as yet adequately equipped in this regard. For the time being, therefore, the career pattern of the working woman is frequently characterised by at least two distinct phases of employment. It need hardly be pointed out that such separations from the labour force entail an interruption in social insurance contributions and result in seriously reduced levels of benefit.

A further problem arises from the employment of women in occupations commonly excluded from social insurance coverage. Domestic work in private homes is one such occupation. In addition, there are the many women who work in family undertakings sharing the workload with their husbands who, as self-employed persons, frequently have the option of contributing to social insurance—a possibility that is denied to their partner-wives. This exclusion is particularly ironic since it is the wife who, statistically at any rate, is likely to survive by some years her partner-husband and herself become solely responsible for the management of the family undertaking. In her advanced years she will be entitled only to the benefits of a dependent wife, although she has in fact been as much of a worker as her self-employed late husband.

Long-term contingencies

It is in the field of old-age pensions that the urgent need for reform is most evident. Here, the traditional assumption—that women need no protection in their own right in their advanced years since they already benefit from the coverage made available to them as dependants of their wage-earning husbands—is compounded by the assumption that women do not bear financial responsibilities for dependants of their own. These assumptions disregard the facts of contemporary life.

Women workers who support themselves—whether it is because they are single, separated, widowed or deserted; whether it is because they are divorced in a society where the break-up of marriage has become relatively common; or whether it is because their husbands' wages are insufficient to meet the family needs—all these make up the vast majority of women in the labour force. Besides, in many instances these same women have to protect dependent children. Nevertheless, because of outdated customs and traditions, there are still numerous obstacles to the achievement of equality of benefits in existing old-age programmes.

The most obvious difference in old-age pension provisions concerns the age of retirement, which is not uncommonly as much as five years lower for women workers than for men. Sometimes this differential is referred to as an advantage for women workers. This is to ignore the fact that, where the level of the pension is based on the number of years of contributions, a five-year reduction inevitably lowers the pensions available to women workers.

In private pension programmes the diminution of the period of contributions is often further exacerbated by the requirement that women employees are not eligible for membership until they have completed a period of employment exceeding that required of their male colleagues. Thus, the woman worker's span of pensionable employment is further reduced and the total number of years during which she may contribute occasionally falls short of that of her male colleague by as much as ten years.

In addition to these handicaps, it must be recalled that a woman worker outlives her male colleague by an average of some seven years. Thus, although she has to live on her pension for considerably longer than a man, she is denied the opportunity to build up substantial equity for herself.

Old-age pensions are not, of course, provided solely through public social security programmes; often they are supplemented by private insurance plans. The differential treatment of women is sometimes considerably more blatant in the latter than in the former. It is not unusual, for example, for an employer to provide insurance protection for his workers under a private pension plan intended solely and exclusively for male workers, the women workers in the same establishment remaining completely unprotected.

Complicating the whole situation is the fact that, in the private sector, old-age pensions are based on life tables which are calculated on the basis of sex. This practice is stoutly defended by the insurance industry and by actuaries, although the defence may spring more from tradition than from actuarial necessity. For the fact remains that in some countries, where the life expectancy of certain groups—for example the Black community in the United States—was actuarially different from that of the rest of the community to the disadvantage of the minority, differential rates were abandoned on grounds of public policy, actuarial calculations notwithstanding.

Perhaps the time has come to state that public policy will no longer tolerate old-age pension plans that provide less protection for one half of the population than for the other solely on the grounds that the other half has proved to be physically more vulnerable to the perils of living. Actuarial calculation is not necessarily the preferred instrument for the achievement of social justice in the last quarter of the twentieth century.

If old-age pension systems discriminate against women wage earners, they do so to an even greater degree against women who are supposedly protected by virtue of being dependants of male wage earners. For the excessively low level of pensions provided to the widows of deceased wage earners is hardly consistent with the basic principles of social security. The notion that the living costs of one adult are one-half of those of two is erroneous; yet in many instances a widow's pension is even less than one-half of the entitlement of her late husband.

That a widow in these circumstances may seek and be entitled to social assistance is an unsatisfactory answer; indeed, such an expedient is unacceptable to the spouse of a former independent, self-supporting member of the community. It also flies in the face of the insurance principle that a single contingency should not have to be covered under several headings in order to achieve minimum protection. If a widow in her advanced years is obliged to seek social assistance to supplement her old-age pension, it cannot be claimed that she was adequately insured.

The transitional benefit which is occasionally provided to a widow in the period immediately following the death of her husband can hardly be viewed as anything more than first aid. For its effect is merely to cover up, at the time of crisis, the extent of the financial adjustment which she will perforce be obliged to make to the paltry pension to which she will subsequently be entitled.

Another aspect of dependency deserves notice, namely the situation of the widower. For, with all its limitations, protection as a dependant is usually available only to the widow, whereas the widower is left either with no rights at all or with rights that are subject to stringent conditions (i.e. proven dependency, disablement or the like). This may be looked upon as discrimination against the husband, which it undoubtedly is: but it clearly stems from discrimination inherent in the pensions earned by women. Canada recently eradicated this form of discrimination from its Pension Plan.

As in the case of the widower, so in that of surviving children: benefits under pension insurance may be refused when the pension is earned by a woman worker.

71

Deficiencies in social security affecting women are not limited to old age but are to be found in most if not all contingencies. An example is provided by long-term disablement. Here again, there is substantial discrimination against married women who are supposedly protected by virtue of being the dependants of their wage-earning husbands. Once more, the problem stems from the notion that the woman who works in her own home or in a family undertaking is not actively employed.

Thus a disabled housewife is not entitled to disablement benefits on the same conditions as a disabled worker. She is not entitled to benefits which have any relationship to her working capacity, although this factor may well be crucial within the home. No measurement is made of the extent of the loss in economic terms of the services and goods she normally provides, albeit without remuneration, nor of her potential for resuming full activity. Yet all of these are matters which are weighed and are significant in connection with disablement benefits for the gainfully employed.

To deny disablement benefits to a woman who works shoulder to shoulder with her husband in a family undertaking in the same circumstances as would give him full entitlement is both unjust and uneconomic. To deny to a housewife the same benefits provided to disabled workers, particularly the opportunities for rehabilitation and training which are built into long-term disability programmes, is equally unjust and uneconomic, for the loss to a family of the services of the disabled housewife may be as catastrophic as would be that of the earnings of the breadwinner.

Short-term contingencies

These then are some examples of the inferior status of women under social security programmes covering long-term contingencies. The treatment they receive under programmes covering short-term contingencies is just as discriminatory, particularly in so far as the levels of benefits are concerned.

Short-term contingencies in respect of which women are particularly vulnerable because of their characteristic pattern of employment are those of unemployment and sickness. Owing in no small part to the fact that working women do not yet consistently enjoy an uninterrupted work career, that full-time work is not always feasible for them and that, in all circumstances, their wages are low, the level of short-term benefits to which they may be entitled is also relatively low, if indeed they are entitled to any.

The status of women under unemployment insurance is a particularly sensitive one. For the very fact that a woman is married may even have the effect of depriving her of the benefits to which she would otherwise be entitled by virtue of her unemployment insurance contributions. The law does not operate in a vacuum; it takes effect through directives conceived and applied by administrators and embodying their particular interpretations of it. Married women who lose their jobs are often viewed as housewives, i.e. dependants, rather than as unemployed persons, and their entitlement to unemployment benefits may be questioned on those grounds.

Indeed, the reported unemployment rates for women workers are often understated having regard to other incontrovertible evidence of unemployment for the simple reason that many married women workers tend to " give up " on their legitimate claim to being unemployed out of a sense of frustration. Society has still not accepted the concept that a married woman worker is economically handicapped, in just the same way as a man, when her earnings have been cut off. Statistically, she reverts from the category of unemployed worker to that of housewife.

When a married woman worker applies for unemployment benefit, she may also face the problem of being required to produce special evidence of her bona fide status. A male applicant is rarely asked who is looking after his young children or whether his wife has a job. Yet a married woman may be refused unemployment benefit on the grounds that she is not legitimately available for employment since she has young children to care for at home or that her husband is employed.

In the case of cash sickness benefits, as in that of unemployment benefits, a woman worker is regarded as being in a different category from a man. Here again, it may be difficult for the administrator of the programme to accept as fact that a working wife's wage is as significant to family income as a working husband's, and its loss due to illness is rarely taken as seriously. Yet when the wife falls ill, the hardship to the family may in fact be greater since it loses not only her earnings but also her services within the home.

Where public cash sickness programmes are supplemented by private insurance, the inequities become even greater, for it is not unusual for private insurance companies to set premium levels for women far in excess of those for men, regardless of relevant morbidity data. The insurance industry claims that these differentials are based on experience, despite the fact that only a small percentage of their business relates to women workers and even this is limited to the selected few who have found the means of paying excessive premium rates or having them paid on their behalf.

Private cash sickness insurance often also provides only limited coverage of illness associated with pregnancy or confinement, or even excludes such illness from coverage entirely. Indeed, it was precisely to fill this gap that certain public programmes had to be developed.

The protection made available through social security in the event of maternity is still limited, however. It does not, for example, include income maintenance for a woman worker who because of pregnancy is obliged by law to leave an occupation deemed to be dangerous to her health or to that of her unborn child, or both. While international and national laws now prohibit the employment of a pregnant woman in certain such occupations, including those involving the risk of exposure to ionising radiations and to benzene, social security does not protect her from the consequent loss of earnings, which occurs long before the period for which income maintenance at the time of confinement is provided.

Some necessary reforms

Apart from the fact that, in coming years, certain aspects of social security will need to be revised—if for no other reason than that society itself is constantly evolving—a thoroughgoing revision of all aspects of social security as it exists today is obviously needed to ensure that one-half of the adult population in industrial societies is no longer deprived of the kind of protection that its designers intended to provide for all. For whether women are occupied as wage earners, or as unpaid workers in the home or the family undertaking, or in occupations commonly excluded from social security such as private domestic service and family undertakings, they must be assured precisely the same protection, without limitation or reservation due to whatever assumption, as are male wage earners or the self-employed.

It is no longer morally acceptable, under social security, to provide protection on a different basis to a woman who has been deserted by her husband and one who is separated from him; to discriminate between a divorced woman and a widow; to differentiate between a middle-aged and an aged widow; to ignore a former wife, depriving her of the protection afforded to her successor; to cut off from health benefits a woman who is no longer even a dependant because she is deserted, separated or divorced; nor, in fact, to treat all " dependent " wives as a class and in a manner that recognises no distinctions in their real status.

One solution which might well be considered by social planners is that of eliminating completely the concept of dependency as applied to the marriage partner who is not gainfully employed. Such an approach would conform more closely to the growing acceptance of man and wife as socially and economically equal partners and would eradicate many of the anomalies which have grown up throughout the system. There are few who would argue against such an approach if a solution could be found to the problem of financing social security thus redesigned.

Social security had its roots in the need for protection against loss of earnings. At the time when systems were developing, the breadwinner was generally the man, and his wife and family depended entirely on him for financial support. Subsequently, the concept of family responsibility, including responsibility for survivors and, along with it, the principle of dependency, were woven into the fabric of social security. When women entered the labour force and themselves became wage earners, the old attitude that regarded the wife as a dependant—only a secondary bread-winner as it were—continued to colour social security programmes. From this arose such anomalies as the working wife's old-age insurance contribution not encompassing any survivors' pensions or the working wife's contribution to health insurance excluding her family.

The present problem is to devise a just system of social security which will apply equally to gainfully employed women and those working in the home and in family undertakings without financial gain. For the fact remains that all women work, in spite of the prevalent and long-standing social view that a woman who carries out all her own domestic tasks is not a woman who works. The irony of this state of affairs is that the goods and services she produces are reckoned to be of economic value when produced under an employment contract but of no economic value when produced under a marriage contract.

If the value of goods and services produced by housewives in the home could be assigned an imputed economic value and a corresponding contribution paid to social insurance, then the major obstacle to the inclusion of the vast majority of women in wage-related social insurance as independent persons instead of dependants would have been removed. Stated in these simplistic terms, it would appear that the answer could be found. But the problem of how to measure unpaid domestic services in the home is not an easy one; nor is it a new one, for it has been examined by economists for decades in connection with the calculation of the national product.

The classical and initially accepted criterion for measuring the value of services produced by a nation was that the value of services which people render to themselves and their families should be excluded from the reckoning. Among these services, of course, was unpaid housework.

Unpaid housework was not the only activity to be excluded by the application of this criterion. However, in other cases of a similar nature, it was subsequently agreed that exceptions would have to be made; for, though the measuring rod of money was not literally applicable to them, the value of the production involved could not be overlooked. For example, in the case of farmers who consume some of their own produce, and real estate dealers who occupy some of their own lodgings, economists conceded that it was possible to impute a monetary value to the goods or services involved and thus to include them in the national product. Clearly, therefore, the original principle of totally excluding the value of services which people render to themselves has not been adhered to in all circumstances. Nevertheless, it continues to be applied to housework as well as to other unpaid services carried out by women in family undertakings.

For the economists grappling with this problem, the main difficulty appears to be that of measuring the volume of production and assessing its value.

75

Although the precise extent of unpaid domestic services in industrialised countries is not known, it is obvious from such estimates as have been made, particularly where these have been based on the market price of equivalent paid domestic services, that they represent a substantial percentage of national income. Even if estimates were to be based on a purely arbitrary figure below the market rate, they would probably still represent a significant percentage of national income. But whatever method were to be used, a clear distinction would have to be drawn between activities related to the maintenance of the home and those that are merely part of the general business of living, the latter, of course, being excluded from the calculation.

The search for an economic measure of the value of goods and services produced by the housewife without remuneration is an important condition for the inclusion of women who are not gainfully employed outside the home, or who are employed without remuneration in family undertakings, within the scope of earnings-related social security. Closely connected is the problem of how to redefine the notion of " active labour force " so as to include such women. The present definition, limited as it is to remunerated labour, excludes millions of women who work and produce without wages, a state of affairs without parallel in the case of men who work.

The International Labour Office itself, in its *Year book of labour statistics*, states that—

the activity rates for females are frequently not comparable internationally, since in many countries relatively large numbers of women assist on farms or in other family enterprises without pay, and there are differences from one country to another in the criteria adopted for determining the extent to which such workers are to be counted among the economically active.

This cautionary note raises the issue succinctly, for it illustrates the lack of consistency in statistical methods when faced with the incontrovertible fact that innumerable women perform productive work without wages. It appears, therefore, that social justice as well as statistical and economic good sense would be served by revision of the present definition of the active labour force so as to include people who produce goods and services, be it with or without remuneration.

Such a redefinition would have repercussions beyond the field of social security. But it would make it possible to bring these unpaid workers within the scope of wage-related social security, thus eliminating one of its major discriminatory aspects.

There remains the problem of financing: for how can unpaid workers make a contribution to social security analogous to that derived from the remuneration of wage earners?

It should not be beyond the wit of social planners to work out a means of achieving this that would be both economically feasible and politically acceptable. A variety of possible solutions might be examined in the light of individual national programmes, including such devices as the use of preferential income tax arrangements, special allocations within a family allowance system in the case of mothers who are not gainfully employed, or government contributions instead of individual contributions, to mention only a few.

It will obviously not be easy to provide independent protection within the framework of social security for women who do not receive a wage for their productive work. From the possible financing methods suggested above, it is equally obvious that patching up traditional wage-related systems is not necessarily the best way of going about it. For while it is possible to impute a wage and to broaden the concept of active labour force and, by these means, to bring under the protective umbrella of wage-related systems women who work as housewives, partners in family enterprises, farmers and others, better and less cumbersome solutions have been shown to exist. The development of social security universally available to all, providing uniform benefits, seems capable of achieving precisely those objectives so difficult to achieve under wage-related programmes.

There is little question that the greatest measure of justice for women within the present framework of social security is to be found in public programmes that are not related to earnings and are not designed primarily for those considered to be members of the active labour force as defined by international consensus. Where old-age and disability pensions are provided to all at uniform rates; where health care is provided on equal terms to all, regardless of employment status; where family allowances are based on family size only and are payable to the mother; in such a system, social security protection of women becomes a reality. For, in these circumstances, the personal status of a woman has no material effect on her social security status. Single or married, separated or deserted, divorced or widowed, legal wife or common-law spouse, she is not subjected to the patchwork patterns of entitlement to which she is exposed as a dependant under wage-related plans.

The rapidly changing status of women in contemporary society lends a sense of urgency to the need for change in social security, so that legislation and programmes meet the circumstances of today instead of reflecting those of an era now rapidly retreating into history. Clearly the adoption of universal plans which provide uniform benefits would appear to offer the most satisfactory solution. But even the unsatisfactory aspects of wage-related plans are capable of remedy if the universal schemes are not acceptable. One way or another, however, the status of women in relation to social security must be assured, not on the basis of dependency, but with independent and equal entitlement and benefits.

(Bibliography overleaf)

BIBLIOGRAPHY

Ackley, Gardner: *Macroeconomic theory* (New York, Macmillan, 1961), pp. 55-56.

Bergmann, Barbara R., and Adelman, Irma: " The 1973 Report of the President's Council of Economic Advisers: the economic role of women ", in *American Economic Review* (Menasha (Wisconsin)), Sep. 1973, pp. 509-514.

Bowley, A. L.: " The definition of national income ", in *Economic Journal* (London), Mar. 1922, p. 3.

Clark, Colin: " The economics of house-work ", in *Bulletin of the Oxford University Institute of Statistics* (Oxford), May 1958, pp. 205-211.

Craig, Isabel, and Tomes, Igor: " Origins and activities of the ILO Committee of Social Security Experts ", in *International Social Security Review* (Geneva, International Social Security Association), No. 4, 1969, pp. 505-530.

Dernburg, Thomas F., and McDougall, Duncan M.: *Macro-economics* (New York, McGraw-Hill, 1960, revised 1963), pp. 34-35.

Franklin, Paula A.: " The disabled widow ", in *Social Security Bulletin* (Washington, US Department of Health, Education, and Welfare), Jan. 1975, pp. 20-27.

Gelber, Sylva M.: " The labor force, the GNP, and unpaid housekeeping service ", in *Labor Developments Abroad* (Washington, US Department of Labor), Aug. 1970, pp. 12-15.

ILO: *Equality of opportunity and treatment for women workers*, Report VIII, International Labour Conference, 60th Session, 1975 (Geneva, 1974).

— *The cost of social security*, Seventh International Inquiry, 1964-1966 (Geneva, 1972).

— *Year book of labour statistics, 1969* (Geneva, 1969), table 1.

International Social Security Association: *Women and social security*, Studies and Research No. 5 (Geneva, 1973).

Laroque, Pierre: "Women's rights and widows' pensions", appearing below.

Marshall, Alfred: *Principles of economics* (London, Macmillan, 8th ed., 1920).

Pigou, A. C.: *The economics of welfare* (London, Macmillan, 4th ed., 1932).

Rys, Vladimir: " Problems of social security planning in industrialised and developing countries ", in *International Social Security Review*, Nos. 2-3, 1974, pp. 314-346.

Shamseddine, Ahmad Hussein: " GNP imputations of the value of housewives' services ", in *Economic and Business Bulletin* (Philadelphia, Temple University), Summer 1968, pp. 52-61.

United Nations: *Report on international definition and measurement of standards and levels of living* (New York, 1954), pp. 21-22.

United States Senate, Committee on Labor and Public Welfare, Subcommittee on Health: *Medical care systems in industrialised countries: a study of some aspects*, prepared by the International Labor Organization, 93d Congress, 2d Session (Washington, US Government Printing Office, 1974).

US Department of Health, Education, and Welfare, Social Security Administration, Office of Research and Statistics: *Social security programs throughout the world, 1973* (Washington, US Government Printing Office, 1974), pp. vii-xxv.

— " Women and social security—study of the situation in five countries ", in *International Social Security Review*, Nos. 1-2, 1973, pp. 73-133.

Women's Rights and Widows' Pensions

Pierre LAROQUE [1]

T HE RULES governing widows' pensions under the legal systems of different countries depend on a combination of three factors.

The first is the place of woman in the family and in society. The need to assist a woman in the event of her husband's death is very widely recognised, but a corresponding need is much less often admitted for a widower. This is because a woman was regarded in the past as her husband's dependant and that attitude is still very common today.

The second factor relates to material difficulties created by the death of the head of the family. The dependent widow and children must receive sufficient benefit for their maintenance when there is no longer a breadwinner.

The third factor is connected with the wider question of old age. It is well known that the average life-span of a woman is longer in most countries than that of a man, and that a woman is generally younger than her husband. Thus many women survive their husbands. If a woman has had no paid occupation because she has devoted herself entirely to her home, or if she worked for too short a time or was too poorly paid to gain entitlement to an adequate retirement pension, the death of her husband may entail a considerable drop in her standard of living, or even total indigence, if she does not receive suitable benefit.

It is obvious that the first of these three factors is the most important, for it is because the wife is wholly or partly dependent on her husband during his life that she finds herself in a difficult situation when he dies. In a society where there was full legal and economic equality between the sexes and the wife shared in the same way and to the same extent as the husband in the expenses of the household the problem of widowhood would appear in a completely different light.

It would not of course be eliminated, for the death of a partner in a marriage always creates a great moral and material upheaval that any modern system of social security must seek to alleviate. The solutions would be different, however, depending on the prevailing conception of

---

[1] Chairman of the Social Section of the Council of State, France.

the relations between husband and wife and in particular on the role of the wife.

The existing systems of social security were conceived and developed in terms of the more or less tacitly accepted notion of the dependent position of women in the family. On the other hand, the present trend of thought in all modern countries is guided by the growing belief in equality between the sexes and by the suppression of discrimination between men and women. It may be asked, then, whether the time has not come to reconsider the principles governing widows' pension schemes.

The law as it stands

Provisions governing widows' pensions are as variable as national social security schemes. Moreover, within a single country the rules may vary according to the husband's occupation or the circumstances of his death. Any account of the situation is thus largely arbitrary. With this proviso, existing schemes can be very roughly grouped in accordance with the principal features described below.

Widows' pensions are one element of survivors' benefit. The same legislation covers the situation of the widow, orphans, and sometimes the parents or even less immediate relations who were dependent on the deceased. It is always a question of partially making up for the disappearance of the income derived from the activity of the head of the family. The widow is the most important of the survivors, but her situation is not fundamentally different from that of the others.

The question of survivors' rights, and so those of the widow, arises when the husband, on his death, was receiving an old-age pension or fulfilled the conditions entitling him to one. This is the normal case. The rules applying to survivors are then seen as an integral part of the old-age scheme, and the same legislation and institutions provide for old-age pensions and widows' pensions. The widow's pension is generally calculated in terms of the old-age pension that the husband was receiving or would have been entitled to at the date of his death. The widow has a right deriving from that of her husband, and it is sometimes said that she receives a " reversionary pension ".

It can happen, however, that the husband dies through illness or accident or is killed in a war before having qualified for an old-age pension. In such circumstances survivors' pensions may be provided for under legislation governing employment injury, war pension and general invalidity schemes. The amount to which the widow is entitled usually varies with the cause of her husband's death, generally being greater if death was due to an employment injury or service to the State, as in time of war, than if it was due to a non-employment injury. Here again the rate is mostly fixed in relation to the husband's earnings.

There is also considerable variety in the conditions governing the granting and maintenance of the pensions. These conditions are sometimes very generous: the widow receives the pension whatever her age and continues to draw it for the rest of her life. Sometimes, on the other hand, the pension is granted only if the widow is over a certain age or has young dependent children and then only for a limited period. Nearly always, the pension is stopped if the widow remarries.

All these rules, despite their differences, show how much the situation of the widow depends on that of her husband. Not only the conditions of entitlement but also the methods of calculating and paying the pension are governed by the constant concern to maintain the woman in a situation broadly corresponding to that which she would have had if she had continued to depend on her husband. The international labour Conventions concerning death of the breadwinner and employment injury or establishing minimum standards of social security naturally reflect the trends of national legislation.

It should be stressed that these approaches, though they are indicative of a turn of mind and social structures deeply rooted in the past, are often justified, or at least partly so, by the present preoccupations of the population concerned.

In the first place, all present-day social security systems aim at meeting the need for security of those who work for a living, and the worker, whether he is an employee or an independent worker, does not distinguish between his own and his family's security. He has no feeling of security if he has no guarantee that his wife and children will be shielded from want in the event of his death. This aspect of the need for security has become increasingly important in recent years. There are many contributory factors: the rise in the standard of living, the growing role of insurance, job instability due in particular to frequent transfers, and the weakening of the guarantees constituted in the past by mutual help within the family all make the risk of the breadwinner's death more threatening. The higher the occupational and social level, the more keenly this danger is felt. The great expansion of the services sector in relation to agriculture and industry constantly adds to the social groups that feel it most keenly, and insurance schemes for managers and executive staff accordingly attach special importance to the rights of survivors. The protection of widows thus remains a very topical question.

In the second place, the husband's death always causes a great upheaval in the life of the widow and it cannot fail to affect her standard of living. There must be compensation for the loss involved and this compensation is one of the natural objects of every social security scheme.

In the third place, it is often pointed out in support of a widow's rights that the contributions paid by the husband for his retirement are an absolute loss if he dies without being able to enjoy his right to a pension or when he has enjoyed it only for a short period. In the event of the husband's death, the widow's pension would be the normal return for his contributions.

These numerous considerations seem to provide a solid foundation for the rules that continue to govern the situation of widows in relation to social security legislation and institutions.

Grounds for criticism

It is no less true, however, that these rules seem today more and more open to question in so far as they are based on the idea of the woman's dependence on her husband and sanction an inequality between the sexes that appears less and less justified.

It is true that the dependent situation of the woman in the family is still widely accepted, but this attitude is becoming less common every day. Modern legislation on the family is increasingly positive in confirming the equality of the marriage partners in respect both of property rights and of relations with the children and succession rights. Increasing numbers of married women have a job, and national legislation and international instruments (such as the Equal Remuneration Convention, 1951 (No. 100), of the ILO and the European Social Charter) specify that women are entitled to the same pay as men not only for the same work but also for different work of equal value. The average earnings of women are certainly still lower than those of men, but progress in the education and vocational training of women and, once more, the expansion of the services sector, where female labour is dominant, are rapidly leading towards equality. It is becoming increasingly common for the earnings of a woman to be as high as those of her husband or even higher. A Swedish periodical, indeed, recently reported the case of a young couple who, realising that the earnings and career prospects of the wife were better than those of the husband, decided that she alone should go on with her job while he should devote himself entirely to the household and bringing up the children. Although this may be an exceptional and extreme case, the mere fact of its being possible shows the extent of the changes taking place.

While these changes reject all inequality between the sexes, no national legislation or international instrument yet places husband and wife on an equal footing in respect of survivors' rights. Whereas the notion of a widow's pension is generally accepted a widower's pension remains very exceptional and, when provision is made for it at all, it is confined to invalid widowers who were dependent on their wives. This discrepancy—another based on the idea of the wife's natural dependence on her husband—is becoming less and less justified and cannot be maintained much longer.

The very notions that seemed to provide a modern basis for the traditional widows' pension schemes do not stand up to serious examination.

The need for security, which underlies all social security schemes, is, to say the least of it, quite as much a family as an individual need. No individual can feel himself secure if he knows that those dependent on him live in uncertainty of the future and may be thrown into indigence by his death. Nothing can be called social security today that does not provide protection for survivors and at the same time protection for the spouse and dependent children against sickness. Once husband and wife can both have a job, moreover, it is impossible to understand why widow and widower should be treated differently. A married woman receiving higher pay than her husband is just as much concerned about his insecurity in the event of her death as a husband is about the insecurity of his wife if he should leave her widowed.

As to the loss for which the pension provides some compensation, that suffered by the man whose wife dies is often as great as, if not greater than, that suffered by the woman who becomes a widow. This is so not only because the earnings of the wife can be as much as, or more than, those of the husband but also because the part played by the woman in running the home and bringing up the children is an essential element in the standard of living of the household in addition to the financial contribution resulting from her occupation. On the other hand, the death of the husband, though it naturally results in an upheaval of her daily life, may cause the widow no long-term financial loss. In such circumstances the pension, if it is payable without limit of time, cannot be justified in terms of compensation for a loss suffered.

The argument, so often used, about contributions having been paid, though it has a considerable psychological effect, is the result of confused thinking. It would be valid only if the pension were, as it is too often thought to be, a reimbursement of the funded value of the contributions received from the insured person throughout his active life. This is obviously not the case. Even under a funded system, once the funding is collective and not individual, the contributions paid are calculated in terms of the pensions to be granted and on the basis of mortality tables. A scheme that provides for widows' pensions thus calls for higher contributions than one that does not. In neither event, however, are the pensions a reimbursement of the contributions paid, which are determined not individually but in such a way as to meet each year a liability assessed by actuarial calculation. This is all the truer under a pay-as-you-go system: the contributions received each year are immediately used to pay what is due on current pensions. They are an expression of the solidarity of active and contributing workers with retired persons. If a worker dies without being able to receive the pension that his contributions would have entitled him to, this does not in itself entitle his widow to claim that the contributions he has paid should be restored to her in the form of a pension.

If the problem of widows' rights is to be clearly understood, the last traces of the old idea of individual insurance that still linger must be removed. We must look resolutely to the future and reason in terms of family and social changes that are gradually eliminating what is left of inequality between the sexes and the notion of dependence of a woman on her husband.

Outline of a system of widows' financial rights

The rights to be accorded widows must be defined not on the basis of theoretical or legal considerations deriving from the marital status they have lost but on that of the needs resulting from widowhood. Investigations have already been carried out in this connection, particularly in the Federal Republic of Germany, but they have not yet led to changes in legislation.[1]

The normal goal is to maintain for the widow a standard of living comparable to that which she enjoyed while her husband was alive—in other words to compensate for the cessation of his earnings.

For the sake of simplicity the question of supporting children in the home will be left aside. It will be assumed that their maintenance is covered by family allowances or orphans' pensions or allowances and that it does not affect the widow's standard of living.

Necessity of temporary aid

At the beginning widowhood involves a complete upheaval of the conditions of the household. The husband's contribution disappears but family expenditure does not go down correspondingly. The house or flat remains the same, for a time at least, and the general expenses of running it continue without reduction. Nor is this all, for additional expenses may arise through the frequently great changes that have to be made in the surviving spouse's way of living. These happen, moreover, at a time when the psychological and spiritual distress of the survivors makes them particularly painful. Time is always needed for the widow to adapt her living conditions to the new situation.

To face its material consequences she requires temporary assistance. Under present legislation this often takes the form of a lump sum, which may be paid at a flat rate or on the basis of the last earnings of the deceased (for example, three months' or a year's earnings). Such a lump

---

[1] For the various possibilities that have been considered in the Federal Republic of Germany see, for example, the article by Horst Fenge on widows' pensions and the reform of social security for women in *Soziale Arbeit*, No. 2, 1970, pp. 49-59.

sum is generally provided not just for the benefit of a widow but more broadly for that of the closest dependants at the time of death, including a widower, children, parents, and even less immediate relations.

Accordingly a grant of this type, to which a widow has a natural entitlement, implies no dependence of the wife on the husband and fully respects the rights of women.

The widow's chances of maintaining a suitable standard of living

When this critical period is over the question is how to enable the widow to maintain an appropriate standard of living. Let us consider, first of all, the case of a widow who has not reached the age entitling her to an old-age pension, where the problem is to ensure the maintenance not of an elderly person but of a person young enough to have a job.

The responses offered by the legislation in force range from refusal to provide the widow with any kind of aid to provision of an income enabling her to achieve a standard of living which is sometimes higher than that of the household before the breadwinner's death. The variety of responses is due to historical circumstances and the unequal strength of the pressure groups influencing public opinion and the public authorities. It seldom follows any logical pattern.

Separate consideration must be accorded legislation based on a more or less confused notion of responsibility towards the widow whose husband has died as a result of activities carried out in the interests of the community—whether through employment injury, active military service, or an injury or illness otherwise due to war. The grants and allowances provided for in such circumstances are based less on concern to maintain the widow's standard of living than on the notion of compensating her for an exceptional burden that the community has placed on her, and they reflect at least in part a collective responsibility derived from equality in the face of public duty. It may seem legitimate that the benefit accorded, which is intended to compensate both material loss and moral prejudice—in fact the total upheaval in the woman's way of life—should sometimes place her in a more favourable situation than she was in while her husband was living.

Setting aside these special cases to concentrate strictly on the question of maintaining a widow's standard of living, the principle must be that a woman who is of an age to have a job should normally ensure her livelihood in this way. There are, however, several variants.

The first is that of the widow who before her husband's death already had a job which enabled her to contribute to the resources of the household and who goes on with her job, or of the widow who, although she had no job while her husband was alive, finds paid work within a reasonable time as a result of previously acquired vocational training. If

Women Workers and Society

her earnings allow her to maintain a standard of living comparable to that which she enjoyed before, there is no reason to pay her any pension or allowance at all—unless, of course, there are dependent children whom she has to maintain and educate. Once the critical period immediately following her husband's death is over, a widow in this situation is not very differently placed from an unmarried woman.

It may be, however, that the widow has not had a job while her husband was alive, and that she lacks the vocational training that would enable her to find one. It is then legitimate, and even necessary, to provide her with maintenance during the period of readaptation, on the condition that this period is actually devoted to efforts to acquire training and a paid activity. For this purpose a temporary pension or allowance should be paid to the woman for a year or two.

In either of the cases just considered it is quite possible, of course, that the widow's job, whether obtained immediately following the death of her husband or after a period of readaptation, will not provide her with sufficient income to maintain the standard of living she enjoyed when her husband was alive. This happens whenever the husband's earnings were greater than the wife's, either because his qualifications were higher or because women are often paid at a lower rate than men. This problem is difficult to solve, for there is no obvious reason why a widow should be treated more generously than an unmarried woman. Furthermore, if there is compensation for the drop in the standard of living of a widow, a widower whose occupational earnings are lower than those of his wife should also, though the situation is much less common, be compensated for the drop in his standard of living due to his wife's having died before him.

It follows then, from the independence of women and equality of the sexes, that, subject once again to relief of the burden due to the existence of dependent children, a woman who is of a suitable age to have a job and who is helped to resume her occupation or to find a new one must earn her living from it and so ensure her personal independence. Where readaptation is difficult the widow's income should be ensured through the machinery for helping the unemployed.

Widows' old-age pensions

This personal independence must also be an element in the situation of the woman who becomes a widow at an age that normally gives entitlement to an old-age pension.

The essential problem here is to get away from any notion of a right attached to widowhood as such, of a reversionary pension, of a woman's right being based on that of her husband, and so to eliminate as far as possible the principle of a woman's dependence on her husband. A woman, like a man, should in all circumstances have a personal right to an old-age

86

pension. This is achieved in legislation under which all, without distinction of sex, are entitled to an old-age pension at a certain age and is true of the basic pensions of the Scandinavian countries. Broadly speaking, however, old-age pension schemes, when establishing the right to the pension and the starting date and amount, take into consideration the period during which the person concerned has had a job, the period during which he has paid contributions and the earnings on which the contributions have been based. A woman can receive a pension of a satisfactory amount in her own right only if the time she has spent on bringing up her children and running her home can be counted on her behalf as well as the time she has been able to devote to a job. It is all the more reasonable that this should be done as the bringing up of children and the running of a home are essential tasks which, if not directly recompensed in money, contribute no less substantially to the economic development and the welfare of the community in general.

The following factors should thus be taken into account in establishing a woman's right to a pension and in calculating the amount: *(a)* the years during which she has had a job (this presents no problem); *(b)* the years she has devoted in her home to bringing up her young children (no contribution should be demanded, but she might be regarded as having received, during the corresponding periods, fictitious remuneration equal to a fraction, perhaps half, of her husband's earnings); *(c)* the years she has devoted to her home in the absence of young children (here a contribution should be required, and it might be calculated on the basis of a fraction, perhaps half, of the earnings of her husband, who would be expected to pay it).

In this way a woman would be entitled to an old-age pension at the normal age on the grounds of her own activity, both domestic and occupational and irrespective of the death or survival of her husband. The very idea of a widow's pension would disappear.

Nevertheless this would not solve all the problems of creating a perfect social security scheme.

One outstanding problem is that of a married woman without an occupation who on becoming a widow is too young to be entitled to an old-age pension but too old to hope to take up or resume a job. Without prejudice to the possibility of unemployment assistance, the right to an early pension should be accorded her, for she is in circumstances that would justify a lowering of the age of entitlement to an old-age pension.

The most serious problem occurs when the old-age pension granted a woman under the terms outlined above is too small to ensure for her a standard of living corresponding to that which she enjoyed while her husband was alive. The earnings of husband and wife are often very unequal and the pensions they are entitled to are thus also likely to be very unequal. For the present at any rate it is generally the earnings of the woman that are lower, and a widow reduced to her own pension and nothing else finds that her standard of living has dropped, perhaps considerably. The same situation can arise if the woman's pension is based wholly or partly on the years spent in her home, and this solution is out of keeping with the concern for security that underlies the relevant legislation.

The answer to this problem might be found in insisting on the family nature of the standard of living that is to be maintained and deciding that when the husband or wife dies the survivor's old-age pension would never be less than half the amount of the old-age pensions they were receiving or would have been entitled to receive together. This rule would naturally apply irrespective of sex, and so to the pension of the man who becomes a widower as much as to that of the woman who becomes a widow, though in fact it is the woman who would generally benefit from it. This would show clearly that a woman's independence of her husband by no means excludes family solidarity but that this is understood as implying relations of complete equality between the partners.

In short it would seem that current trends as regards women's rights must normally lead to the disappearance of widows' pensions. If the notion of widowhood retains a social sense this can only be based on respect for the equality of husband and wife, of widower and widow, and strictly confined to situations where widowhood gives rise to special needs, in other words, first during the critical period immediately following the death of the spouse, secondly where there is need of early entitlement to an old-age pension, and thirdly where the widow's or widower's old-age pension has to be increased because it is less than half the amount of the two pensions taken together.

* * *

The ideas expressed here may cause some surprise. It is certain that they depart widely from present trends of thought. It is also certain that to give effect to them would call for long periods of study and longer periods of transition. But it is precisely because of this that they call for urgent consideration. Ideas change so fast today that we are seldom abreast of economic and social realities. The transformations required by changing ideas must be worked out in advance if legislation and institutions are not to become quickly out of date and the essential reforms are not to be overtaken by events even before they can be put into effect.

Equality of Remuneration for Men and Women in the Member States of the EEC

Evelyne SULLEROT [1]

The meaning of equality of remuneration

BEFORE ASKING OURSELVES whether equality of remuneration exists or how it works, we have to be quite clear in our minds what the expression means. It is a curious fact that the institutions which do most to shape public opinion have never attempted this task of definition. Public opinion is of course very much preoccupied at present with the idea of " equal pay for equal work ": the new feminist movements have adopted it as a slogan and women everywhere are determined that the principle shall be respected. In Europe their demands are very forthrightly expressed and it is gratifying to see that the slow mobilisation of opinion which began after the Second World War has progressed steadily. Women are now mindful of their rights and quick to claim them. However, this does not mean that they are always well informed. For example, there is much misunderstanding regarding the expression " equal pay for equal work " itself. We must therefore endeavour to define both the term *equal work* and the term *equal pay*.

A definition of equal work

The ILO Equal Remuneration Convention, 1951 (No. 100), refers to " work of equal value ", whereas the Treaty of Rome, by which the European Economic Community was established, refers to " equal work " (Article 119). However, neither gives a precise definition of the term. The Treaty of Rome merely provides that piece-work is to be remunerated on the basis of the same unit of measurement and that pay for time-rated work must be the same for the same job.

---

[1] Sociologist and member of the Economic and Social Council, France. The present article is largely based on a paper prepared for the Meeting of Experts on Equality of Remuneration convened in Geneva by the ILO in May 1974.

The public is not much enlightened by journalists who sometimes compare the remuneration received by men and women working in the same industry, for example banking or insurance or textiles, without reference to differences in skills, seniority or the jobs performed, or compare men and women workers in large categories possessing some common attribute, e.g. all men and women manual workers or all male and female executive staff, again without taking into account differences of industry, skill level, seniority or hours worked per week.

These comparisons are certainly not very valuable as proof of the application or non-application of Article 119, even if they give an idea (however difficult to interpret) of the position of women in the workforce, concentrated as they are among the lower paid.

The only clarifications of this very vague notion of equal work have been provided by jurisprudence, at least in Italy and the Federal Republic of Germany. It appears that:

— when men and women are employed on time-rated work it is not admissible to pay a reduced wage to women on the grounds of their lower output, because remuneration by the hour or week is based not on the result obtained but on the period of time during which the company commands the services of the worker; and

— the notion of equal work cannot be made subject to the economic equivalence of the work done but must be defined by reference to scientific job-evaluation criteria.[1]

In other words it is the jobs performed and not the results obtained which may justify equality of remuneration. Moreover, the fact that social legislation may make female labour more expensive than male labour must not have any bearing on the matter.

Generally speaking, the narrowest approach is that adopted by the Benelux countries, which regard as equal only jobs actually performed by both men and women, while the broadest is that of the trade unions, which calculate the average male and female earnings in a given industry. Both approaches are open to criticism. Jobs done by men and women alike can be taken over entirely by the latter, whereupon it can be claimed that they are not comparable with men's jobs and can be paid at a lower rate. On the other hand, to look at the average pay of men and women as such runs the risk of emphasising differentials which may have nothing to do with sex. As has been jokingly pointed out, one can always find wage differences between groups of workers, for example the fair-haired may not earn the same as the dark-haired or the brown-eyed the same as the blue-eyed, but this does not mean that the differences are due to the colour of the hair or of the eyes.

---

[1] See Commission of the European Communities: *Report of the Commission to the Council on the application of the principle of equal pay for men and women: situation on 31 December 1972* (Brussels, doc. SEC(73) 3000 final, 18 July 1973), p. 12.

To sum up, then, it may be said that in spite of the slightly different wording in the Rome Treaty the EEC has arrived at a broad interpretation of " equal work " more or less the same as that of ILO Convention No. 100.

A definition of equal pay

On this point Article 119 of the Rome Treaty is more explicit. It reads: " ' Pay ' means the ordinary basic or minimum wage or salary and any other consideration, whether in cash or in kind, which the worker receives, directly or indirectly, in respect of his employment from his employer."

However, the words " any other consideration . . . which the worker receives . . . indirectly " have caused problems. The question has arisen whether certain social benefits provided under a welfare system can be regarded as such considerations. For example, although there is no discrimination in the pensions systems of most of the EEC countries, they do not appear to serve women as effectively as men in the Netherlands. A survey in that country showed that, as of 1 January 1969, women were excluded from 25 per cent of the pension funds of the undertakings examined and that in other funds, even where their remuneration was identical, they could hope to draw only 89.6 per cent of the pension received by men. Before the United Kingdom entered the EEC, pensions there were lower for women because of their longer life expectancy even if they had made the same contributions throughout their working life.

On 25 May 1971, however, in Case 80/70, the Court of Justice of the European Communities ruled that no reference could be made to social security (and pensions) systems in applying Article 119 of the Rome Treaty. The only systems or benefits falling under the provisions of the Article were those negotiated within the undertaking or industry concerned. Thus no benefits resulting from the general social security system can be taken into account in applying Article 119 because they are not the subject of collective bargaining. On the other hand, everything discussed and agreed during such negotiations can be included. In practice, the remuneration counting for these purposes is that fixed by the collective agreement, whether based on time or piece rates.

The principle of non-discrimination must obviously apply to the statutory minimum wage (resolution of the Conference of Member States of 30 December 1961). In this respect, the principle of equality of the sexes is respected in all member countries where a minimum wage is provided for by legislation (i.e. France, Luxembourg and the Netherlands). No exception is possible in France. In Luxembourg the same rates have applied to men and women since 1963. In the Netherlands the College of State Mediators first laid down that men and women doing the same job under the same conditions in the same undertaking should

the same minimum wage. The Act of 27 November 1968 [1], which
nto force on 23 February 1969, replaced these provisions by one
shing a single minimum wage rate applicable to all workers except
those under 24 years of age, 65 or over, or working not more than a third
of the normal working hours. In this connection it should be noted that
women workers under 24 form a much larger proportion of the female
labour force (almost 60 per cent) than do men under 24 of the male
labour force (less than 25 per cent). The last remaining exemptions,
which had been granted in respect of certain jobs carried out exclusively
by women, were cancelled in 1972.

Notwithstanding the above, the information generally published on
remuneration according to sex is not strictly comparable. Sometimes the
figures relate to gross hourly earnings, in which case no allowance is
made for working hours, overtime or bonuses. Sometimes, mainly in the
United Kingdom, they relate to weekly earnings and take the number of
hours worked into account. And at other times, especially in the case of
workers in the tertiary sector, they relate to monthly earnings, sometimes
gross, sometimes net.

It goes without saying that comparisons based on these data are
meaningful only for each particular case and in the light of the definitions
given to the term remuneration; no conclusion whatsoever can be drawn
from a comparison of these different situations. For example, an OECD
working paper [2] attempts a synoptic review of female earnings as a
percentage of male earnings in various countries (Australia, Belgium,
Canada, Denmark, Finland, France, Japan, Sweden and the United
States), but the basis of calculation varies from case to case:

— average weekly pay of full-time employees over 21 years of age;

— average annual pay of workers in private industry;

— average hourly pay in certain occupations;

— average hourly pay in industry;

— average monthly pay of full-time workers (unspecified sector);

— average annual pay (unspecified sector);

— average hourly pay (unspecified sector).

These data are obviously so disparate that they cannot be compared. The
calculations are based sometimes on gross and sometimes on net income;
the reference period is sometimes hourly, sometimes weekly, sometimes
monthly and sometimes annual; in some cases the categories of worker
compared are imprecise; some are limited to industry, some to white-
collar workers, and so on.

---

[1] See ILO: *Legislative Series*, 1968—Neth. 1.

[2] OECD: *The role of women in the economy* (Paris, doc. MS/S/73.3, 16 Nov. 1973),
table 23, p. 61.

The comparisons published by the press or broadcast on television without any details or indication of source only create confusion in the public mind. This confusion is magnified by the fact that each pressure group seizes on only those figures which best support its claims.

Statistical data on wages in EEC member countries

Standardising the data

While it is difficult enough to define the field of application for the principle of equal pay, even greater difficulties arise in attempting to standardise the data for a group of countries with very different social backgrounds in order to permit study and comparison of the extent to which the principle is applied. It is to the credit of the Statistical Office of the European Communities (SOEC) that it makes such attempts and also carries out standardised wage surveys every six years. The results of the most recent surveys have not yet been published and if complete data are required it is necessary to turn to those of 1966.

The methods used in these standardised surveys reflect the complexity of the problem: some examples of the efforts made to clarify the situation are given below.

MANUAL WORKERS

Excluded from this category are foremen, gang leaders performing supervisory duties, apprentices (even if engaged in production work), male or female family workers and homeworkers. Manual workers are classified according to three skill levels.

Skilled workers are all those who, by virtue of their specialised knowledge and abilities, do jobs which are considered more difficult, diversified or responsible than usual. Such skills may have been acquired by training leading to a diploma, apprenticeship, long service, etc. It will be seen that this category must differ considerably from one industry to another and from one country to another, and that it in fact embraces a wide range of skill levels.

Semi-skilled workers are those employed on specialised but less difficult, repetitive tasks involving less responsibility and not requiring diversified occupational skills. They normally acquire their knowledge and the necessary abilities in a few months and are sometimes referred to in collective agreements as production workers.

Unskilled workers are those employed on simple tasks not calling for any special training. They are often referred to as labourers or mates.

SALARIED AND SIMILAR WORKERS

It is even more difficult to define clearly and in generally applicable terms this huge mass of workers (including many women) who have nothing in common except the fact that they receive a salary and possess a written employment contract. The 1966 wage survey covered only manual workers in industry. The 1972 survey, the results of which are still being analysed, covered both manual workers and white-collar staff in industry. The latter were found to be so disparate that it was necessary to divide them into six categories even after excluding apprentices, family workers, homeworkers and top management.[1] These categories were:

— senior executives with general responsibilities;
— planning personnel;
— junior executives;
— lower-grade white-collar staff;
— supervisors in charge of a large group or several groups of workers;
— supervisors in charge of a small group of workers.

The definition of " monthly salary " has also given rise to many difficulties because it is important that these surveys should be comparable and that they should throw sufficient light on the earnings of persons paid on a monthly basis to permit the inclusion in 1978 of salaried employees in the tertiary sector (wholesale and retail trades, banks and insurance companies). Despite the years which have elapsed, the methods used in the 1966 study continue to be of interest as regards:

— the representation in graph form of the differences between men's and women's wages;
— the efforts made to refine the approach to the problem of sexual discrimination by successively eliminating the factors which falsify comparisons, i.e. by ascertaining the earnings of men and women in comparable age groups, with similar skills and seniority in particular industries;
— the representation in graph form of male and female earnings differentials according to skill level.

Some results of the survey

MALE AND FEMALE EARNINGS

For each country included in the accompanying graphs the gross hourly earnings received in industry are shown along the abscissa and the percentage of men and women in each pay group is shown on the ordinate. It will be observed that:

— in all countries the curve for women is distinctly farther to the left than that for men, showing that most women receive the lowest pay;

---

[1] For more detailed information on these six categories, see *Questionnaire et les notes explicatives pour l'enquête sur la structure et la répartition des salaires* (SOEC, doc. 2511/71f, Oct. 1972).

PAY RATES OF MEN AND WOMEN, ALL INDUSTRIES

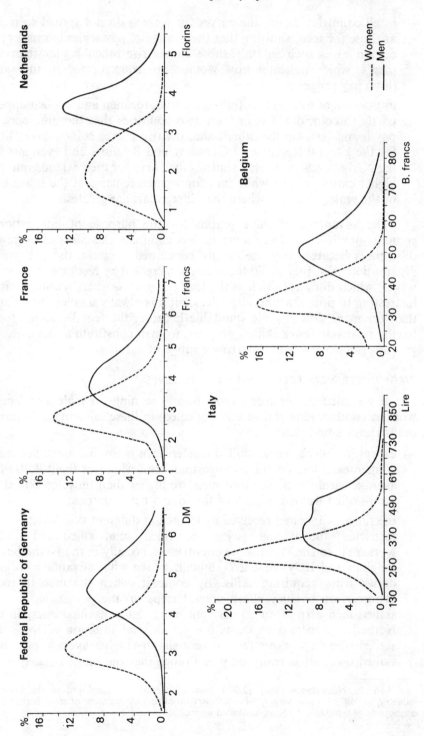

— in all countries, again, the curves for women do not spread so much as those for men, showing that their range of pay scales is smaller; in certain cases such as Italy these curves rise much higher than the men's, which indicates how women are concentrated in the same (low) pay range;

— in the case of France and Italy the curves for men and women appear partly to coincide; it is in these two countries that the difference in pay is smallest. On the other hand, the two curves coincide very little for the Federal Republic of Germany and Belgium, and even less for the Netherlands: in these countries the curve for men extends into the higher earnings zone while that for women remains at the lower end of the scale, so this is where the differentials are greatest.

The advantage of these graphs for the purpose of international comparisons is clear. They more or less eliminate the effect of currency differences because they are chiefly concerned to show the pattern of distribution. And they avoid the distortion created by recourse to average wages, which does not disclose the true range of workers' earnings. It is interesting to note that the wage dispersion is always smaller for women than for men. This is understandable because, the female labour force having relatively fewer skilled workers, women constitute a more homogeneous population with a narrower range of earnings.

WAGE DIFFERENCES ACCORDING TO SKILL LEVEL

If we calculate the mean gross hourly earnings of male and female workers (skilled, semi-skilled and unskilled) in these same manufacturing industries, we find that:

— except in France, where skilled women earn more than unskilled men, women earn less on the average than men whatever their skills: the average earnings of unskilled men are higher than those of skilled or semi-skilled women in each of the four other countries;

— the range of incomes received by women at different skill levels is very restricted; the average pay of unskilled, semi-skilled and skilled workers is so similar in some countries (especially in the Netherlands, Belgium and Italy) that it is difficult to see what advantage women derive from acquiring skills. By contrast, when the men in these countries do so they climb several steps up the pay scale, so that skilled men earn 20 to 30 per cent more than unskilled ones. In the Netherlands there even exists the paradoxical situation whereby unskilled women workers receive very slightly higher average pay than skilled ones.[1] It is really only in France that the range is fairly wide

---

[1] In the Netherlands many skilled women workers are employed in the clothing industry, which pays low wages, whereas electronics, a new industry offering higher pay, employs large numbers of young, unskilled women.

and that it appears worth while for a woman to acquire skills, though the range is still much wider for men. A direct consequence is that the pay differences according to sex are much greater in the case of skilled workers than in that of unskilled, as can be seen from table 1.

TABLE 1. WOMEN'S EARNINGS AS A PERCENTAGE OF MEN'S BY SKILL LEVEL

(All manufacturing industries)

Skill level	Belgium	France	Germany (Fed. Rep.)	Italy	Netherlands
Skilled	66.8	74.2	73.2	70.6	59.9
Semi-skilled	71.3	80.6	74.4	76.0	60.1
Unskilled	75.0	84.4	78.2	90.9	68.7

Source: Commission des CE: *Rapport de la Commission au Conseil sur l'état d'application au 31 décembre 1968 du principe d'égalité entre rémunérations masculines et féminines* (Brussels, doc. SEC (70)2338 final, 18 June 1970), Ch. II, pp. 8-9.

AN EXAMPLE: THE TEXTILE INDUSTRY

In some industries which employ both male and female labour (clothing, textiles and food) efforts have been made to carry the analysis further.

In the textile industry, for example, which employs more women than men in Italy (65.8 per cent), in the Federal Republic of Germany (59.6 per cent) and in France (56.9 per cent) a little less than half as many in Belgium (45.2 per cent) and relatively few in the Netherlands (27.9 per cent), the composition of the female labour force is closer to that of the male than in the manufacturing industries as a whole (there are more semi-skilled and skilled women, except in the Federal Republic of Germany). The differences in pay are smaller than in the manufacturing industries as a whole (see table 2).

TABLE 2. WOMEN'S EARNINGS AS A PERCENTAGE OF MEN'S IN THE TEXTILE INDUSTRY

Belgium	France	Germany (Fed. Rep.)	Italy	Netherlands
75.2	83.0	79.5	80.8	61.5

Source: As for table 1, Ch. II, p. 12.

Once again, however, the differentials are greatest at the highest skill level, as can be seen from table 3.

TABLE 3. EARNINGS OF WOMEN TEXTILE WORKERS AS A PERCENTAGE OF MEN'S
BY SKILL LEVEL

Skill level	Belgium	France	Germany (Fed. Rep.)	Italy	Netherlands
Skilled	72.5	80.3	84.3	78.0	63.4
Semi-skilled	76.5	87.3	86.2	83.5	64.8
Unskilled	81.3	90.2	84.8	86.6	69.7

Source: As for table 1, Ch. II, p. 13.

If we adjusted for differences in skills, seniority (in general, men have longer service) and age (women are mostly either very young or, if middle-aged, have little seniority, as they have only recently resumed work), we would find that the wage differentials between men and women are very much reduced or even non-existent. They are to a large extent structural in nature. If we knew precisely to what extent, we should be able to determine whether there really is a differential due to sex, independent of these other factors, and if so how large it is. The amount of calculation required for this purpose would be enormous, however. It would be necessary to study at least the hourly earnings, country by country, for men and women workers (i) of the same age, (ii) with the same skills, (iii) with the same seniority, (iv) paid on the same basis, (v) working in the same branch of industry, and (vi) in undertakings of comparable size. Despite the approximate nature of some of the definitions used, we should then be in a better position to estimate the effect of the sex factor. In practice, however, if we applied only four of these six criteria to different industries, we should need over 6,000 tables per country!

It is for this reason that only one attempt has been made, using the textile industry and taking into account only age groups, approximate seniority and three levels of skill. The pay differentials were then found to be much narrower, but the samples used for the calculations very soon become too limited in a survey of this type.

In addition, a complete survey was carried out in the cotton-spinning industry for the occupation of winder (men and women), taking all the other criteria together (age, seniority, etc.). This disclosed much smaller differentials, the women's earnings being 99.7 per cent of the men's in France, 92.6 per cent in the Federal Republic of Germany, 87.8 per cent in Italy, 82.7 per cent in Belgium, and 75.7 per cent in the Netherlands.

Equality of remuneration in national legislation

The original time limit established for implementation of the principle of equal pay in the EEC member States was very short (equality had to be achieved by 31 December 1962). Looking back, this may have been naively optimistic, but it turned out to be useful inasmuch as it encouraged rapid action in at least two fields, namely:

— elimination of discrimination in respect of statutory minimum wages; and

— the revision of collective agreements to eliminate different job classifications for men and women.

A new time-table divided into three phases (30 June 1962, 30 June 1963 and 31 December 1964) was then drawn up. As complete equality still did not seem to have been achieved in any country, the Commission subsequently requested governments, employers and unions on several occasions to complete a detailed questionnaire on the progress made, as well as launching the SOEC surveys mentioned earlier.

At the outset France, the Federal Republic of Germany, Italy and Luxembourg possessed legal instruments which, although inadequate, guaranteed women workers equal rights, while Belgium and the Netherlands still had no general legal standards for women workers. Let us take a brief glance at each case in turn.

In Belgium there were no relevant texts until 1967. The Royal Order of 24 October 1967 [1], which was repealed by the Act of 16 March 1971 [2], provided that " any female employee shall be entitled to institute legal proceedings in the competent court to demand the application of the principle of equal pay for equal work ". In addition, trade unions can also take legal action to defend the rights of their members, even against the latter's wishes.

In France the principle of equal pay for equal work was established by the measures adopted in 1945 to fix wage rates and again in 1950 at the time of the return to freely negotiated rates, and also by the wording of collective agreements. Nevertheless, appeal was difficult and the preamble of the Constitution seemed to be inadequate as a legal instrument. On 22 December 1972 a new Act [3] was passed which clarifies the notion of equal remuneration, establishes a clear legal basis for appeals to the courts and provides for enforcement. Any stipulation in wage regulations or a collective agreement that violates the principle of equality is thus rendered void. An order issued by the Council of State on 27 March 1973 lays down the procedure to be followed and establishes

---

[1] ILO: *Legislative Series*, 1967—Bel. 4.

[2] Ibid., 1971—Bel. 2.

[3] Ibid., 1972—Fr. 3.

the penalties applicable to employers who violate the principle of equality. These penalties are sufficient to act as an effective deterrent. The establishment in June 1974 of a Secretariat of State for Women's Affairs responsible directly to the Prime Minister has made it possible to go more deeply into individual cases and to speed up official procedures.

In the Federal Republic of Germany the Constitution of 1949 provides that men and women have equal rights. The new Works Constitution Act [1], which came into force on 19 January 1972, reiterated the ban on discrimination and automatically rendered void all agreements which introduced such discrimination.

In Italy article 37 of the Constitution of 1948 provides that women shall have the same rights and, for equal work, the same pay as men. This provision gives a subjective right to equality of pay which can be invoked in legal proceedings. In addition, specific provisions exist for civil servants and certain other occupational groups. In 1973 the Chamber of Deputies passed a law regulating home work, a type of employment often used to evade the equal pay obligation. Under this law, home work has to be paid at the rates laid down for piece-work in the relevant collective agreements. If there are none, the rates are to be fixed by a regional joint commission or the director of the regional labour office. Violations of this law are punishable with heavy fines.

In Luxembourg all agreements have had to comply with the principle of equality since the Act of 12 June 1945 came into force. The Act of 23 June 1963 reaffirmed the ban on discrimination as regards public service personnel. However, it appears to be difficult for women workers not covered by a collective agreement to uphold their legal rights. In 1973 draft regulations were prepared by the Government to fill such gaps in the legislation. In the Netherlands no general legal provisions or regulations have been adopted. Consequently, the right to equal pay can be obtained only through collective agreements or the contract of employment. The Netherlands ratified Convention No. 100 in 1972 and the Social and Economic Council was asked to advise on the manner in which the principle of equality could best be guaranteed. The response (in 1973) was a unanimous recommendation of legislative action, which should make it possible to institute legal proceedings when all other means have failed.

As matters stand, the public authorities of these countries can declare void all agreements containing discriminatory provisions, with the exception of the Netherlands, where collective agreements which do not respect the equal pay principle have been made binding *erga omnes*.

In the Federal Republic of Germany and the Netherlands no legal provision is made for administrative inspection. In Italy the labour inspectorate has only a supervisory role; in Belgium penal sanctions are

---

[1] ILO: *Legislative Series*, 1972—Ger.F.R. 1.

laid down for failure to observe collective agreements; in France and Luxembourg the labour inspectorate is responsible for checking the implementation of the principle of equality (but the trade unions have complained that there are not enough labour inspectors).

In the three new member States of the EEC efforts have also been made to apply Article 119 of the Rome Treaty.

In Denmark single scales were established for time rates and piece rates in the national joint agreement of 28 March 1973. The hourly rate has been increased for jobs performed solely by unskilled women, and a joint commission is to be set up which will replace the present sliding-scale system.

In Ireland a national agreement reached in 1972 provided for a reduction in the differences between men's and women's wages and on 3 July 1973 the Government presented a Bill to Parliament on equal pay for men and women.

In the United Kingdom the Equal Pay Act of 1970 [1] provides for equality of remuneration by the end of 1975. The existing differences had to be reduced by a third in 1973; however, although the Equal Pay Act authorised the Secretary of State for Employment to bring the remuneration of women workers up to 90 per cent of comparable remuneration for men by the end of 1973, the Government stated in January 1973 that it did not not intend to take such action.

Generally speaking, the differences in the remuneration of men and women are larger in the three new member countries than in the six old ones.

Difficulties encountered in reducing inequality

Collective agreements

While it is essential for women workers to be protected individually by legislation, the protection afforded by collective agreements is also indispensable. However, a number of situations can arise which account for the slowness of progress in this field. Let us consider three of these.

(1) Women workers in certain occupations or regions are not covered by collective agreements at all. This situation was still very frequent in 1968, especially in branches employing a high proportion of women, such as brewing, retailing and domestic service. By the end of 1972 the situation had improved and was approximately as follows:

— in the Federal Republic of Germany between 500,000 and 1 million workers (men and women) were not covered by collective agreements;

— in France there were cases of non-coverage in retailing, in mixed and stock farming in 13 départements, and in the liberal professions;

---

[1] ILO: *Legislative Series*, 1970—UK 1.

101

— in Italy there were gaps in the coverage of craftsmen, domestic servants, etc.;

— in Belgium it was thought that the number of women workers not covered by agreements was very small;

— in the Netherlands the situation was less satisfactory, 20-25 per cent of wage earners not being covered by collective agreements;

— in Luxembourg there were gaps in the food and timber sectors.

Replies on this point have not yet been received from the new member States.

(2) Some collective agreements do not guarantee non-discrimination between men and women as regards wages. If the Commission's report on the application of the principle of equal pay presented in July 1973 recommends employers and trade unions to include in all collective agreements a clause indicating practical ways of applying the principle of equal pay and a procedure for the settlement of any difficulties [1], it is because many agreements still do not cover this point.

(3) Some agreements still specify different pay rates for women and men, either for time-rated work or for piece-work, but their number has decreased to the point where there are now very few left. In Belgium, however, there remain wage differences of about 5 per cent in a few industries employing less than 1,000 women, while in the Netherlands there is still discrimination in collective agreements covering bakeries, ready-made clothing, ceramics, footwear, textiles and laundries. As for the new member countries, discriminatory clauses existed in some British and Irish agreements at the time the Community was enlarged. The " social report " now being prepared will show what has happened since. At all events married women, who were previously not eligible for employment in the Irish civil service, have been admitted since 1 July 1973.

Job classification

Within the various trades and occupations—and sometimes even within the terms of collective agreements—provision is made for a system of job classification which may indirectly introduce discrimination against women.

Certain jobs (nursing, welfare work, etc.) tend to be reserved for women. It may be wondered whether there is anything intrinsically feminine about such jobs, or whether the fact that people think so is not just due to custom. The report on the application of Article 119 published in 1970 contained statements by the Federal German Government, which considered work in the food and clothing industries and in commerce to

---

[1] *Report of the Commission . . . 31 December 1972*, op. cit., p. 42.

be more suitable for women " in view of their physical constitution ".[1]
We may ask ourselves whether this suggestion is really relevant. In
making the same point with reference to agricultural work carried out
solely by women (e.g. the harvesting of jasmine and olives), the Italian
Government refers more correctly to tradition.[2] The Netherlands Government appears to support this viewpoint when it refers to the " well-
known " predominance of women workers in certain specified occupations.[3]

In the Federal Republic of Germany, in particular, the separation of
work into " light " and " heavy " categories has made it possible insidiously to re-establish discrimination without referring to women. It
has even been referred to as the " horizontal " method of discrimination;
the " vertical " method consisting of creating categories with rates of
remuneration lower than those of labourers and which, by definition, are
reserved for women.

There is a tendency to consider that, since muscular strength is not
required for " light work ", there is no need to assess the difficulty of the
work in terms of the speed at which it is done or the special dexterity or
knowledge required. Since 1969 the Federal German Government and
the two sides of industry have had an agreement to try to find a way of
solving this problem. There is, for example, talk of eliminating the light
work category in the chemical industry in 1975. However, it is still widely
employed. In France it does not exist and the criteria used in job
classification include accuracy, dexterity and speed. However, the trade
unions point out that the concentration of women in certain workshops
makes it impossible to compare their performance directly with that of
men workers, and that the subdivision of women's jobs combined with
the link between pay and output results in a sort of " dequalification ".

In Italy four categories were originally established for men and three
for women, who were excluded from the upper category. An agreement
was reached to change this state of affairs, and since the end of 1964 there
have been five categories without distinction of sex for both white-collar
and manual workers. In 1972 further progress was made towards a single
classification system more favourable to women.

In the Netherlands minimum wage provisions applicable to all have
made it possible to identify jobs described as " non-mixed ". At the
end of 1971 a survey of 50,000 undertakings showed that 24,000 men and
60,000 women were paid at or below the minimum rate. This proportion
of women is remarkable in a country where few women work.

In Italy home work has been the most generalised form of indirect
discrimination. According to some estimates, this kind of employment,

---

[1] *Rapport de la Commission... au 31 décembre 1968*, op. cit., Ch. I, p. 37.
[2] Ibid., p. 83.
[3] Ibid., p. 108.

which is constantly increasing, affects 1½ million workers, 75 per cent of whom are women. The vast majority of them are considered self-employed, but are in fact disguised wage earners. Various draft laws have been presented to Parliament with a view to improving this situation.

Progress and its limits

In preceding sections of this article we have seen that there has been constant progress as regards both legislation and the practical results achieved. It is an important fact that the differences between the remuneration of men and women workers in EEC member States have continually decreased, especially in the countries where they were formerly largest. Between 1960 and 1966, the year in which the wage survey took place, progress was considerable.

However, some differentials still remain and it is disturbing to note that they have decreased very little in the country where they were smallest to start with, namely France. France made the inclusion of Article 119 a condition of signing the Treaty of Rome. Although humanitarian principles were also invoked, the French demand seems to have been inspired mainly by the fact that the country's competitive capacity was diminished because, unlike its neighbours, it did not underpay women workers. The Treaty instituted a means of combating sex-based discrimination with regard to pay in the six EEC countries, and this certainly produced results. However, although in countries where differentials of 30-40 per cent had existed these were reduced to 10-15 per cent, there was no spectacular improvement in France, where the original differentials were of the order of 10 per cent. It was as though once the differences in discrimination had been reduced, the EEC countries were settling for a situation in which they would continue to practise discrimination on a uniform if more modest scale. This state of affairs, which I denounced in 1971 [1], has since been improved by various legislative measures. The public has also become more conscious of the problem, and the trade unions, which in the early phases were not particularly active in this field, no doubt because there were few women in the union hierarchy, are now adopting a more determined stand.

Nevertheless, despite steady progress, there remain significant wage differentials, by no means all of which are due to sex-based discrimination. Let us consider some of the main causes for their continued existence. These fall into two main groups, the objective causes and those based on prejudice, defensive attitudes and tradition. The latter are very difficult to combat.

---

[1] Commission of the European Communities: *The employment of women and the problems it raises in the Member States of the European Community*, Report by Evelyne Sullerot (Luxembourg, Office for Official Publications of the European Communities).

Objective causes

These are related to the specific role and needs of women. Proportionally speaking, there are far more young women and girls at work than there are young men and youths. Many of them stop work either upon getting married or when the first or second child is born, or for other reasons. The first consequence of this is that women have less seniority, which is an important factor in remuneration and promotion. It also means that they are less skilled. As a rule, few women manage to reach the higher skill grades. There are all sorts of reasons for this, for example inadequate career guidance and the lesser interest their families and the State take in their vocational training.

Much more often than men women work in small enterprises, whereas pay is generally better in firms with a larger labour force. This happens because, with an eye to their household and family tasks, they tend to seek work near home.

A further point which affects the figures for those paid on a monthly basis is that women—again because of their family obligations—work fewer hours than men. For all workers together, the difference ranges from six to ten hours per week according to country.

Finally and perhaps most important, women are not equally distributed among the various branches of economic activity but tend to be concentrated in a small number of trades and occupations.

All these factors have an effect on pay, although one cannot really speak of sexual discrimination. Out of 76 complaints made by women workers to the Secretariat of State for Women's Affairs in France alleging sexual discrimination with respect to pay, for example, only one proved to be well-founded and was followed up. In all the other cases the employee who supposed herself to be discriminated against either did not have the same qualifications or seniority as her male colleagues or else did not work the same number of hours or carry out the same tasks.

Many of these characteristics of female employment stem from a state of affairs which one may regret but which is sometimes freely chosen by the women themselves—and therefore difficult to change.

Sexual prejudices and defensive attitudes

If there is such a thing as " women's jobs ", ranging from the clothing industry to typing, it is simply because a long tradition pushes young girls who could do something else into these occupations. This situation suits both their employers, who can group them together and underpay them, and their families, who keep parroting the old saw that while waiting to find a husband a girl should choose a " truly feminine " occupation " which will be useful to her later ". Even though this attitude is rapidly changing, its effects are still felt. Moreover, women themselves have a real taste for certain types of work (e.g. paramedical professions, social work, making clothes and teaching) and a certain indifference or even antipathy for others such as building and metalworking trades and technology generally. It is difficult to decide how far such inclinations are the product of education and tradition. Although these latter must have a major influence, this does not make it any easier to initiate change without coercive measures. Yet it cannot be denied that the feminisation of jobs is the prime cause of pay differentials. Mixed jobs are always relatively better paid than those carried out mainly or entirely by women, while those which are exclusively done by men are better paid still.

Sexual prejudice comes into play at the time of recruitment, especially if a post of responsibility or a job usually done by men is to be filled. In all EEC countries but especially those suffering from underemployment there is a tendency to employ the man when a man and a woman with equal qualifications are in competition. Finding employment is even more difficult for mothers of families, especially if their children are young.

Sexual prejudice also affects promotion. Upgrading, recycling and training courses are offered more rarely to women than men, even if they have the same legal entitlement. In workshops proficiency tests to obtain a higher skill grading are often offered to men only, and employers would be embarrassed if a woman applied even though entitled to do so.

The protection given to women workers also makes it more difficult for them to obtain employment and promotion. Employers sometimes hesitate to take on a worker who has to be granted long periods of maternity leave, flexible or reduced working hours, exemption from night work, etc. This conflict between necessary protection and equally necessary freedom is one of the more delicate aspects of the position of women in the labour force.

Fears inspired by the economic situation

It must be remembered that in addition to the above reasons for the persistence of earnings differentials between men and women, which are more or less independent of economic conditions, a difficult employment situation always has more serious effects on a vulnerable group such as women workers. In Italy, for example, the position of women homeworkers—who are in fact " dequalified " and unprotected wage earners—has deteriorated because the market is sluggish and men are given priority in recruitment.

If we are to judge by the tragic example of the 1929-34 depression, a serious economic crisis would have a disastrous effect on the pay of women. At that time the minimum wages legislation in the United States, for example, excluded those doing " light work ", and therefore deprived most women of protection against the collapse of pay rates. The most deplorable practices were observed. We need guarantees that the existing machinery is sufficient to prevent another such collapse in the event of a crisis, otherwise the progress so far achieved will be seriously compromised. It is to be hoped that the existence of Article 119 and the measures to which it has given rise represent the beginning of an irreversible process.

The future

Action needed on behalf of women

It will not be easy to eliminate the differences between the earnings of men and women which stem from a certain life-style on the part of the latter, for the good reason that it is difficult to determine how far women's choices are deliberate and how far dictated by tradition. If they interrupt their careers to bring up children, work a shorter week, take supposedly suitable jobs, find employment in small firms, are satisfied with lower qualifications and build up less seniority than their male counterparts, then clearly all this will have an effect on their pay packets. Is there anything to be done about it?

With the best will in the world one could hardly oblige women to choose different jobs, work longer hours, seek employment in larger firms, and so on. Thus the only solution is to operate indirectly by trying to change the factors which lead women to behave contrary to their career interests. For example, much could be done by providing effective and inexpensive social facilities to lighten their household duties, or by improving and diversifying their vocational guidance and training.

Here we shall do no more than mention recurrent education and training, since they are not the subject of this article. Nevertheless, it should be pointed out that France and the Federal Republic of Germany now make recurrent training available to all wage earners. This is particularly valuable for women whose family life often leads them to cease work or change jobs, perhaps to follow their husbands. However, there are still very few women who undergo such training, and in France little is done to retrain women who wish to return to work.

Finally, more information should be made available to women to teach them how to look for work and analyse employment contracts, to publicise the existence and content of collective agreements (the women workers they protect rarely know much about them) and to explain how to combat discrimination.

Current action

As noted above, there has been progress in equal pay legislation but certain countries still have an effort to make in this direction. Moreover, studies still need to be carried out everywhere with a view to defining jobs

107

and pay scales more precisely. To this end the EEC's "Article 119 Special Group" requested a number of independent consultants to conduct job classification studies which uncovered cases of indirect discrimination. The conclusions of these studies have been used in preparing a memorandum to be discussed by the Group, whose mandate is to watch over the implementation of the equal pay principle. Following these discussions a memorandum serving as a basis for proposals to eliminate such indirect discrimination will be sent to the trade union organisations. The Commission's ad hoc Committee on Women's Problems is following the progress of this research very closely.

* * *

In the specific field of wage discrimination on grounds of sex the EEC member States have achieved steady and remarkable progress. The provisions of Article 119 have been gradually embodied in national legislation, showing that when a group of countries are confronted by an egalitarian text they can react in a spirit of constant mutual emulation.

Nevertheless the problem is not yet solved, and everywhere in Western Europe (as in Eastern Europe and the United States) the typical qualities of women—especially dexterity and a flair for human contacts—are not remunerated as they should be. It may be that post-industrial society, which will make less and less use of physical strength and create more employment in the tertiary sector, will be more favourable for women than the industrial society has been, but this improvement may well be limited.

An economic crisis would no doubt partly compromise the results already achieved, but attitudes have nevertheless evolved and it is possible that the move towards equality of remuneration will continue even under difficult conditions. In any case, it calls for a concerted effort by governments and social partners (employers and trade unions). The existence of the EEC machinery has made possible some very important surveys (which will be repeated), the formation of working groups, and the preparation of reports which have spurred on progress and co-ordination. The results have been sufficiently encouraging to spur on further efforts.

For all these reasons the EEC Commission, faced with an employment crisis which bids fair to last a long time, considered it a matter of importance to send member States two important directives concerning women workers.

The first [1] concerns approximation of the legislation of member States with regard to the principle of equal pay. Member States are

---

[1] Directive dated 27 January 1975 (doc. R/243/75 (soc 14)).

requested to ensure that all forms of discrimination are eliminated or excluded from job classification systems; to introduce procedures whereby women workers who consider themselves victims of discrimination can assert their rights; to repeal or declare void all legislation, regulations, contracts or administrative practices contrary to the principle of equality of remuneration; and to give adequate publicity to existing and future measures relating to application of the directive. They have one year in which to comply and must convey all relevant information to the Commission within two years so that the latter can report to the Council.

The second directive [1] is still more important inasmuch as it goes further, seeking to establish true equality of treatment between male and female workers with respect to access to employment, training and promotion, and working conditions. This lengthy document sets out the present position and the many different measures which need to be taken in the fields of recruiting, access to employment, promotion, upgrading of jobs in feminised sectors, regional development planning, raising the age limits for entering certain jobs, teaching, vocational training, guidance and further vocational training for the reintegration of women after interruptions in their careers, grants, accommodation for girls and women under training, educational leave, flexible working hours, crèches, care and assistance in the home, social security, and so on. Indeed, the Council considers that equality of remuneration is " only one element of equality between men and women at work ", and that it would be desirable for the other elements, namely working conditions, social security, dismissal procedures and access to employment, training and promotion, to be the subject of a similar legal instrument.

The Commission recognises that the recent economic crisis has changed the situation and that other problems have arisen which may weaken the will to achieve equality. Nevertheless it affirms: " . . . the urgency of the problem of equal treatment in employment persists. In spite of the economic difficulties a beginning should be made towards its resolution without delay."

The fact that these texts should have been produced despite the anxiety caused by the employment crisis in the EEC member countries, and that they should be at once more specific and wider in scope than those dealing solely with equal remuneration, is highly significant. After a long period of semi-indifference, the aspirations and awareness of women, both individually and collectively, have begun to burgeon even more rapidly than the undeniable improvements in their situation on the employment market. The Council thinks that their claims will prevail even at a time of economic difficulty and is determined to give a lead. Only the future will show whether the impetus thus given to the move-

---

[1] Directive dated 12 February 1975 (doc. COM(75) 36 final).

ment for sexual equality will be speeded up or held back when it comes to implementation in the individual member States. The answer lies with the governments and social partners of the nine countries in question—but also with a new partner, namely feminine public opinion.

———————

Women's Wages in Japan and the Question of Equal Pay

Nobuko TAKAHASHI [1]

I N 1967 Japan, as a Member of the International Labour Organisation, ratified the ILO's Equal Remuneration Convention, 1951 (No. 100). The purpose of this article is to describe the content of Japanese legislation relating to the principle of equal pay for men and women (section II), the impact of the Japanese system of employment and remuneration on the application of the principle (section III) and some of the existing differences between men's and women's earnings (section IV). It closes with some remarks on the measures required to approach the still distant target of equal pay (section V). We start, however, with a brief note on the historical antecedents of Japanese legislation on the question of equal pay.

I. Historical background

Prior to the Meiji Revolution of 1868 Japan was a preponderantly agricultural country. Women's employment was confined almost exclusively to work on the land and to cottage industries. Practically the only other jobs open to women were as domestic servants, barmaids and entertainers.

By the end of the nineteenth century Japan had developed a large-scale system of factory production, especially in the textile industries, which employed large numbers of women and girls. A movement to protect factory women and children had been initiated as early as in 1882; but it was not until three decades later that it culminated in legislation. This was the Factory Act of 28 March 1911 [2], which prescribed, inter alia,

---

[1] Commissioner of the Japanese Labour Insurance Appeal Committee, and former Director-General, Women's and Minors' Bureau, Ministry of Labour, Tokyo.

[2] See *Bulletin of the International Labour Office* (Basle, International Association for Labour Legislation), Vol. VI, No. 3, 1911, pp. 267-270. A consolidated English version of the Act of 1911 and of an amending Act No. 33 of 29 March 1923 is given in *Legislative Series* (Geneva, ILO), 1923—Jap. 1. For further amending Acts No. 21 of 27 March 1929 and No. 19 of 29 March 1935, see ibid., 1929—Jap. 1 and 1935—Jap. 3.

111

the minimum age of employment of young persons and the maximum hours of work for young persons and women.

By that time much progress had been made also in the provision of secondary and higher education for girls, many of whom took up non-manual and professional occupations as doctors, teachers, office clerks, telephone operators and shop assistants.

During the 1920s advocates of women's rights, including equal pay for men and women, made considerable headway; but, owing to the hostilities that lasted from 1931 to 1945, the principle of equal pay did not become embodied in legislation until after the Second World War.

II. Legislation for equal pay

It was in the Labour Standards Act of 1947 [1] that the principle of equal wages for men and women was first laid down in a legislative text. Echoing article 14 of Japan's new Constitution of 3 November 1946, which proclaims that " there shall be no discrimination in political, economic or social relations because of . . . sex ", section 4 of the Labour Standards Act prohibits employers from discriminating between men and women, to the disadvantage of women workers, in matters of wages. Employers violating this prohibition are liable to penalties (section 119).

In September 1947 the Labour Standards Bureau, which had been set up under the terms of section 97 of the Labour Standards Act, issued a " notice " explaining that the purpose of section 4 of the Act was to improve the social and economic status of women workers, which had generally been inferior to that of men under a feudalistic system of national economy, by abolishing wage discrimination against them.

The Labour Standards Act also provided for enforcement of its provisions by means of a network of inspectorates, including not only the central Labour Standards Bureau referred to above but also Labour Standards Offices and Labour Standards Inspection Offices in each prefecture. There are at present 350 Inspection Offices, staffed by 3,000 inspectors who visit employers' premises on a regular basis. In addition, workers can apply directly to the Labour Standards Inspection Offices for remedy of working conditions falling short of the standards laid down by the Act. Such an application is followed by an immediate visit of inspection to the enterprise concerned, which is then required to make whatever adjustments are found to be necessary.

Furthermore, the Women's and Minors' Bureau [2], which is responsible for the improvement of the conditions of work of women and

---

[1] Act No. 49 of 5 April 1947. An English text of the Act, reproduced from the English edition of the Japanese *Official Gazette*, is published in *Legislative Series*, 1947—Jap. 3.

[2] Both the Labour Standards Bureau and the Women's and Minors' Bureau were set up within the Ministry of Labour at the time of its establishment in September 1947.

minors and of the status of women, was assigned by the Labour Standards Act specific functions regarding the administration of the provisions of the Act relating to women and young persons—interpretation, co-operation with the inspectorate and investigation of premises. In that capacity, the Bureau is directly concerned with the application and promotion of the principle of equal pay for men and women.

In the notice issued in September 1947 to which reference was made above, the Labour Standards Bureau gave an interpretation of the meaning of " equal pay ". It declared that " differentiation of wages by reason of differences in individual efficiency shall not be unlawful but differentiation by reason of the efficiency of women workers being in general and on the average lower than that of male workers shall be unlawful ". The term " wages " means all the contractual payments including bonuses and allowances (section 11) and is furthermore interpreted as including the system of payment or method of calculation as shown by a notice issued by the Women's and Minors' Bureau in November 1950, which laid down that it was unlawful to use different systems of payment for female and male workers—for example, to pay women a daily wage and men a monthly salary in cases where a woman's job, efficiency, age, length of service, etc., were the same as a man's.

For some time after the adoption of the Labour Standards Act there were fairly frequent violations of the provision relating to equal pay. This was partly because employers had not yet grasped its implications and partly because, during a period of depression due to a war-ravaged national economy, they did not feel able to raise the level of women's wages. As the years went by, the Act came to be understood and accepted as a result of the Government's inspection activities and educational programmes and of the work of trade unions, as well as of an improvement in the national economy. There was a rapid shrinking in the number of cases of infringement. Since 1958 there have been only about ten cases a year.

All this does not mean, however, that the principle of equal pay is thoroughly observed in Japan, and that women workers have the happy impression that they are always equally paid. On the contrary, there is quite strong feeling among women workers that they are not fairly paid. The following paragraphs will explain the situation.

In individual Japanese establishments women's job titles are very often different from men's. Even when they are categorised under the same titles, the actual work is often different, though the difference may be very slight. This nominal difference in work accounts for the difference of wage. Consequently it is not unusual for the initial wages for a boy and a girl doing apparently the same work in a certain factory to differ because, for example, the size of the parts handled is not quite the same, or because the boy may occasionally carry something heavy or has greater responsibilities or expectations for the future. The disparity grows as the years go on and periodical wage rises are granted.

Further, the concept of " work of equal value " is not entirely familiar to Japanese society, where the peculiar " seniority wage system " prevails. This will be described in the following section. Under this system, the wage of an individual worker is largely decided by his personal characteristics, e.g. age, length of service, educational background and family situation, rather than by the content or quality of his work. The result is that women workers do not much mind being paid less than their male colleagues if they are younger or have a shorter period of service, less education or less family responsibility, even if they do the same work.

In this way wage disparities between men and women are widespread and accepted, though often unwillingly, by women workers. In one respect it might be said that the Japanese concept of " work of equal value " is very strict, for it requires exact sameness of work and personal situation; if a single element is different, the principle of equal pay may not be applicable. For example, in the above-mentioned notice of the Women's and Minors' Bureau issued in November 1950, it is precisely laid down that " it is unlawful to use a different system of payment—in cases where *a woman's job, hours of work, duty, efficiency, skills and knowledge, age, length of service, etc., are the same as a man's* ". This strictness in the interpretation of " work of equal value " may also account for the fact that violations of the law are very infrequent.

There are two other legislative texts bearing on the question of equal pay for men and women. One is the National Public Services Act No. 120 of 21 October 1947, which provides for " equal treatment of both sexes ". This requirement applies also to local public services.[1]

The other legislative text is the Working Women's Welfare Act No. 113 of 16 June 1972.[2] This Act, the purpose of which is to promote the welfare of working women and to improve their status, lays down the fundamental principle that women workers shall not suffer from any discriminatory treatment by reason of their being women. The Act applies to all establishments and is to be enforced by the Women's and Minors' Bureau of the Ministry of Labour.

III. Employment and wage practices in Japan

Japan's system of employment is marked by three characteristic features. One is that the worker commits himself to lifelong employment with a single employer. Another is that wages are based on length of service. The third feature is the system of enterprise unionism.

---

[1] Act No. 261 of 13 December 1950.
[2] See *Legislative Series*, 1972—Jap. 1.

This system of employment was investigated by a team of three Examiners [1] appointed by the Organisation for Economic Co-operation and Development (OECD), who visited Japan in November and December 1970. Most of the following brief description of the system is quoted from their report.[2]

(1) *Lifetime commitment.* As a rule, Japanese enterprises—at any rate the larger firms—recruit their workers straight from school or university, train them throughout their period of employment and keep them on their payrolls until the age of retirement. In other words,

the worker commits himself to lifetime employment with a single employer who endeavours to provide him with lifetime job security, subject to ordinary good behaviour, until compulsory retirement, usually at the age of 55. He is free to quit, but is unlikely to do so due to a combination of economic self-interest, psychological pressure, etc. As a result, there has been little inter-firm labour mobility in most of the modern sector, at least in big firms. . . . Mobility within the firm is in principle unlimited, virtually determined only by individual adaptability, although subject in large measure to the level of education on entry.

(2) *Seniority wage system.* In Japanese enterprises there is a prevailing practice of determining the individual worker's wage level mainly on the basis of length of service, regardless of his job content or job performance. The wage is usually raised at fixed intervals once or twice a year even though the worker's job content or his position in the firm may not have changed since his last wage increase. Seniority is not, however,

the only factor determining wage differentials in an enterprise. Persons with different educational backgrounds start at different levels, and the steepness of the seniority ladder is higher for those with higher education. Age as such is also a determining factor. . . . Promotion and some form of informal merit rating (but very seldom piece-rate incentives) also influence the . . . increases. Individual family responsibilities may also be taken into consideration.

(3) *Enterprise unionism.* The enterprise union " is the principal form that trade unionism has taken in the postwar years, displacing craft and industrial unionism of the prewar period ". Wages are determined by " collective bargaining . . . between the individual enterprise and the enterprise union ". Consequently, the wage level for a particular job in a particular industry can vary widely with the enterprise, higher wages being paid by larger enterprises with higher productivity and better organised unions. It is also arrangements reached by the two parties that determine a variety of fringe benefits, including severance pay, allowances of many kinds, housing accommodation, welfare facilities and recreation

---

[1] One from the Federal Republic of Germany's Ministry of Labour and Social Affairs, one from the United States Department of Labor and one from the OECD's secretariat.

[2] " Report by the Examiners " (especially pp. 98-100), in OECD: *Manpower policy in Japan* (Paris, 1973).

facilities, which can be summed up in the OECD Manpower and Social Affairs Committee's phrase " enterprise-based social policy ".[1]

Japan's practice of lifetime employment and the seniority wage system existed before the Second World War. It is said to have begun in government-operated factories and in the major private enterprises, which, as a result of the introduction of technology from abroad and because there was not enough trained labour to meet their needs, hired young unskilled workers and trained them within the enterprise into skilled workers, retaining them in their own firms and gradually raising their wages according to age and length of service. The practice spread widely because, in the social environment of prewar Japan, it was considered an effective means of ensuring workers' loyalty to the enterprise.[2]

After the Second World War this system of employment tended to become even more firmly entrenched. One reason was that the depression and the insufficiency of employment opportunities that followed the war caused workers, who were fearful of unemployment, to resist staff reductions and to demand from their employers lifetime security of tenure of their jobs. Another reason was that a decline in real wages in that period, by prompting demands for increases in money wages according to age to meet the different cost of living of the various age groups, led to a greatly accelerated development of the seniority wage system and enterprise unionism. Thus, " building upon certain prewar habits and tendencies ", Japan's employment system " is, in its more elaborate postwar form, a joint creation of employers and workers in special circumstances of the postwar period with a view to mutual benefits to employers and to the members of the enterprise unions ".[3]

Nevertheless, Japan's employment system has been undergoing some modifications in recent years in consequence of a shortage of labour and especially of young workers. Enterprises have had to raise the wages of young workers and have also begun to recruit some of their staff outside the ranks of school leavers and new graduates, with the result that present wage practice is " no longer purely automatic but is being gradually harmonised with the work performance or ability of the worker ".[4]

Before considering the effects on women workers of the employment and wage practices that have now been briefly described, there are two further aspects of the wage system that should be noted.

One is that wage levels vary widely—though diminishingly in recent years—both with the age of the worker (as is to be expected in view of the

---

[1] OECD, op. cit., p. 13.

[2] " Employment and wage practices ", annex to " Report by the Japanese authorities ", in OECD, op. cit., p. 87.

[3] General observations of OECD's Manpower and Social Affairs Committee on the Japanese employment system, in OECD, op. cit., p. 10.

[4] " Employment and wage practices ", op. cit., p. 89.

seniority wage system) and with the size of the enterprise. For example, in 1970 the average wage of boilermen aged 40-49 was 50 per cent higher than that of boilermen aged 20-24, while the wage of a boilerman in an undertaking employing 1,000 or more workers was on average 20 per cent higher than that of a boilerman of the same age in an undertaking employing only 10-99 workers.[1]

The other feature of the wage system is that the wage packet consists of a number of components. The basic portion of the individual wage is composed of (i) remuneration directly related to the demands of the work performed and (ii) remuneration based on personal factors such as the worker's age, length of service, experience and educational attainments. This basic wage is supplemented by a variety of allowances such as " duty " allowances (e.g. for extra responsibilities or special working conditions) and those for living costs (see table 1). The latter include family allowances, commuting allowances, regional allowances, housing allowances, allowances for children's education, etc.—all of which have little to do with the worker's actual job performance. The larger firms tend to provide many more and larger allowances. In 1972 family allowances were provided by 89.5 per cent of the firms employing 1,000 or more workers and by 64.2 per cent of those employing 30-99, with a ratio of two to one in favour of the larger firms in the average amount of allowance per worker.[2]

There are several respects in which Japanese employment and wage practices have unfavourable effects on the wages of women workers. In general, the turnover of women workers tends to be fairly high owing to interruptions by marriage and the raising of a family, so that a female worker may not stay long enough in a firm to obtain full advantage from rises in wages based on length of service. Moreover, in a firm where the male workers are supposed to commit themselves to lifelong service, a woman is likely to be regarded as a temporary, or stopgap, worker. Employers tend to be reluctant to give women an expensive training and hesitate to put them on the ladder of promotion leading to positions of responsibility, fearing that they may leave before they have, as it were, paid back the employers' investment in them. Thus a woman worker is likely to be assigned a simple job and, even if she eventually stays a longer time with the firm, to remain an auxiliary worker with comparatively little responsibility and a comparatively low wage.

Furthermore, as " the young are . . . ' cheaper ' than the old "[3] under the seniority system, employers will tend to encourage female workers to leave after a certain period of service and before the increases

---

[1] Ministry of Labour: *Basic survey of wage structure, 1970* (Tokyo, 1971) (Japanese only).

[2] Ministry of Labour: *General survey on wages and working hours system, 1972* (Tokyo, Sep. 1973) (Japanese only).

[3] " Report by the Examiners ", op. cit., p. 99.

TABLE 1. PERCENTAGE DISTRIBUTION OF COMPONENTS OF AVERAGE MONTHLY
CASH EARNINGS, SEPTEMBER 1971

(Enterprises with 30 or more employees)

Component of earnings	Percentage distribution	
Total earnings	100.0	
Regular earnings (excluding overtime)	89.8 = 100.0	
Basic wage	83.5	
Wage based on job-related factors		(27.2)
Wage based on personal factors		(15.4)
Wage based on a combination of factors		(40.9)
Incentive wage	5.0	
Duty allowances	3.8	
Allowances for living costs	6.0	
Attendance allowance	1.2	
Other allowances	0.5	
Overtime and miscellaneous irregular earnings	10.2	

Source: Ministry of Labour: *General survey on wages and working hours system*, op. cit.

in their wages deviate too far from the development of their work capacities. As this attitude is sometimes shared by the male workers, cases are occasionally reported of agreements for compulsory retirement of women workers at a very early age or on marriage.

The complex composition of the wage packet can also work to the detriment of women workers. It can lead to a lawful differentiation between a woman's and a man's wage by giving a woman worker a lower remuneration based on the personal factors referred to above and few allowances. The allowances for living costs, in particular, tend to widen the disparity, inasmuch as they are generally paid to heads of households.

There is thus no denying the fact that, in some respects, the Japanese employment and wage system has unfavourable effects on the wages of women workers.

IV. Earnings of women workers

The average earnings of women workers in Japan are only about half those of men, although the ratio is gradually rising. Thus, by 1972, the arithmetic mean of the total monthly cash earnings of women workers, expressed as a percentage of the corresponding earnings of male workers, had risen from 42.8 in 1960 to 50.2. In the case of contractual cash

TABLE 2. PERCENTAGE DISTRIBUTION OF MALE AND FEMALE EMPLOYEES BY
LEVEL OF EARNINGS, JUNE 1972

Earnings [1] ('000 yen)	Women	Men	Earnings [1] ('000 yen)	Women	Men
Under 20	1.38	0.05	70-80	2.90	12.67
20-25	3.22	0.13	80-90	1.68	12.32
25-30	6.28	0.32	90-100	0.84	10.93
30-35	10.37	0.76	100-120	0.85	15.00
35-40	13.76	1.51	120-140	0.39	7.83
40-45	16.64	2.82	140-160	0.20	3.63
45-50	15.68	4.14	160-180	0.12	1.75
50-60	18.72	11.30	180-200	0.06	0.85
60-70	6.67	12.55	200 +	0.11	1.29

[1] Monthly contractual cash earnings.

Source: Ministry of Labour: *Basic survey of wage structure, 1972* (Tokyo, June 1973) (Japanese only).

earnings [1] only, i.e. excluding special cash payments [2], the percentage rose from 43.5 in 1960 to 50.8 by 1972.[3]

Apart from the disparity in the average, there is a conspicuous difference in the pattern of distribution of men's and women's earnings. As shown in table 2, women's earnings are concentrated in the lower brackets, whereas men's range widely from the lower to the higher brackets. And while men's earnings show a remarkable rise with increase in age, women's remain at about the same level after the age of 30 (see table 3).

The wide disparity between women's and men's earnings is largely due, as in other countries, to a concentration of women in certain low-wage branches of manufacturing and in clerical jobs; but also to some extent to certain peculiar features of the Japanese wage system. The main factors accounting for the disparity may be considered under the following headings: (1) occupational distribution of men and women workers, (2) hours worked by men and women, (3) special characteristics of women workers, and (4) social attitudes to women's work.

[1] Earnings (including overtime payments) regularly paid every month on the basis of the conditions stipulated in the contract between employer and worker.

[2] Marriage allowance, end-of-year allowance, etc., as well as bonuses.

[3] Ministry of Labour: *Monthly Labour Survey* (Tokyo), Mar. 1961 and Nov. 1973 (Japanese only).

TABLE 3. AVERAGE EARNINGS BY AGE GROUP AND SEX, JUNE 1972

Age group	Average earnings [1] (yen)	
	Women	Men
Under 18	36 300	38 400
18-19	41 500	50 400
20-24	46 600	63 000
25-29	49 500	79 200
30-34	46 200	94 400
35-39	45 100	102 800
40-49	48 200	109 600
50-59	48 500	104 000
60 +	43 300	70 500
All age groups	46 200	88 200

[1] Monthly contractual cash earnings.

Source: Ministry of Labour: *Basic survey of wage structure, 1972*, op. cit.

Occupational distribution of men and women workers

Of the 11 million women who were in employment in 1970 (see table 4) rather more than half (52.2 per cent) were in white-collar jobs, about a third (34.0 per cent) in blue-collar jobs and about a seventh (13.8 per cent) in catering, domestic and other service occupations, the corresponding proportions of the 23 million men in employment being, respectively, two-fifths (41.8 per cent), rather over a half (52.4 per cent) and less than 3 per cent. Most of the female white-collar employees were clerical workers, only 2 per cent of them occupying managerial posts, whereas a fifth of the male white-collar employees were managers or officials. Of the female professional workers, more than a third were nurses, another third being teachers, especially in kindergartens and primary schools. On the other hand, more than a third of the male professional workers were technicians and engineers, while most of the men in the teaching profession were teachers in secondary schools and higher education institutions. As for the production workers, a majority of the female operatives were employed in light industries, whereas a large proportion of the male blue-collar workers were in heavy industries, half of them being, presumably, skilled workers.

These data reveal the concentration of women in low-paid jobs. Moreover, jobs as nurses, teachers in kindergartens, weavers and spinners, which are traditionally the preserve of women, tend to be given

TABLE 4. PERCENTAGE DISTRIBUTION OF MALE AND FEMALE EMPLOYEES BY
MAJOR OCCUPATIONAL GROUPS AND SELECTED OCCUPATIONS, 1970

Major occupational group or selected occupation	Males		Females	
Professional and technical workers	7.9		9.9	
Engineers and technicians		2.9		0.09
Nurses, midwives and crèche staff		0.02		3.9
Professors and teachers		2.7		3.4
Kindergarten teachers		(0.01)		(0.4)
Primary school teachers		(0.8)		(1.7)
Secondary school teachers		(0.7)		(0.5)
High school teachers		(0.8)		(0.4)
College and university professors		(0.3)		(0.1)
Managers and officials	8.4		0.8	
Clerical and related workers	15.9		30.7	
Sales workers	9.6		10.8	
Farmers, lumbermen and fishermen	1.6		0.8	
Workers in mining and quarrying	0.5		0.06	
Transport and communication workers	8.7		2.0	
Communication workers		0.6		1.4
Production workers	41.6		31.0	
Metalworkers		9.2		2.3
Machine workers		2.0		0.4
Electric machine assembly and repair workers		1.8		3.9
Transportation equipment workers		2.3		0.1
Silk reel and textile workers		0.9		4.8
Garment workers		0.4		3.9
Food and beverage workers		1.0		1.0
Construction workers		7.8		1.4
Labourers		4.0		3.8
Protective service workers	2.8		0.1	
Service workers	2.9		13.8	
Domestic service workers		—		1.0
Personal service workers		2.3		10.9
Total	100.0		100.0	
(In thousands)	22 760		10 920	

Note: The occupational breakdowns are not exhaustive.
Source: Prime Minister's Office: *Population census, 1970.*

121

comparatively low evaluations. Furthermore, a number of highly paid occupations in production and engineering works are monopolised by men because women are debarred from them by law.

Hours worked by men and women

Women work fewer hours than men largely because of statutory limitations on women's overtime work and night work. In 1972 women worked an average of 171.8 hours a month, including 6 hours of overtime, whereas men worked an average of 198.6 hours a month, including 19.4 hours of overtime.[1] As there is a legal obligation to pay 125 per cent for overtime and night work, the difference between men and women in the amount of overtime worked accounts for an appreciable proportion of the difference between men's and women's earnings.[2]

Special characteristics of women workers

Some of the characteristics of women workers have unfavourable effects on their earnings under the Japanese wage system. These include the following:

Age composition. In 1972 half the women workers were under the age of 30, the average age being 31.4, or 3.8 years younger than the male average.[3]

Length of service. In 1972 the average length of service of women workers in the same undertaking was 4.7 years, or 4.5 years less than that of men. The disparity was wider than in the case of age because of the higher turnover rate of women workers. In the 35-39 age group, for instance, women had only 5.8 years of service whereas men had 11.1 years, and in the 40-49 age group women had 7.3 years of service whereas men had 15.5 years.[3] This shows that most mature women are not eligible for the steep increases in wages enjoyed by mature male workers (see table 5).

Educational background. In 1971 the proportions of the total number of women workers who had had higher, secondary and primary education were, respectively, 10, 46 and 43 per cent, the corresponding figures for male workers being 18.5, 39.7 and 41.0 per cent.[4]

Size of establishment. A larger proportion of the total number of women workers than of male workers are employed in smaller enter-

---

[1] *Monthly Labour Survey*, op. cit., Nov. 1973.

[2] In September 1971 overtime payments accounted for 9.8 per cent of contractual cash earnings. See Ministry of Labour: *General survey on wages and working hours system*, op. cit.

[3] Ministry of Labour: *Basic survey of wage structure, 1972*, op. cit.

[4] Prime Minister's Office: *Employment Status Survey* (Tokyo, Mar. 1972).

TABLE 5. AVERAGE LENGTH OF SERVICE IN THE SAME
UNDERTAKING BY AGE GROUP AND SEX, 1972

Age group	Average length of service in years	
	Women	Men
Under 18	1.4	1.3
18-19	1.5	1.5
20-24	3.1	3.3
25-29	5.1	6.1
30-34	5.5	8.8
35-39	5.8	11.1
40-49	7.3	15.5
50-59	8.1	15.5
60 +	9.0	9.5

Source: Ministry of Labour: *Basic survey of wage structure, 1972*, op. cit.

prises. Thus, in 1972, 36 per cent of the female labour force but only 30 per cent of the male was employed in enterprises with 1-29 employees, whereas only 22.6 per cent of the women workers, compared with 28.5 per cent of the male workers, were employed in enterprises with 500 or more employees.[1]

Type of employment. A larger proportion of the total number of women workers than of male workers are non-regular, i.e. temporary workers and workers engaged on daily contracts, who, under the Japanese employment system, have a less stable status—and are paid less—than regular workers. Thus, in 1972, 94.3 per cent of all male workers were regular, whereas in the case of women the proportion was only 85.4 per cent.[1]

Household status. Except for widows and divorced women who are heads of families, women workers are seldom eligible for the allowances for living costs, such as family, housing and children's education allowances. In 1971 these allowances accounted for 4 per cent of regular contractual earnings.[2]

Social attitudes to women's work

Fundamentally, it is the attitude of society towards women's work that is responsible for women's earnings being lower than those of men.

[1] Prime Minister's Office: *Labour Force Survey, 1972. Annual report* (Tokyo, July 1973).
[2] Ministry of Labour: *General survey on wages and working hours system*, op. cit.

Traditional notions of the respective roles of women and men and of the " inferiority " of the female sex consciously or unconsciously limit women's job opportunities, prevent their promotion, and discourage their continuity of service—all of which tend to lower women's earnings, as well as their status at the place of work.

* * *

Real differentials

As has been indicated, the lower level of women's earnings is due to a multiplicity of factors. Since some of them automatically depress women's earnings under the prevailing wage system, the resulting differences have to be eliminated from the wage figures in order to determine real wage differentials by sex.

If overtime payments are excluded, and if only regular contractual earnings for work performed during normal working hours are taken into account, the level of women's wages was equivalent in 1972 to 56.3 per cent of that of men. If allowance is also made for the difference in hours worked by men and women during normal working hours, the figure becomes 57 per cent.[1] If the allowances for living costs that are included in regular contractual earnings could also be excluded the ratio would be even higher, though the exact figures cannot be calculated for lack of data.

Allowance should also be made for differences between men and women with respect to age, length of service, educational background, size of enterprise, etc. For instance, when the wages of men and women of the same age and same length of service are compared, the differences between their earnings dwindle, as shown in figure 1.

Another approach to finding the real differences between men's and women's wages is to recalculate their earnings after weighting the age composition and other characteristics of men and women workers. Using the Paasche formula for this purpose, the following ratios of women's to men's wages are obtained [2]:

weighted length of service:	68.2 per cent
weighted age:	64.2 per cent
weighted size of establishment:	57.6 per cent
weighted educational background:	57.1 per cent
sum of the four items:	61.5 per cent

---

[1] Ministry of Labour: *Basic survey of wage structure*, op. cit. The sample used for this calculation included 60,000 establishments and 1,400,000 employees in eight major industries.

[2] On the basis of figures taken from Ministry of Labour: *Basic survey of wage structure*, op. cit.

FIGURE 1. WOMEN'S CONTRACTUAL CASH EARNINGS AS PERCENTAGE OF
THOSE OF MEN OF SAME AGE AND LENGTH OF SERVICE, 1972

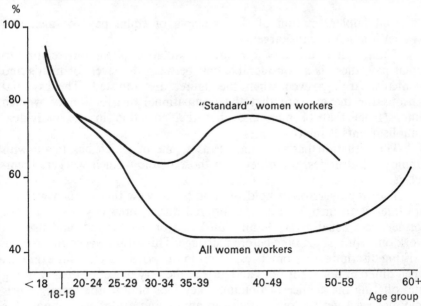

Note: A " standard " worker is one who has been employed by the establishment since leaving school.

As these calculations show, length of service plays a particularly significant role in the apparent difference between men's and women's wages.

Depending on the method of comparison employed, women's wages expressed as a proportion of men's may be summed up as follows:

average of total cash earnings:	50.2 per cent
average of contractual earnings:	50.8 per cent
average of regular contractual earnings:	56.7 per cent
average of hourly earnings:	57.0 per cent
average calculated by the Paasche formula:	57.1-68.2 per cent.

These figures show that the ratio of women's to men's wages is not as low as is implied in the proportion of " 50 per cent " which is commonly used and which is based on the arithmetic means of the total earnings of all men and women workers without taking into account differences in age composition, length of service, size of establishment, etc. Even the figures produced by the Paasche formula are thought to be a little too low, as they are based on regular contractual earnings and not adjusted to differences in the number of hours worked and in allowances.

125

V. Conclusion

Full implementation of the principle of equal pay for men and women is still a distant target.

Though there are very few cases of violation of the law relating to equal pay, there is a considerable gap between the levels of men's and women's earnings even when the figures are adjusted. The essential reasons for the gap are that the occupational distribution of women differs from that of men and that their position in the individual establishments is inferior.

This situation has two main causes, one of which has to do with employers' attitudes, the other with those of the women workers themselves.

The employers often hold the traditional view that women workers are inferior to men, an attitude fostered during prewar years when the former were usually very young, unskilled or uneducated, and used to work only for a short time before marriage. This attitude accounts for the existing discriminatory practices. Firms in the private sector, for example, open different doors for boys and girls at the very outset of their working life, offering the chance of obtaining key jobs only to the former. Girls may not even get the opportunity to apply, and are offered minor jobs instead. Different standards of promotion are applied to male and female workers so that their positions diverge ever more widely as years go on. Women workers are expected to be " young, pretty, dexterous and cheap ", and are discouraged from staying long by written or unwritten contracts of retirement at a certain age, sometimes less than 30, or whenever they get married. Such discriminatory treatment is rather openly practised, as it is not the object of any definite legal prohibition in private enterprises. It is most frequently observed in large establishments which can easily attract highly qualified male workers.

On the other hand, women are often criticised for lacking proper occupational skills and qualifications. There are no institutional obstacles to stop girls getting vocational education and training in present-day Japan. Public schools of all levels are equally open to boys and girls, and the latter do in fact take advantage of their educational opportunities. In 1972, 88 per cent of girls finishing junior high school, which is compulsory, went on to senior high school, as against 86 per cent of boys; and 28 per cent of girls finishing senior high school went on to college or university, the corresponding figure for boys being 30 per cent. Nevertheless, there is a noticeable tendency among the girl students to major in liberal arts rather than such courses as law, economics or engineering, and out of 63,000 trainees in the public vocational training centres which specialise in training manual workers only 12 per cent were women in 1972. Consequently, women enter the labour market with far lower levels of skill and professional qualification. Girl students reply that they would rather remain feminine than trouble themselves studying hard when there is little prospect of getting appropriate employment as a result. Women are also frequently accused of having little sense of responsibility for work, of not displaying initiative, or of having lower morale. They would retort that they are not assigned jobs where they could show and develop their abilities, and that they cannot be high-spirited when they are so discriminated against. Thus there is a kind of vicious circle which needs to be broken somewhere.

In order to widen the occupational opportunities for women and improve their position in the establishment, thus raising their average earnings, it would therefore be necessary, apart from inspection to enforce legislation regarding equal pay, to promote a variety of measures, including the following:

(a) improvement of women's occupational skills and efficiency, providing adequate opportunities for vocational education and training;

(b) amelioration of personnel management practices in enterprises by urging employers to engage women on a basis of equality with men for any job and to give them the same opportunities of training and promotion;

(c) improvement of the wage system by increasing the job performance component and by promoting scientific job analysis and evaluation;

(d) promotion of trade union interest in the implementation of the principle of equal pay, encouraging the more active participation of women workers; and

(e) programmes of assistance to women workers with family responsibilities: these might include the provision of day nurseries, time off for child care, the extension of home-help services, etc., so that women would not suffer the consequences of a decline in efficiency or of involuntary interruptions of work.

During the past decade the Japanese labour administration authorities have shown that they are anxious to see such measures applied, and their efforts have been reflected in a gradual rise in the average earnings of women. The Government also showed its interest in improving the position of women workers by enacting the Working Women's Welfare Act in 1972. This Act, which is intended to ensure that women can harmonise their work with their home life and make the best use of their abilities without any discrimination against them by reason of their sex, provides for measures to promote vocational guidance and training, adequate health protection during pregnancy, time off for child care, welfare facilities, etc.

Following the passing of this Act and in accordance with its requirements, the basic policy with regard to measures for the welfare of women workers was drafted and published by the Minister of Labour in 1973. This document clarified the main policies to be implemented during the following five years. Since then the Ministry of Labour, mainly through the Women's and Minors' Bureau, has been developing programmes laid down in the basic policy, promoting equal treatment by publicity and meetings with employers and workers organised through its local offices in every prefecture in the country. Employers have been gradually accepting the principle since, quite apart from the question of recognising the nation's will embodied in the Act, the shortage of manpower has driven home the need to utilise the potentialities of women workers. Usually through their women's divisions, trade unions have been pursuing campaigns to get the provisions of the Act, including equal treatment, put into practice. Among the improvements achieved, cases of elimination of discriminatory retirement age have already been reported.

However, as the Act has no penalty clauses, there is no guarantee that the principle of equal treatment will be closely observed. Some women workers have been bringing actions alleging unequal treatment, especially with regard to dismissal. They have usually won their cases, but at the expense of much time and trouble. It has been keenly felt by the Bureau and by women's organisations that some specific institution should be set up to promote equal opportunity for women. The Bureau is ready to study this possibility.

It must not be overlooked, however, that the problem of lower wages and the lower status of women at work cannot be settled solely in terms of labour practices, since it forms part of the broader problem of the whole position of women in society and, as such, is affected by general social and cultural factors. Consequently, it is of fundamental importance that the general status of women should be improved. This improvement must be sought simultaneously on every front by promoting equal treatment of boys and girls both at home and at school, by encouraging the development of women's skills and responsibilities, by fostering partnership between husband and wife in the sharing of family responsibilities, by promoting women's participation in civic activities and, in particular, by dispelling prejudices against women working.

It is to the accomplishment of these tasks that the Women's and Minors' Bureau, which as noted earlier has been entrusted with special responsibility for improving the all-round status of women as well as for the administration of the Working Women's Welfare Act, will be devoting its efforts, in co-operation with other governmental agencies and civic organisations, in the years to come.

———————

The Participation of Women in the Labour Force of Latin America: Fertility and Other Factors

Juan C. ELIZAGA [1]

IN MOST LATIN AMERICAN COUNTRIES, only 20 per cent or even fewer of the women and girls over 10 years of age are economically active as the term is used in population censuses, manpower surveys and other socio-economic studies. This situation does not appear to have changed very much between 1950 and 1970. In Brazil, admittedly, the female participation rate increased steadily from 13.6 per cent at the beginning of the period to 18.5 per cent at the end, but this appears to be one of the very few exceptions. On the whole, the rate has remained relatively stable, with bigger changes in the 1950s than in the 1960s, although it is true that the information for the latter decade is very incomplete, data for 1970 being available in respect of only a few countries in the region (see table 1).

When these rates are compared with those for countries of other regions, it can be said that the level of labour force participation of Latin American women is among the lowest in the world. Participation rates by age group recorded in or around 1960 and 1970 show that, between the ages of 15 and 65, the average woman in Latin America worked for a total number of years corresponding to less than 25 per cent of the time theoretically available (see table 2). In Japan, she worked 26 years, i.e. a little more than 50 per cent of the time available. The corresponding average figures for France, England and Wales, and the United States in 1960 were 21.8, 20.2 and 14.8 years respectively. The figures for the socialist countries of eastern Europe are even higher than for Japan: 28 years for Hungary, 32 for Czechoslovakia and 34 for Romania. Some

---

[1] Latin American Demographic Center (CELADE), Santiago de Chile.

TABLE 1. FEMALE PARTICIPATION RATES IN SELECTED LATIN AMERICAN
COUNTRIES
(%)

Country	Lower age limit	Female participation rate [1]		
		1950	1960	1970
Argentina	14	23.4	23.0	.
Brazil	10	13.6	16.5	18.5
Chile	12	25.5	20.9	19.2
Colombia	12	19.1	18.8 [2]	.
Costa Rica	12	16.1	16.0	.
Ecuador	12	33.3	16.7	.
El Salvador	10	16.2	16.5	.
Guatemala	7	11.6	10.4 [2]	.
Mexico	12	12.9	15.6 [3]	16.4
Nicaragua	10	14.1 [4]	18.7	17.0 [5]
Panama	10	20.3	21.0	25.7
Paraguay	10	22.7	22.9	.
Peru	6	.	17.0	.
Uruguay	10	.	23.9	.
Venezuela	10	17.5	17.2	.

[1] Economically active females as percentage of all females above the lower age limit used for the enumeration. [2] 1964. [3] Lower age limit: 8 years. [4] Lower age limit: 14 years. [5] Based on advance census sample data.

of these data refer to 1960 and others to 1970, but on the whole variations over the decade were slight.

The greater participation of women in the industrialised countries is understandable in view of the stage of development reached by their economies and social institutions, the educational level attained by women and the pressing demand for labour. The reasons why female participation rates should be lower in Latin America than in other developing regions (Asia, Africa), where agriculture generally plays a more important part, are less obvious. It is to be noted that the Latin American countries differ from many other developing and even developed countries precisely in that relatively few women work in agriculture. Not only do women constitute a small percentage of the total agricultural labour force, but judging by the differences in rural and urban participation rates, Latin American agriculture offers them far fewer employment opportunities. This holds good for countries with quite different levels of urbanisation. Some of the differences between Latin American countries and agricultural countries in other regions can be explained by the different criteria used in the enumeration of unpaid family workers, but

TABLE 2. MEAN NUMBER OF YEARS WORKED BY WOMEN BETWEEN THE AGES OF 15 AND 65 IN LATIN AMERICA AND OTHER REGIONS, 1960 AND 1970

Country	Mean number of years worked [1]		Country	Mean number of years worked [1]	
	1960	1970		1960	1970
Latin America			Mexico	9.7	10.5
			Nicaragua	11.4	10.2
Temperate South:			Panama	12.2	.
Argentina	11.4	13.7			
Chile	10.7	10.6	*Caribbean:*		
Uruguay	13.8	.	Cuba	9.6 [2]	.
			Dominican Republic	5.7	.
Tropical South:			**Other regions**		
Brazil	8.7	9.9			
Colombia	9.9	.	United States	14.8	.
Ecuador	8.6	.	Czechoslovakia	.	31.9
Peru	11.0	.	England and Wales	20.2	.
Venezuela	9.8	.	France	21.8	21.7
			Hungary	.	27.7
Mexico and Central:			Italy	14.1	.
Costa Rica	8.3	.	Netherlands	13.4	.
El Salvador	9.2	.	Romania	.	34.3
Guatemala	6.4	.	Yugoslavia	19.4	.
Honduras	6.4	.	Japan	26.0 [3]	26.7

[1] It is assumed that the activity rates by age group remain constant over time. [2] 1953. [3] 1955.

Sources: Latin American figures are based on population censuses carried out in or around 1960 and 1970. Data for some countries have been slightly adjusted. Figures for other regions are from United Nations: *Demographic aspects of manpower*, Population Studies No. 33 (New York, 1962; Sales No. 61.XIII.4); and for 1970, from ILO: *Year book of labour statistics, 1972* (Geneva, 1972).

we cannot disregard the influence of cultural factors on the role of women in various rural societies. It is interesting to note that in the home countries of most of the migrants populating Latin America (Spain, Portugal and Italy) the participation rate of women is comparable with the higher rates found in Latin America itself. However that may be, it is advisable in view of the incompleteness of statistics concerning agricultural activities on family farms that the question of women's participation in the labour force should be studied in a narrower focus concentrating on non-agricultural activities. This is what the present article sets out to do.

We can eliminate the effect of regional variations in agricultural and extractive occupations simply and accurately enough by considering only

131

the *urban* female population. This simultaneously permits a comparison of countries with different levels of urbanisation. There are also advantages in restricting the study to women of child-bearing age; not only is their participation greater in these age groups but also and more importantly the problem can in this way be linked with the level of fertility, as will be seen later. Women who are past child-bearing, especially in countries with a relatively " young " population, constitute only a small fraction of the female population of working age. Moreover, as they belong to earlier generations, their formative period is fairly remote from the one whose educational characteristics, fertility and cultural values are now being examined and we therefore cannot expect their attitude to work to correspond to current or even recent conditions. Any change in female participation rates must therefore be brought about by relatively young women, who form the vast majority of the female labour force. This explains the presentation of table 3. It shows that the average number of years worked between the ages of 15 and 44 is about 30 per cent of the time potentially available, except in the case of Colombia where it is approximately half that percentage. As regards Chile, the only country for which data are available for 1960 and 1970, it will be noted that the participation rate declined slightly over that period. If we compare the figures for Latin America—even for countries with large populations, whether highly urbanised (Argentina and Chile) or moderately so (Brazil, Colombia, Mexico and Peru)—with those for industrialised countries, we are once again struck by the wide gap between them as regards the employment of women. For the industrialised countries, instead of taking urban female participation rates *per se*, it was found more convenient to take the rates of highly urbanised countries in which workers depending on agriculture are estimated to account for less than 20 per cent of the population, and where the rates consequently reflect fairly accurately the level of participation in urban activities. In these countries, around 1960, women were economically active for between 30 and 55 per cent of the total time available (in this case between the ages of 15 and 50), a percentage which would be even higher if, as in the case of Latin American countries, we considered the period between the ages of 15 and 44.

The foregoing figures confirm that even when the rural population or agricultural activity is disregarded, female participation rates are still low in Latin America compared with those in other regions generally, and in the industrialised countries in particular. In the present article I shall attempt to interpret and, so far as possible, explain the factors accounting for this state of affairs and for the recent changes which have taken place. One factor that has attracted a great deal of attention in this connection is the influence of fertility. Latin American countries, with a few understandable exceptions, have long had some of the highest fertility levels in the world, comparable only with those certain African countries have

TABLE 3. FEMALE PARTICIPATION RATES BY AGE GROUP IN THE URBAN AREAS
OF SELECTED LATIN AMERICAN COUNTRIES

(%)

Age	Around 1960					Around 1970	
	Argentina	Chile	Colombia	Mexico [1]	Peru	Brazil [2]	Chile
15-19	36.5	27.8	26.8	36.7	30.5	32.5	18.0
20-24	45.1	39.4	23.2	40.9	35.8	41.0	35.8
25-29	33.3	33.7	15.4	30.3	29.6	32.6	32.7
30-34	27.4	28.6	12.6	27.2	26.5	29.2	28.9
35-39	25.2	27.5	11.6	29.3	25.4	27.5	27.1
40-44	24.1	26.9	11.2	30.2	24.7	26.3	26.8
Mean number of years worked [3]	9.6	9.2	5.0	9.7	8.6	9.5	8.5

[1] Rates are for the Federal District only, which then accounted for 30 per cent of the urban population of Mexico. The rates for the urban population as a whole are approximately one-third lower than those given for the Federal District. [2] Calculated by dividing the population in all non-agricultural occupations by the corresponding urban population. These rates therefore over-estimate the true values. However, the proportion of non-agricultural occupations in the rural areas must be small. [3] Between the ages of 15 and 44.

Source: CELADE Data Bank. Census sample data.

been experiencing recently. Suffice it to say, for the moment, that the birth rates in many Latin American countries—and in fairly recent times at that—have been running at over 40 and even 45 per thousand, whereas the industrialised countries and Europe and North America generally have birth rates of around 20 per thousand.

Is there a causal link between this high fertility and the particularly low participation rate of women in Latin America? It is well known that there is a negative correlation between participation and family size, particularly the number and age of children. But this relationship does not mean that fertility can explain all the difference in participation rates, nor even most of them. As fertility is itself inversely related to the level of women's education and the latter is in turn directly related to participation, it is extremely difficult to say which of these various factors depends on which, even supposing that such an attempt to consider them in isolation could be theoretically justified. There are factors in a society—such as the structure of the economy and its stage of development—which could explain, perhaps to a significant degree, the female participation rate, and which are unrelated to the fertility level, at least in the short term. The basic hypothesis of this study is that fertility does not go very far towards accounting for the differences in participation in a society as a whole. It can be and indeed is important for certain groups of

133

women (e.g. married with more than three children) but it is not so for other more numerous groups (e.g. married women without children, or with only one or two), in that fertility can be considered a constant in these latter groups, since it cannot be reduced. It follows that a drop in fertility is not going to result in a direct and immediately significant rise in participation rates, because this calls for other changes (on the labour market and in the quality of the supply of female labour) which would by themselves bring about increased labour force participation, even if fertility did not change.

In the subsequent sections, before finally reverting to the question of fertility, we shall study a number of the factors or conditions affecting female participation at the level of both the individual and society, on the assumption that fertility remains constant. For the individual, these are marital status, education and income; and for society, the structure and stage of development of the economy (implicitly taking into account factors such as urbanisation, modernisation of the various social institutions and the role of women).

Marital status

In Latin America, as in many industrialised countries, the participation rate of single women is several times higher than that of married women. This difference is proportionally larger in the Latin American countries because of the particularly low participation rate of married women. In the age group 20-24, where there is still a large proportion of single women, the ratio of married to single participation rates is about 1 : 5 in Latin America, whilst in some industrialised countries it is as close as 1 : 2 (France) or even 1 : 1 (Bulgaria) (see table 4). These differences acquire real importance from the age of 25 onwards, since the proportion of married women then attains its peak and they constitute the majority of the female population. The labour force participation rate of widowed, separated and divorced women appears to be slightly lower than that of single women, but distinctly higher than that of married women; they become numerically important after the age of 35 or 40. In fact, single, widowed, separated and divorced women together account for as many as 45 or 50 per cent of all women between the ages of 15 and 44. Clearly this immediately reduces to 50 or 55 per cent the population whom lowered fertility levels might encourage to join the labour force. If we deduct from this proportion the number of married women without children or with one or two children, who will barely be affected by possible changes in the social and cultural conditions of women or by family planning policy, it can be seen that the scope for raising female labour force participation rates by changes in fertility is somewhat limited. In Chile, around 1960, where fertility was average by Latin American standards, 47 per cent of

TABLE 4. FEMALE PARTICIPATION RATES BY MARITAL STATUS IN LATIN AMERICA
AND OTHER REGIONS, AROUND 1960

(%)

Country and marital status [1]	Age						
	15-19	20-24	25-29	30-34	35-39	40-44	45-49
Argentina							
Single	37	61	67	67	← 60 →		
Married	8	12	14	14	← 13 →		
Others	34	47	55	58	← 43 →		
Brazil							
Single	26	41	48	← 49 →		← 47 →	
Married	6	8	9	← 8 →		← 6 →	
Others	51	52	42	← 26 →		← 15 →	
Chile							
Single	25	50	57	← 55 →		← 53 →	
Married	5	10	11	← 13 →		← 12 →	
Others	.	36	52	← 51 →		← 41 →	
Chile (1970)							
Single	17	47	58	← 57 →		← 51 →	
Married	6	12	15	← 14 →		← 13 →	
Others	27	45	49	← 54 →		← 43 →	
United States							
Single	29 [2]	73	79	79	79	78	77
Married	28 [2]	34	29	31	37	42	43
Others	53 [2]	69	71	71	74	74	73
France							
Single	35	74	80	78	78	76	75
Married	42	45	36	32	33	35	38
Others	56	74	68	70	71	72	71
Bulgaria							
Single	26	63	83	83	81	78	71
Married	63	75	84	86	88	87	81
Others	68	82	90	92	92	91	82
Japan							
Single	37	81	76	70	71	67	66
Married	37	42	38	44	54	59	58
Others	12	48	74	78	86	83	80

[1] " Married " includes common law wives. " Others " denotes widowed, separated and divorced women.   [2] Rates are for age group 14-19.

Sources: For Latin America, censuses and census samples from the CELADE Data Bank. For the other countries, United Nations: *Demographic yearbook* (New York, 1968).

135

married women between 15 and 44 years of age had two or fewer children, and in Brazil, which had a fairly high fertility of 3.6 children, the corresponding figure in the urban areas in 1970 was 45 per cent. This means that only some 25 per cent of the women between 15 and 44 years of age were in a position to choose between having children and working, supposing the alternatives to be incompatible.

In view of the low participation rate among married women, it appears from what has been said that a reduction in fertility could not lead to more than a very moderate increase in female participation. It seems clear that other conditions, such as an improvement in women's educational standards and an increased demand for women workers, are necessary if the supply of female labour is to rise to levels comparable with those of the industrialised countries.

Education

While it is well known that women's labour force participation rates are positively correlated with their level of education, there is unfortunately very little hard information available on this question as far as Latin America is concerned. Some of the data we do possess are shown in table 5.

The countries to which this information relates, Argentina and Chile, are among those with the highest educational levels in the region and also among those which, for several decades, have had the highest participation rates. From the age group 20-24 onwards, participation clearly varies according to the level of education, and these differences increase with age. In both countries, there appear to be at least two educational " thresholds " beyond which there is a greater probability of participation: a certain amount of secondary education (7 to 12 years) and some university education (13 years or more). The classification used is perhaps not the most appropriate; for example, a classification based on " completed secondary education " and " completed university education " might reveal even more marked disparities. The participation rates of women who have not received any schooling are consistently lower than those of women who have received one to three years of primary education, a fact which is of particular significance for other countries in the region where a large proportion of the female population has not had any formal education at all; it is true, of course, that most of these women belong to the rural population, whose participation follows a pattern of its own and, as already mentioned, is best omitted from the analysis. In Brazil, in 1970, 36 per cent of women aged between 20 and 39 were " without education ", a percentage which logically increases with age. In Peru, in 1961, 45 per cent of women aged between 20 and 29 had no education, whilst in Chile, which had one of the lowest illiteracy levels,

TABLE 5. FEMALE PARTICIPATION RATES BY EDUCATIONAL LEVEL AND AGE IN ARGENTINA AND CHILE, 1960

(%)

Country and number of years' study	Age						
	15-19	20-24	25-29	30-34	35-39	40-44	All ages [1]
Argentina							
None	29.0	20.7	15.7	13.0	14.5	15.9	12.1
1-3	42.0	28.1	18.9	16.0	15.8	16.8	17.8
4-6	41.1	38.2	27.1	22.2	20.5	20.4	23.8
7-12	19.1	57.7	46.5	42.2	44.6	39.3	35.4
13 or more	25.6	45.2	77.5	70.8	62.9	63.8	55.0
Chile							
None	27.8	22.6	15.8	13.7	12.5	15.1	14.5
1-3	30.8	31.7	22.2	20.8	17.1	21.7	22.1
4-6	26.4	33.4	24.4	21.0	19.9	17.9	22.5
7-12	13.3	34.2	33.1	30.3	27.8	25.6	24.2
13 or more	12.5	42.4	59.6	68.0	80.0	76.0	53.4

[1] 15 years and over, without upper limit.

Source: CELADE Data Bank, census sample data.

the corresponding figure was between 12 and 14 per cent. Looking at the other side of the coin—the situation of women with a fairly high level of education, whose participation rate is also generally higher—we find that in Brazil, in 1970, 16 per cent of women aged 20 to 39 had received secondary or higher education; in Peru, in 1961, the proportion was 14 per cent of women aged 20 to 29; and in Chile, in 1960, approximately 30 per cent of women aged 20 to 29.

Generalising from the situation in these countries to the region as a whole and even taking into account progress made in the field of education, it is fairly safe to estimate that around 1970 over 25 per cent of women aged between 20 and 50 were without any education and fewer than 15 per cent had received secondary or higher education, except in a very few countries. Despite the advances made in education during the past 20 or 30 years in all the Latin American countries, therefore, it could not be claimed that the level so far attained is sufficient to enable women to participate in the labour force on a large scale.

Some idea of what can be achieved is clear from the example of Brazil, where in the course of the 1960s, as can be seen in table 6, women's educational standards improved considerably—and it is significant that this coincided with a large increase in their participation rate (see table 1).

TABLE 6. EDUCATIONAL LEVEL OF THE FEMALE POPULATION OF BRAZIL BY AGE, 1960 AND 1970

Age and educational level	% of all women in age group with education shown	
	1960	1970
20-24		
No education	38.0	30.6
Some secondary or higher education	9.7	20.7
25-29		
No education	41.7	35.4
Some secondary or higher education	8.4	15.9
30-34		
No education	43.2	38.1
Some secondary or higher education	7.8	12.8
35-39		
No education	49.3	42.5
Some secondary or higher education	6.3	10.5
All ages 20-39		
No education	42.4	35.8
Some secondary or higher education	8.2	15.7

Note: The intermediate category of women with some degree of primary or related education is not shown here.

Source: Population censuses.

The virtual doubling of the proportion of women having " some secondary or higher education " is the most outstanding feature of this development and certainly the one which contributed most to the increase in female participation rates between 1960 and 1970.

A relatively high educational level, that is to say at least secondary education, considerably enhances women's employment prospects, but it is important that they should be able to find work in non-manual occupations calling for some degree of skill, particularly in those branches which experience has shown to be the most favoured by women in the more developed countries: the liberal professions, office work and selling. The growth of these activities is associated with the expansion of such sectors as social services (education, health, etc.), public administration, banking, insurance, real estate, etc., and certain branches of trade (especially in respect of wage-earning occupations). These are precisely the sectors in which the better-paid jobs are to be found. Hence, although the supply of labour increases with women's qualifications, an increase in effective participation is governed by demand. This aspect of the problem is considered in the next section.

The structure of the economy and its stage of development

The evolution of the economy from the pre-industrial stage to its most highly developed modern forms has been accompanied by important changes in the sectoral distribution of the labour force. Apart from the relative decline of agriculture and the steady advance of the tertiary sector, very significant qualitative changes have occurred in the composition of industry and services. This has had and continues to have a decisive influence on women's participation trends both in the developed countries and even more so in the developing countries.

In a pre-industrial economy or one in which industry is in its infancy, work opportunities exist for women in agriculture, handicrafts and personal services (domestic service, needlework, laundering, ironing, etc.). These occupations, which are compatible with the prevailing low educational level, are generally carried out within the home by unpaid family workers, independent workers or paid domestics. Many of the women performing work of this type do not appear to have been enumerated as workers in the population censuses carried out in Latin American countries from 1950 onwards.[1] This would explain the extremely low participation rates in countries that are predominantly agricultural and have very little industry.

This situation has been gradually evolving over the past decades as industrialisation and modernisation generally have brought about changes in the economic structure of the countries in the region. In a few countries (Argentina, Chile, Brazil) this process began and took shape earlier, between 1914 and 1940, whereas in most of them it did not really start until after the Second World War. The growing displacement of handicrafts by manufacturing (with its higher output per worker), and of the individual worker by companies on the services and trade sectors, and the emergence and expansion of new skilled services (education, health, office work, etc.), radically changed the demand for female labour at least as far as work outside the home and skilled work necessitating a minimum of education were concerned.

This change in sectoral organisation and degree of development of the economy has been accompanied by a progressive change in women's participation patterns. At first, most women were probably not in a position to join the labour force, mainly because they did not have the necessary education and because, as mothers of generally large families, they were not free to work outside the home. It would be difficult to say to what extent women were prevented from taking advantage of the greater opportunities to work in these new fields by discrimination against female labour and the role society assigned to women. In any case, this

---

[1] In almost all these countries, the 1950 censuses were the first to be conducted according to modern methods.

stage was marked by their low level of participation in urban activities, whilst most female workers were occupied in domestic services and other personal services calling for few skills and consequently poorly paid. The latter factor plus limited education explains why a high proportion of women stop working soon after they marry, whether or not they have children.

In a second stage, through which a good many Latin American countries appear to have passed since 1950 or 1960, female participation tends to increase. This is certainly masked somewhat by qualitative changes in the sectoral structure, such as transfers from domestic services and cottage industries to manufacturing industry and more productive manual occupations (restaurants, hotels, health services, commercial cleaning services, etc.). The most outstanding change at the individual level is the improvement in women's education, to which reference has already been made. It would be interesting to be able to establish whether, in those countries of the region that have proceeded furthest in this stage of development, the potential supply of skilled and semi-skilled female labour presently exceeds or falls short of the effective demand, assessing the latter on the basis of the degree of development of the economy in question and bearing in mind that throughout Latin America the male labour force is patently underutilised.

Consequently, in considering recent changes in women's work patterns it is important to observe not only the over-all change reflected in their participation rates but also the changes in the sectoral structure resulting from the differential growth of employment. Before examining the data on this question, however, we have to give some additional thought to the demand for female labour and the response of the women themselves.

It can be said that the probability of participation in the labour force increases with the availability of certain types of work, with the pay offered and the working conditions provided. A woman with a relatively good education is more attracted by non-manual occupations, which offer a level of remuneration more in keeping with her skills and which, by reason of the hours worked and the location and social environment of the workplace, are better adapted to her needs and aspirations. Such a woman will consequently be drawn towards work in the so-called social services (teaching, health, welfare), towards office work in commercial and industrial undertakings and in public administrations, and towards the independent liberal professions. It is precisely in these sectors that women's participation has increased most (see table 7).

Of course, it is not merely a question of the availability of suitable employment opportunities: there are a number of factors apart from education which limit the supply of female labour. Mention is often made of the husband's income (if the woman is married), the family income, the number and age of children and the composition or type of family. No

TABLE 7. PERCENTAGE DISTRIBUTION OF FEMALE LABOUR IN NON-AGRICULTURAL SECTORS

Occupational sector	Around 1960						Around 1970		
	Brazil	Chile	Colombia	Mexico	Peru	Venezuela	Brazil	Chile	Mexico
Agriculture [1]	30.1	4.7	13.2	33.1	31.9	7.6	20.5	3.1	10.9
All non-agriculture	*100.0*	*100.0*	*100.0*	*100.0*	*100.0*	*100.0*	*100.0*	*100.0*	*100.0*
Industry [2]	17.9	20.3	20.5	19.6	25.4	20.3	23.2	19.2	21.4
Trade [3]	6.2	11.5	12.1	21.3	17.1	10.1	9.1	16.8	15.2
Transport [4]	1.6	1.2	1.4	1.4	0.9	1.6	1.3	1.5	0.8
Services	69.1	61.4	61.6	56.4	50.7	64.1	63.1	54.5	51.2
Administrative [5]	*3.0*	*1.7*	*2.8*	.	*1.9*	*5.8*	*3.3*	.	
Social [6]	*15.3*	*13.5*	*12.7*	.	*16.4*	*19.1*	*20.1*	.	
Public [7]	.	*9.0*				*6.5*	*3.4*	.	
Domestic	*36.9*	*35.5*	*44.7*	.	*30.6*	*31.7*	*34.3*	.	
Other	*13.9*	*1.7*	*1.4*		*1.8*	*1.0*	*2.0*	.	
Other occupations [8]	5.2	5.6	4.4	1.3	5.9	3.9	3.3	8.0	10.9

[1] Percentage of total female labour force; includes extractive industries. [2] Includes construction and basic services [3] Includes banking, insurance, etc. [4] Includes communications and warehousing. [5] Includes armed and security forces. [6] Includes teaching, health and welfare services. [7] Miscellaneous personal services. [8] Includes poorly defined and unspecified occupations.

Source: Population censuses.

study has yet been made which isolates the effect of the husband's income on female participation in the Latin American countries. The participation of young women (say, less than 20 years old) is probably inversely related to family income, in that parents who are well off can afford to extend the schooling of their children (the somewhat longer-term effect of which may be to increase participation). Again, as we shall see in the next section, participation is inversely related to the number of children, a relationship which can vary according to the type of family. For example, in a nuclear family, responsibility for the care of the children falls entirely on the mother, whereas in an extended family, in which the couple lives with the parents of one of the spouses or with other relatives, this responsibility may be delegated to some of these while the wife is at work. The presence of children and relatives is of importance when the woman is deciding whether to work or not, in that she weighs the " advantages " of caring for the children (and looking after the household in general) against the advantages of the income from an occupation and any personal satisfaction she may derive from performing it. The lower the " opportunity cost ", the more probable it is that she will go out to work. If the sacrifice involved is large, she probably will not work unless the level of income and the various other satisfactions provide adequate compensation, in which case she may engage a domestic servant to help her in the home. To sum up, the decisive—and closely related—factors shaping the supply of female labour are, other things being equal, educational level, type of occupation and remuneration.

Examination of the figures available from the latest censuses on the distribution of non-agricultural female labour shows (cf. table 7) that the sectors which account for most of this labour force are, in order of importance, domestic services (30 to 45 per cent), industry (19 to 25 per cent), social services (13 to 20 per cent) and trade (9 to 17 per cent). These figures relate to the six Latin American countries with the largest populations (excluding Argentina) which have reached a relatively advanced stage of urbanisation (Chile and Venezuela) or are at an intermediate stage but developing rapidly (Brazil, Colombia, Mexico and Peru). Unfortunately, the information for 1970 is very incomplete; that from the 1960 censuses is much fuller.

From a qualitative point of view each of the four occupational sectors mentioned above has its own trend and significance. Domestic services, the largest sector, are tending to contract as the economy develops, although there are differences between countries which apparently do not correspond strictly to the degree of development attained. The proportion of women working in industry differs little from country to country and there were no very significant changes between 1960 and 1970. It is possible that in some cases (Peru) the higher-than-average figure has less to do with the implantation of modern industry than with the availability of " female " occupations in typical handicraft industries.

In others (Brazil), where a considerable increase was recorded during the decade, the possibility cannot be excluded that this was due partly to changes on the census classification criteria.

Trade and the social services are the most important sources of the increasing demand for female labour. It is particularly the social services which are creating most employment opportunities for women. In the countries examined, this sector already employed a large proportion of the non-agricultural female labour force in 1960 and its share has certainly increased since then (in Brazil, it rose from 15.3 to 20.1 per cent during the decade). Public administration is another field suitable for women, even if the numbers it can absorb are rather limited; nevertheless, in some countries (Venezuela, 6 per cent) conditions appear to be particularly favourable.

The participation of women workers in trade is open to various interpretations. In some countries (Mexico, 1960 and Peru, 1961) this sector was probably swollen by the presence of own-account retailers. This hypothesis appears to be confirmed by a comparison of the Mexican figures for 1960 and 1970: by the latter year the relative importance of trade had fallen sharply, a reduction that was balanced to a large extent by the increase recorded for the poorly defined or unspecified occupations (" other occupations "). On the other hand, there are grounds for believing that the expansion of this sector in some countries (Brazil, Chile) is due to the modernisation of commercial activities.[1]

From a comparison of the figures in tables 3 and 7, one could conclude, although not with certainty, that the countries with the highest participation rates for women between 15 and 44 years of age are also those in which the relative importance of the key sectors mentioned is greatest.[2]

It would be useful to be able to check, in addition, the correlation between participation in these key sectors and certain characteristics of the women concerned, such as age, marital status, education and income. The 1970 census for Brazil is fairly rich in this type of information, which is worth examining briefly.

Comparing the sectoral participation rates for various age groups with the average rate for all age groups, we find that in the social services

[1] In Brazil, the high growth rate of the labour force (both sexes) over the period 1960-70 in industry, trade and services (at the expense of the agricultural sector) coincided with an increase in the proportion of women working in the more modern sectors. In Chile, the fastest-growing sector was trade, both in general and as regards women's participation. As this is the sector with the highest rate of employment growth (both sexes) in Colombia, Peru and Venezuela, it can be assumed that female participation in trade will have grown significantly in these countries.

[2] Although table 3 provides no data for Venezuela, there is reason to believe that participation rates are relatively high among the urban female population. Similarly, it can be assumed that the key sectors account for a large fraction of the female labour force in Argentina, which was not included in table 7.

the participation rate is higher than the average between the ages of 25 and 39 (almost 30 per cent of economically active women in these age groups work in this sector); in public administration, it is higher between the ages of 30 and 39; in trade, there are few variations between the age groups; whereas in industry and personal services (mainly provided by domestic servants), the participation rate is higher than average in the youngest age groups (15-24 years).

The foregoing comparison indicates generally higher rates of participation among women over 25 years old, most of whom are married or were formerly married and are now widowed, separated or divorced. The sector with the largest proportion of married women is that of the social services (35 per cent, as against 17 per cent of single women and an even smaller percentage of women of other marital status). The other sector in which married women are particularly numerous is public administration. Single women, on the other hand, tend to work rather in industry and in personal services; the latter sector is the only one in which widowed, separated and divorced women are found in any numbers (probably owing in part to the presence in this group of lower-class " separated " women who previously lived as common law wives). One may reasonably conclude that married women, and probably some of the widowed, separated and divorced ones as well, tend to seek employment in specific occupations which are suited to their educational attainments and offer advantages as regards income and working conditions.

This last statement can be verified to some extent by reference to the data on the monthly incomes of women working in the various sectors—still for Brazil—in 1970. These show that the distribution of women by income differs fairly considerably between the social services and public administration sectors on the one hand and personal services, industry and trade on the other. About 70 per cent of the women working in the personal services sector declared monthly incomes of less than 100 cruzeiros. The proportion of women who declared less than 200 cruzeiros a month, by sector, was as follows: industry, 80 per cent; trade, 66 per cent; social services, 45 per cent; public administration, 30 per cent. The differences between these last four sectors stand out even more clearly when we look at the distribution pattern as a whole, because it can then be seen that the majority of women in industry and trade are in the lower half of the income scale.

Fertility

One of the most striking features of female employment in Latin America, as has already been pointed out, is the low participation rate of married women, so low that even in countries where it is high in relation to the average for the region, it would have to be doubled to reach the level recorded in many industrialised countries. The difference between

TABLE 8. FEMALE PARTICIPATION RATES BY AGE AND BY NUMBER OF CHILDREN,
1960
(%)

Age	Number of children [1]			
	0	1-2	3-4	5-7
Argentina				
15-19	36.6	7.0	.	.
20-29	53.4	12.1	6.6	6.1
30-39	48.3	15.0	11.4	9.3
40-49	40.4	15.2	12.1	11.5
Brazil				
15-19	24.9	7.4	6.9	.
20-29	36.7	11.2	8.1	7.7
30-39	38.7	17.8	13.2	10.8
40-49	34.6	20.3	15.9	13.2
Chile				
15-19	23.8	17.6	.	.
20-29	47.6	22.5	7.0	6.0
30-39	47.8	28.3	14.0	8.8
40-49	39.6	24.6	19.7	13.0
Chile [2]				
	0	1	2	3
20-24	16.2	11.1	6.3	3.8
25-29	21.4	20.5	13.3	7.9
30-34	22.0	22.4	17.2	12.3
35-39	18.5	20.9	17.5	14.2
40-44	18.3	19.4	17.6	14.2
45-49	17.8	17.9	15.4	12.8

[1] Children born alive, irrespective of the mother's marital status.   [2] 1960 census figures relating exclusively to married women.

Source: Unless otherwise stated, CELADE Data Bank, census sample data.

single women and others in this respect is considerable even in the capital cities: in Buenos Aires, for example, a fairly recent fertility survey disclosed a participation rate of 70 per cent for single women compared with only 25 per cent for married women.

At the same time, the latter's participation varies considerably according to the number of children they have. The figures for Chile (1960) suggest that the participation rate of childless women hardly differs at all from that of women with only one child. The influence of family size

TABLE 9. PARTICIPATION RATES OF MARRIED WOMEN [1] BY AGE, NUMBER OF
CHILDREN AND EDUCATIONAL LEVEL IN THE METROPOLITAN AREA
OF SANTIAGO DE CHILE, 1970

(%)

Age of mother and number of children [2]	Number of years' education					
	0	1-3	4-5	6	7-11	12 or more
25-29						
1-2	22.3	15.9	21.7	18.8	15.4	40.8
3-4	16.7	4.8	5.8	5.9	9.8	21.0
5 or more	5.0	4.8	6.5	5.1	6.5	11.1
30-34						
1-2	33.3	17.2	15.1	20.5	20.9	45.3
3-4	20.0	9.6	8.8	8.8	10.3	32.5
5 or more	4.2	6.9	10.2	8.0	11.0	13.3
35-39						
1-2	14.3	20.7	19.7	16.8	23.9	48.0
3-4	3.6	13.4	14.4	14.2	15.7	39.7
5 or more	17.5	11.1	8.2	10.0	9.4	21.1

[1] Includes common law wives.   [2] Children born alive.

Source: 1970 population census, 5 per cent sample from provisional figures. As it is a sample, the margin of error in the rates for some groups may be large.

seems to show up as from the second child and to be particularly marked for women aged under 30 with three or more children (see table 8). Consequently, any expectation of greater participation by married women, as a result of a rapid change in fertility, decreases considerably on the birth of the third, fourth or fifth child. This is not merely because fewer mothers of three or more children work than do those with two or fewer children, but also because it is difficult to see why the latter should reduce their family size still further, or to conceive of a policy with this as its goal. It is worth stressing here what has already been said earlier: that married women between the ages of 15 and 44 with three or more children represent only a little over 50 per cent of all married women, even in high-fertility countries like Brazil.

Table 8 shows the participation rates of women by age and by number of children in three countries with different levels of fertility: low (Argentina), medium (Chile) and high (Brazil). There are noticeable differences in the figures for mothers with 1-2, 3-4 and 5-7 children; but the gap tends to narrow as the age of the woman increases, probably owing to the growing average age of the younger children.

The participation of women with a given number of children increases with the mother's educational level. The figures available for Chile support this hypothesis. The data given in table 9, which are for the metropolitan area of Santiago and are based on a 5 per cent sample from the 1970 census, show that—

(i) in the age groups 25-29, 30-34 and 35-39, the participation rate of women with 1-2 and 3-4 children increases with the mother's educational level, especially once she has had at least some secondary schooling (7-11 years);

(ii) the differences between women with 1-2 and 3-4 children generally remain more or less constant;

(iii) the participation of women with 5 or more children does not increase much with the mother's educational level, except among women aged between 35 and 39, a fact which may be related to the age of the children.

* * *

The foregoing comments, taken together with those made in the previous sections, lead us to conclude that a substantial increase in the participation rates of married women would be possible only if the following conditions were met: improvements in educational standards, structural changes and modernisation of the economy, and a reduction in family size. The preceding analysis suggests that the first two conditions are by far the most important. This reasoning is obviously true in respect of single women, and it is further strengthened if it is conceded that education and economic development have a long- or medium-term influence on fertility.

In conclusion, it is worth pointing out that there are signs that since 1960 fertility has begun to fall in a few Latin American countries. Nevertheless, with the exception of Chile and Costa Rica, where the decline appears to have been of the order of 25 per cent, there is no clear evidence of a significant reduction. In Brazil—judging by the data from the latest censuses—if there has been any reduction, it has been slight; the average number of children for mothers between 20 and 29 years of age remained practically unchanged at three between 1960 and 1970, whereas the average number of children for mothers between 30 and 39 years of age fell from 5.3 to 5.1. In Mexico, still according to census data, mothers aged between 20 and 29 continued to have an average of about 3.3 children over the same period. An approximate idea of the fertility situation in Peru and Venezuela may be had from the fact that around 1961 the average number of children of mothers aged between 20 and 39 was somewhat larger than that found in Brazil at about the same date. Consequently, in accordance with known fertility trends, no favourable influence in female participation rates was to be expected during the past decade. Moreover, as has already been seen, female participation has actually decreased in Chile, one of the few countries where there has been a sharp drop in fertility (although it should not be overlooked that this is a case where positive qualitative changes have occurred in the composition of the female labour force).

Trends in Women's Employment in the USSR

Svetlana TURCHANINOVA [1]

FULL EQUALITY for women in every field of economic, social and political activity is one of the basic principles of the Soviet State. As far as economic and social equality is concerned, the surest guarantee is seen to lie in women's widespread participation in the production process, which not only gives them financial independence but promotes the all-round development of their personality and allows them to play a full part in the life of the community.

The Government, for its part, follows a consistent policy of encouraging women's massive involvement in economic activity through a variety of practical measures. These include a wide range of social welfare benefits, special occupational safety measures for working women and steady improvement of their working conditions, extensive educational facilities and increased family allowances.

These factors combined account for women's large share of the total labour force (51 per cent), with the world's highest proportion in production management (63 per cent), scientific occupations (49 per cent), cultural activities (73 per cent) and the arts (45 per cent). The provisions mentioned above, supplemented by the state maternity and child welfare scheme, go a long way towards resolving the fundamental problem facing working women, that of reconciling their careers with their role as mothers and their all-round personal development. If this problem is to disappear altogether, we shall have to take even fuller account of the specific features and requirements of women's employment in the context of the scientific and technological revolution, and to eliminate whatever inequality still lingers on in their home life. This inequality is being steadily eradicated by rising standards of living and expanding social services catering for family needs and various aspects of child care.

Every five-year plan contains provisions to improve women's working conditions and lighten their domestic burden. The 1971-75 plan, for example, fixed the maternity benefit for all working women at the level of

---

[1] Chief of Department, Central Trade Union College, Moscow.

their full earnings regardless of length of service; the period of paid leave for looking after a sick child was extended; and children's allowances for families in the lower income brackets, introduced on 1 November 1974, are running at an annual figure of 1,800 million roubles. The aggregate expenditure under the national budget for maternity benefits and family allowances, and for tuition and maintenance in kindergartens and other children's institutions, exceeded 14,300 million roubles in 1973. During that year there were 10.5 million children attending pre-school institutions.[1]

Women's labour force participation

A feature of the employment situation in the USSR is the high proportion—86 per cent—of able-bodied women of working age who work in the various sectors of the national economy. In 1959 the proportion was 75 per cent. The total female labour force, both manual and non-manual, increased from 28 to 46 million between 1959 and 1970 alone, and has now risen to over 51 million.[2]

The female labour force was swollen both by women reaching working age and by those entering productive employment from what is known as the domestic economy (housekeeping and cultivating private plots). The composition of the Soviet labour force was long affected by the considerable surplus of females resulting from the heavy male casualties of the Second World War. In 1959 women, primarily of working age, outnumbered the men by 20.7 million. The situation had substantially changed by 1970, when there was even a small male surplus in the 16-24 age group. The numbers of women and men aged 25 to 39 were near to parity, and it was only among those aged 40 and over that there was still a surplus of women.

During the 1960s women accounted for 60 per cent of the growth of the labour force, so it is not surprising that their share of total employment should have risen from 47 per cent at the beginning of the decade to 51 per cent at the end.[2]

The fast rates of female employment growth in 1965-70 were due to a high demand for labour which outpaced the growth of the working-age population. Another contributory pull factor was a series of social and economic measures, particularly increased basic rates of remuneration in every economic sector (machine-tool operators, for instance, received pay increases of 15 per cent on average) and a 25 per cent tax cut for the lower-paid groups.

Meanwhile, the growing material and intellectual needs of the population arising from the availability of better education, expanded home-building programmes and increased output of durables acted as push

---

[1] *Vestnik Statistiki* (Moscow), 1975, No. 1, pp. 91 and 93.

[2] Ibid., p. 86.

factors in inducing families to raise their aggregate take-home pay by having more of their members, primarily housewives, enter productive employment.

Over the past five years, however, most of the new recruits to the labour force have been supplied by the rising generation, in equal proportions of males and females.

The 1970 national census showed 7.5 per cent of all women of working age, or 5.9 million in absolute figures, to be employed in the domestic economy as against 25.4 per cent in 1959.[1] Women's employment in the domestic economy, above all as housewives, is seen in present-day Soviet society as necessary not only for the individual mother but also for the proper rearing of a new generation, and hence, at least for the time being, as an indispensable element of a rational employment system. But this confinement to the domestic economy of a certain number of women for a certain period of time does not in any way signify that they are for ever withdrawn from productive employment. The typical Soviet woman today is not a housewife permanently chained to her kitchen sink, nursery or garden plot but a full citizen active in productive employment and interrupting it only for a while to bear and look after her children.

The optimal level of women's employment obviously depends on a number of demographic factors such as the birth rate and the size of families which can markedly affect their capacity to engage in productive employment. For example, in the Soviet Central Asian republics, with their high birth rates and typically large families, female participation rates are lower than the national average.

Patterns of female employment

The past 10 to 15 years have seen not only increased numbers of women in employment and their higher proportion of the total labour force but also significant shifts in their sectoral and occupational distribution.

It can be seen from the table that women in the USSR are well represented in every economic sector, particularly in the key " production " sectors (industrial production—especially manufacturing—agriculture and forestry, transport and communications, etc.) which occupy two-thirds of the female labour force. In fact this proportion has declined somewhat over the period covered by the table as the result of higher productivity achieved in the output of material goods and consequent lower labour requirements. The workers thus released are shifted from one production sector to another or absorbed by the social, cultural and

[1] Calculation based on data in *Vestnik Statistiki*, 1973, No. 1, p. 80.

PERCENTAGE DISTRIBUTION OF WOMEN WORKERS BY ECONOMIC SECTOR,
1960 AND 1974

Sector	Share of total labour force		Share of female labour force	
	1960	1974 (estimate)	1960	1974 (estimate)
All women workers	**47**	**51**	**100**	**100**
" Production " sectors :				
Industrial production	45	49	35.0	32.0
Agriculture	41	44	9.5	8.8
Forestry	21	21	0.3	0.2
Transport	24	24	5.1	4.2
Communications	64	68	1.6	2.0
Construction	30	29	6.4	5.8
Retail trade and public catering	66	76	10.6	12.7
Other " production " sectors	45	49	0.7	1.1
" Non-production " sectors :				
Municipal and personal services	53	53	3.5	3.8
Health, physical education and social services	85	85	10.1	9.4
Education and culture	70	73	11.5	12.7
Entertainment	36	45	0.4	0.4
Research and auxiliary services	42	49	2.5	3.6
Banking and state insurance	68	81	0.6	0.7
Government and economic administrative bodies, co-operative and civic organisations	51	63	2.2	2.6

Source: *Vestnik Statistiki*, 1975, No. 1, pp. 86-87.

welfare services. The number of women employed in agriculture has been going down in the past 10 to 15 years, while that of women workers in industry, transport and other production sectors has been rising slowly. Nevertheless, the *proportion* of the total female labour force employed in industrial production dropped from 35 to 32 per cent during these years (see table).

The percentage distribution of male and female employees varies widely from sector to sector, depending, primarily, on the working conditions and job content in each. Male labour predominates in the extractive industries, transport, construction, forestry and other sectors involving arduous and hazardous work wholly or partially proscribed to women by the existing legislation. The proportion of women workers in those sectors is no higher than 30 per cent. The over-all male/female labour ratio in the production sectors was close to 55/45 in 1974, while in non-production activity female labour accounted for nearly 69 per cent of the total.

The rising proportion of women workers is characteristic both of the national economy as a whole and of most of its sectors individually. Their share has now stabilised in forestry and transport, public health, municipal and personal services, while shrinking slightly in construction.

Industrial women workers

The largest occupational group of Soviet women at the present time is in industrial production, which in 1974 employed 16 million women or almost one-third of the entire female labour force. Nearly half of all industrial workers are women.

The level of women's employment and the content of their jobs in industry are decisively influenced by technological progress and, above all, by the mechanisation and automation of production processes. Increased mechanisation is reducing the demand for manual labour, improving the industrial environment and thereby opening up occupations which were formerly inaccessible to women. At the same time, advances in science and technology are modifying the structure of industrial production, with manufacturing industries gaining ground at the expense of the extractive industries, where working conditions are more difficult. Rapid headway has been made over the past decade in the industries contributing most to technological progress (electronics, electrical and radio engineering, instrument-making, chemicals, etc.) as well as in consumer goods industries (light industry, food and printing, to name just a few).

The distribution of female labour within industry is uneven. As of 1 January 1970 nearly 70 per cent of all women industrial workers were employed in three branches: engineering, light industry and food, according to the figures of the USSR Central Statistical Board.

Engineering employs the most women—over 33 per cent of the total industrial female workforce—and their numbers are still rising, particularly in electrical engineering, ball-bearing production and other comparatively new branches. This is a direct result of the increasingly favourable working conditions created by ever greater mechanisation and automation.

Light industry comes second, employing over 20 per cent of the industrial female workforce. About 10 per cent work in food factories, 6.8 per cent in chemical plants, and close on 5 per cent in the building materials industry.

The predominance of men in some and of women in other branches—due to disparities in the prevailing working conditions—has led certain industrial occupations to be classified as " male " or " female ". After all, it is quite natural that the proportion of female labour in coalmining, forestry and electric power should be under 25 per cent, as against 83 per cent in light industry and between 30 and 50 per cent in engineering and metalworking, building materials, pulp and paper, and woodworking.

Soviet labour legislation proscribes or restricts women's employment in processes and occupations potentially hazardous to the female organism. A " List of specially heavy and dangerous processes and occupations in which women must not be employed " was inserted in the Labour Code as early as 1932, when the Soviet national economy was still in its infancy.[1] It has since been supplemented and amended on many occasions with a view to protecting greater numbers of women against the health risks involved in such work. In principle limitations of this sort are imposed on women's employment by the urban placement offices [2] as well as by enterprises when hiring or training workers. In fact the restrictions are applied still earlier, at all stages of training and even on entry to colleges and universities, technical and vocational training schools. The latter, for instance, allow girls to be trained in only 714 out of the total of 1,100 trades. Nearly all geological prospecting and mining occupations are outside the girls' training programmes at vocational schools; the only one in coalmining open to girls is that of control panel operator at the pit head or in strip mining. Wherever access to an occupation is restricted or prohibited for women, however, it is exclusively on the grounds of their psycho-physiological characteristics and health protection requirements; in all other cases the choice of occupation is determined by individual interest and vocational training.

The balance of male and female labour is being slowly evened up in most industries. As progress continues to be made in manufacturing, particularly through advances in mechanisation and automation bringing fundamental improvements in conditions of work and safety, the proportion of women workers in the traditionally "male" sectors is growing. This is to be observed in the oil extracting and refining industries, coalmining, iron and steel and non-ferrous metallurgy, and engineering, in all of which women's share of the total workforce is slowly rising. That of male workers is increasing, meanwhile, in the traditionally " female " sectors, as technological progress calls for more fitters to set up transfer machines and automated equipment, and more repair workers, both of which occupations are at present mainly filled by men. By the same

---

[1] ILO: *Legislative Series*, 1932—Russ. 5A. See also " Normativnye akty po ispolzovaniyu trudovykh resursov ", in *Yuridicheskaya Literatura* (Moscow), 1972, pp. 555-565.

[2] These are operated by the state manpower allocation committees of the Councils of Ministers in the various republics.

token, the proportion of women has somewhat declined in the chemical, textile and garment industries.

As the key sectors advanced technologically, the structure of the female labour force changed and women's employment in machine maintenance considerably increased. The number of women workers in mechanised jobs in Soviet industrial undertakings more than quadrupled between 1939 and 1959. The subsequent 15 years have also witnessed a rapid growth of women's employment in skilled machine maintenance jobs. Between 1965 and 1972, for example, while the over-all industrial female labour force in the Russian Federation (the largest of the Soviet republics) rose by 12 per cent, the proportion engaged in mechanised jobs went up by nearly 22 per cent and that in automated occupations by 67 per cent. Certain individual occupations showed a still faster rate of growth in women's employment: more than a threefold increase in the number of women fitters supervising and monitoring automated equipment, a 180 per cent increase in the numbers operating remote-controlled equipment, etc. Women's share of the total workforce engaged in mechanised and automated occupations relating to the supervision and control of equipment and machinery is also rising: 77 per cent of transfer machine operators and 42 per cent of automated plant engineers and mechanics are now women. This accounts for the higher over-all level of women's employment in mechanised jobs, with nearly half of all women workers engaged in automated and mechanised occupations.

It is interesting to note the present balance and trends of women's employment in basic and auxiliary industrial occupations.[1] Over 60 per cent of women are in basic and fewer than 40 per cent in auxiliary jobs, as against a 44/56 ratio for men.[2] A significant feature, however, is that in textiles and other light industries with a large proportion of female employees women workers are employed mostly in basic production jobs while the auxiliary work is mainly done by men. In industries like ore- and coalmining with comparatively few women workers (under 30 per cent) female labour is employed primarily in auxiliary operations. In industries with average rates of female employment (30 to 50 per cent) its distribution between basic and auxiliary operations varies widely, yet averages something like a one-to-one ratio, particularly in engineering. It is noteworthy that male workers are supplying the bulk of the growing numbers of auxiliary employees in the Russian Federation's industries, while the basic jobs are being primarily filled by women.

---

[1] The Central Statistical Board of the USSR divides industrial occupations into " basic " and " auxiliary " according to function. Basic occupations are those concerned directly with the actual production of industrial goods, while auxiliary occupations are those which *serve* " basic " production, e.g. plant maintenance and repair work, technical supervision, loading and haulage, power supply.

[2] Calculated by the Central Research Laboratory of the State Committee on Labour Resource Utilisation of the Council of Ministers of the Russian Federation.

Professional women workers

The practical application of scientific and technological advances is not only diminishing the need for sheer physical strength [1] but also progressively " intellectualising " the entire field of labour and enhancing the significance of entrepreneurial, organisational and managerial functions. The type of employment engaged in by women today accurately reflects the changes taking place in the pattern of work and job content in the USSR. Women have long ceased to be the " back-up " workforce they were in the early years of Soviet government when they were employed mostly in unskilled jobs. Their extensive participation in all sectors of the national economy as specialists, production managers and as skilled workers generally is one of the most characteristic features of the present-day employment scene in the USSR. Women account, for instance, for 48 per cent of all designers, 44 per cent of engineers, 59 per cent of technicians. The number of women executives and professional workers is steadily growing: 32 per cent of supervisory and management staff are now women. Over 500,000 work as factory and state farm directors, co-operative farm chairmen, construction project superintendents and office and department chiefs. Growing numbers of women work as agricultural specialists: 40 per cent of graduate agronomists, veterinarians and livestock experts are women.

Turning to the political and judicial scene, 475 women were elected to the Supreme Soviet of the USSR in 1974, or 31 per cent of the total membership. Women constitute 36 per cent of the deputies to the Supreme Soviets of the constituent and autonomous republics of the Union, and 47 per cent of those to the local Workers' Soviets. Over 32 per cent of all judges and nearly 50 per cent of people's assessors in 1974 were women.

There are 559,000 women working as physicians in the health services, making up 70 per cent of the medical profession, and 1.7 million are employed in education—71 per cent of the total teaching staff.[2] They are well established in science, too, constituting about 49 per cent of all scientific workers. There are women members of the academies, both full and corresponding, professors, assistant professors, senior research officers, chiefs of major scientific laboratories and research establishments.

---

[1] For example, the present Ninth Five-Year National Economic Development Plan (1971-75) provided for the output of mechanised loading and warehouse handling equipment to be increased by 76 per cent compared with the previous five-year period. The output of plant for light industry and the food industry is being doubled, food factories being re-equipped with fully mechanised and automated transfer machines which supersede manual labour altogether both in basic and in auxiliary operations. All this widens the range of work accessible to women and improves the conditions in which it is performed. The process of mechanising auxiliary operations leads to some women workers being transferred to other operations after retraining.

[2] *Vestnik Statistiki*, 1975, No. 1, pp. 89 and 84-85.

The proportion of women among research staffs has been growing fast over the past 10 to 15 years: it more than trebled from 128,700 to 439,000 between 1960 and 1973, while the number of women having taken a science degree increased by 150 per cent.

It is not only in the sciences, however, that women's employment in highly skilled occupations has grown over the past decade. The number of women engineers increased by 320 per cent, that of mechanical engineers by 210 per cent and that of designers and technologists by 130 per cent between the two latest national censuses of 1959 and 1970.

Proof of the higher " quality " of women's employment is provided by the rising number of women engaged in intellectual work, the shift from physical towards intellectual occupations, the growing number of women specialists with higher and secondary specialised training (discussed in the next section), and so on. The number of women intellectual workers rose from 33.5 per cent of the total in 1939 to 54 per cent in 1959 and 59 per cent in 1970. There has, besides, been a substantial change in the distribution of women between physical and intellectual occupations, the latter accounting for a mere 13.6 per cent of all working women in 1939 but rising to 23 per cent in 1959 and to over 30 per cent in 1970.

Education and training

A factor contributing to the increased employment of women in intellectual jobs has been their rising level of general education and vocational training. Nearly 10 million women with higher and secondary specialised training (59 per cent of all those so qualified) were employed in the Soviet national economy in 1970. This is to say that one in every five working women, counting both manual and non-manual workers, was a specialist with higher or secondary education.

Particularly notable headway in women's education has been made in the republics of Soviet Central Asia, the Transcaucasus and in the country's eastern regions where as few as 10 per cent of all women could read or write in the 1920s and 1930s.

The general educational standards of men and women in the USSR today are practically equal. There are 737 men and 739 women per 1,000 workers who have received a secondary or higher education. Only the older generations (those over 50) still reveal disparities in general educational standards. Among young people (under 30) the women's level of general education is higher than the men's, and women workers are now improving their skill level at almost the same rate as male workers.

The Soviet public education system offers unlimited opportunities for women to study on a par with men, to undergo vocational training and advance in their chosen profession.

Women's equality in all phases and forms of training has been codified in the basic principles governing legislation in the USSR and its constituent republics, which proclaim the fundamental right of all Soviet citizens regardless of sex, race or nationality to equal access to education, to eight-year schooling and to free tuition in every form of training. Identical syllabuses for all students, ruling out any discrimination against women in their choice of trade or occupation (apart from the restrictions noted earlier), are yet another factor ensuring equal educational opportunities to men and women.

Free tuition at all levels of training means that no Soviet family has to worry about which of its children (a son or a daughter) can afford to go on studying after school. The choice of calling and the type of specialised training undergone depend on the youngster's own abilities and preferences. The attitudes towards female education, fostered by the mass media and reinforced by legally guaranteed access to education, encourage girls and women to study and advance in their profession. A further contributing factor is that the State guarantees security of employment according to one's occupational preference and skill rating, equal opportunities for professional advancement and equal pay for equal work to all trainees of either sex having qualified for any trade or profession in any public educational establishment.

The eight years of schooling currently provided are being raised to ten, as specified in the present five-year plan (1971-75). General education is provided at schools, at technical vocational schools offering a ten-year course, and at technical colleges. Most Soviet girls first attend general secondary schools and then choose the trade or profession for which their further education will equip them. Sociological surveys have shown that women industrial workers under 30 have an average of 9.8 years of schooling.

This is not the place to dwell upon the vocational and technical training system which, as we have seen, is essentially the same for both sexes.[1] Suffice it to say that the inter-enterprise training institutions providing on-the-job training and the technical vocational schools providing a full secondary education along with occupational training are particularly suitable for girls because they are through with their studies and can start work before the time comes for them to shoulder their family responsibilities. They will by then normally have become accustomed to the higher income and sufficiently interested in their jobs to keep the interruption of their employment fairly short. More than 20 million people receive on-the-job training every year: a third of them are women. All workers follow a course of retraining or vocational upgrading once every three to five years on average. In light industry undertakings, for example, one in every four women workers does so each year.

---

[1] A recent summary description, albeit focusing on the rural areas, appeared in A. Petrov: " Rural vocational training in the USSR ", in *International Labour Review*, Oct. 1974.

Some outstanding problems

The very considerable successes already achieved in women's vocational training do not mean that there are no more problems left to solve in this field. There is in particular a need for further improvement in the skill level of women industrial workers. Whereas women's work is in general equal to men's in respect of complexity, nevertheless the skills and performance ratings of women employees still lag behind in certain occupational groups and undertakings. This is because, above all, women's housekeeping tasks have yet to be fully rationalised. For all the substantial progress made in the provision of personal services, public catering and government-maintained facilities for pre-school children, there are still a good many household chores a working married woman has to do. She has only from two-thirds to half as much spare time as her husband, and because on-the-job training and retraining require an extra investment of time and effort they are less accessible to women workers with small children to look after and a greater share of the housework to do. Relevant surveys have shown that the professional advancement of women under 30 is slower than that of men of the same age.

The need to give women more leisure time and expand their vocational training opportunities is being tackled both nationally and locally, that is, at factory level.

This is being done, above all, by reducing the time working women have to spend on housework and child care—through improved personal services, more extensive public catering, better shopping facilities and housing and other amenities needed to raise the standard of living.

The 1975 national budget, for instance, provides for 923 million roubles to be spent on the extension and development of personal services, 15,200 million roubles on housing, with a total of 21,500 million roubles being allocated to finance the entire range of measures designed to increase the people's well-being.

Much is also being done by the enterprises themselves, as already noted, to improve women workers' living and working conditions. There is an on-going enterprise-funded programme for improving the working environment and conditions, extending mechanisation and social services, and building modern residential complexes complete with all kinds of cultural and welfare facilities, kindergartens, crèches, boarding houses, shopping centres, medical centres, etc.

A good deal of occupational safety research affecting women workers is also under way, notably with a view to revising the list of processes and occupations prohibited to women and the permissible stress limits. The emergence of new industries and trades, the changing levels of mechanisation and automation, and the introduction of new processing techniques, chemicals, etc., call for thorough measurement of the effects on the female organism. On the other hand, the advantages of mechanisation and automation along with progress in occupational safety and health have already made some of the proscribed trades and occupations safe for women.

Great emphasis is being laid on modernising industrial safety facilities, the current five-year plan providing for the installation or reconstruction of 300,000 ventilating units, the building of washrooms, toilets, etc., covering 15 million square metres of industrial floor space, over 10,000 health care centres, etc.[1] These efforts are to be continued. Special consideration is being given at factory level to the needs of pregnant women workers and nursing mothers. Under present legislation they are allowed shorter working hours, transferred to lighter work whenever necessary, and completely exempted from overtime working while continuing to draw their previous average earnings.

A feature of recent years has been the increased consideration given to female ergonomic standards in machine and plant design (practically all industrial plant and machinery used to be made predominantly for male workers to operate). These standards are observed, for example, in the manufacture of all the 80 types of looms and weaving machines produced in the USSR at the present time.[2] Similar measures taken in other sectors of the economy will go a long way towards creating optimal working conditions for the women they employ. By guaranteeing women not just the right to work but a free choice of occupation and full opportunities for advancement and promotion, the Soviet Government is doing much to help them combine their careers with their maternal and other domestic roles. Indeed the assistance furnished in this way is a major component of the Soviet social programme for constantly improving the working people's standard of living and facilitating their harmonious all-round development.

---

[1] Y. S. Yakushin: *Narodnoe blagosostoyanie v devyatoy pyatiletke* (Moscow, Ekonomika, 1973), p. 38.

[2] See *Okhrana Truda i Sotsialnoe Strakhovanie* (Moscow), 1973, No. 1, p. 2.

Sexual Equality in the Labour Market

Some Experiences and Views of the Nordic Countries

Anna-Greta LEIJON [1]

IN THIS ARTICLE I attempt to show what progress we have made in the Nordic countries with regard to the equality of the sexes in the labour market. I shall also discuss various ILO Conventions and Recommendations and explain why the Nordic countries have ratified certain Conventions but not others. Finally I shall have a number of suggestions to offer concerning the great task that lies ahead of us.

My specific examples are taken from Sweden. This is because I am familiar with Swedish conditions. It does not imply that public opinion on this issue and the solutions adopted are the same in all the Nordic countries, though there are many points of resemblance between our various ways of approaching and tackling problems, and I would venture to say that the differences between the Nordic countries are smaller than the differences between them and many other countries.

Three fundamental principles

The principles that the Swedish Government regards as fundamental in order to promote equality between men and women are these:

(1) Priority must be given to efforts to achieve equality between groups and between individuals in the society. The individual's position in society is determined by the prevailing economic and social conditions, as well as by sex. The achievement of equality between men and women must, therefore, form part of the general struggle to achieve equality in society. In the campaign for equality between men and women, priority must be given to measures which strengthen the status of those women

---

[1] Assistant Minister of Labour, Sweden.

who are worst off with regard to education, training, employment and income, and who also lack all influence in society.

This principle must be duly considered in development policy and planning.

(2) Women must have the same right as men to employment, regardless of marital status.

The reason for this is that a strong position in the labour market considerably enhances a woman's opportunities for active participation in the community and in public life. It also gives her economic independence and social security as well as proving beneficial for her family. Furthermore, it gives her increased potential for influencing society by participation in trade union activities. This experience will deepen her interest in taking an active part in political and other organisations.

(3) Women and men must participate in working life on equal terms, which is not possible today. Working conditions have to be adapted more closely to the tasks to which workers must (and should be entitled to) attend parallel to their working careers, particularly the demands of parenthood. But this aim cannot be achieved either so long as women still have to bear the main burden of looking after homes and children; so long as women—but seldom men—spend a number of years away from the labour market while their children are growing up; so long as large groups of women continue to work part time; and so long as the labour market remains divided into " male " and " female " occupations. This is turn means that a change in the traditional role of women must be accompanied by a change in the traditional role of men. In a society that is really committed to principles of solidarity and equality, a new role characterised by similar opportunities and responsibilities for men and women will be the norm.

For women the change must primarily take the form of increased opportunities for employment and political participation, while for men it must entail increased responsibilities (and greater satisfaction) in the home and with their children.

Apart from these three principles, there are others which are equally important but which are so well known and so widely conceded that I need not elaborate on them. I am thinking for instance of equal rights to education and training and equal participation in trade union and political activities.

More and more women gainfully employed

In the Nordic countries, as elsewhere in the world, the twentieth century has witnessed sweeping changes in the labour market. It is above all the situation of women that has been transformed. In Sweden the number of women in the labour market practically doubled between 1950 and 1970, while the number of married women in gainful employment quadrupled. The forecasts indicate that we can expect this trend to continue. During the past few years women in Sweden have been entering the labour market at a rate of 50,000 to 70,000 per year (our total population being 8 million and our total labour force 4 million, of whom 1.6 million are women). Women have accounted for practically the entire labour force increment, and they are more or less our sole remaining labour resource that has not yet been fully tapped: 66.5 per cent of all women in Sweden between the ages of 16 and 64 are now employed, the corresponding figure for men being 87.0 per cent.

The labour force participation rate of married women working at least half time has increased as follows:

Year	1950	1960	1965	1970	1973
%	16	26	37	45	47

The proportion of women in the labour force having children under 7 has risen from 37 per cent in 1965 to 57 per cent in 1974.

In Norway the participation rate among married women remained low for a considerable time, but here too things have moved very fast in the past 15 years. Whereas only 10 per cent of married women were gainfully employed in 1960, the figure today is two or three times that number. (The category " gainfully employed " includes persons declaring earnings from their own gainful employment as their principal source of income.) According to the Norwegian labour force surveys (which include women working part time), the corresponding rate is now 41 per cent. Finland has long had a very large proportion of married women in the labour market. The participation rates of such women in Finland and Sweden are now practically level, even though part-time employment is far less common in Finland than in Sweden.

Women are no longer a reserve in our labour market which can be manipulated like a concertina to the rhythm of cyclic fluctuations. Even during our latest recession the number of women in employment continued to rise. Instead of withdrawing from the labour force, as they had done in earlier recessions, their ranks continued to grow both absolutely and relatively. It remains to be seen whether this tendency will persist during the next recession, but it was encouraging to note that nobody spoke of women as a threat to men's employment and that nobody queried their right to look for employment in a period of economic difficulty.

Owing among other things to their increased participation in employment, however, women are also coming to account for a larger share of the unemployed. The interesting thing is that a great deal of unemployment among women arises from the formal registration with employment offices of women who formerly were only " latent " applicants for employment (" would apply for a job if there were any to be had "). But there are still a great many latent applicants for employment who during the 1970s will be calling on society to help them exercise their right to work.

I would like to quote one small example to show how this transition from concealed to open unemployment functions in reality. In September 1972 it was announced that the Swedish Government and the big textile firm of Algots had concluded an agreement for the establishment of factories in three northern Swedish municipalities. A thousand new employment opportunities were to be provided by the company in the course of five years. This decision was announced on a Saturday. The following Monday, when the employment office opened, the telephone exchange was jammed with applications for the new jobs. In two days 281 women had registered their interest and by the end of the first week 453 women had done so. In August, before the decision was announced, there had been 493 women registered as unemployed in the county concerned. One month after the decision, in October, this figure had risen to 762. Active measures in the labour market increase employment, but they also raise the expectations of many people who did not previously believe they had any real chance of finding work. In this way, paradoxically enough, increasing job opportunities can result in higher unemployment figures.

All this reflects a new attitude on the part of men and women towards the idea of women in the labour market. It is no longer a matter of course for men to have first refusal of jobs even when jobs are hard to come by. Women's self-confidence has risen. A woman will be less afraid of venturing into the labour market after a long period as a full-time housewife if she looks around her and sees other women doing the same thing and succeeding. The participation rate of women can be expected to go on rising during the years ahead.

Male and female labour markets

The fact remains, however, that we still have a segregated labour market, or more exactly we have one labour market where men predominate and another where women predominate. I would like to quote what is said on this point in the ILO report to this year's session of the International Labour Conference.[1]

As has often been emphasised [the labelling of certain jobs as " men's work " and of others as " women's work "] is both dangerous and discriminatory. It leads to recruitment based on sex rather than on capacity, and it perpetuates unproven beliefs about women's abilities and inabilities as workers. It places unjust barriers in the way of their opportunities for advancement. It creates a situation in which work traditionally done by men commands higher pay and prestige while that traditionally

[1] ILO: *Equality of opportunity and treatment for women workers,* Report VIII, International Labour Conference, 60th Session, Geneva, 1975, p. 20.

done by women is accorded lower pay and prestige and is consistently undervalued. It has no inherent logic.

Clear examples of all this are to be seen in Sweden. Women choose among 25 occupations, men choose among 300. The female sector comprises nursing occupations, office work and retail trade. Women also have shorter working days than men, and 36.6 per cent of all women in the labour market work part time (fewer than 35 hours per week) as against a mere 2.4 per cent of the men.

Traditional female occupations are valued less highly than men's jobs. The hourly rates of pay of female industrial workers, expressed as a percentage of the men's rates, have developed as follows:

Year	1960	1964	1970	1974
%	70	75	83	86

The segregated labour market and the lower rates of pay received by women do not imply that the traditional female occupations are easier or that working conditions in them are specially adapted. For instance, nursing entails at least the same amount of heavy lifting as many typically male occupations that are usually regarded as heavy jobs. And in the whole of the nursing sector, which is completely dependent on female labour, no efforts have been made to safeguard women against night work as has been done in industry. It is therefore only natural to ask whether the special rules applied to women in this respect in industry have really been prompted by consideration for women's interests.

Measures to promote equality

It goes without saying that our labour market policy must in principle be the same for everybody, regardless of sex. But even a policy on these lines can have discriminatory effects. Formerly, for instance, most relief work projects in Sweden were organised in the construction and road-building sectors, so that in practice unemployed women did not enjoy the same rights as men to relief employment. Since then changes have occurred in this sphere and in others besides, but we have also come to realise that special measures may have to be taken to enable women in the labour market to attain true equality and overcome such handicaps as insufficient education, limited experience of the labour market following several years at home, and so on.

This attitude is not our private property. It is shared by, among others, the ILO report cited earlier. The mere prevention of discrimination is not enough: equality of status must be actively promoted.

A number of special measures of this kind have been proposed by the Advisory Council on Equality between Men and Women [1] that the

---

[1] Similar bodies have been established in Finland and Norway.

Swedish Government has set up and whose chairman I am. The Council is attached to the Prime Minister's Office and is broadly representative of government departments, major trade unions, women's associations, as well as women from all parts of Sweden and in all kinds of occupations.

So far the efforts of the Council have been concentrated on improving women's status in the labour market. A few of the steps taken by the Government on the recommendation of the Council and constituting a kind of positive discrimination—i.e. in *favour* of women—are listed below:

— A substantial number of new positions have been created in the public employment offices whose incumbents are responsible exclusively for improving the provision of good job opportunities for women.

— Within the framework of regional development policy, measures have been undertaken to counteract the traditional division of male and female occupations. Companies that are being established or expanded in regions where there is a shortage of employment opportunities can be granted government loans and subsidies only if they recruit at least 40 per cent of each sex.

— Our Advisory Council has started a regional pilot project which now covers six out of Sweden's 24 counties. The goal of the project, which includes extensive training, is to introduce women into industries with a vast majority of male workers. A large number of women have been employed under this project, for instance in engineering and in the wood industry. They have also proved to the sceptics, both men and women, that women can cope with all kinds of industrial jobs. Prejudice against women in traditionally male jobs is disappearing. The pilot project has influenced other companies with a similar manpower structure to employ more women. During the past year, when 70,000 women entered the labour market, 15,000 of them were engaged for what used to be regarded as typically male jobs. Another positive effect of the project is that in many cases the working environment has been improved for all workers in the companies.

— The Government, as an employer, has a great responsibility for creating equal opportunities for women and men within the civil service. To this end a special government committee has been set up and will present its proposals this year. The Government is shortly going to set up another committee which will examine to what extent military posts, and civilian posts serving the military, could be held by women.

What is known in the Nordic countries as " labour market training " is one of the best aids that society can offer to women wishing for gainful employment. In Sweden this training is available to anybody who is unemployed or in danger of becoming so and who cannot obtain permanent employment. Certain courses training people for occupations with a severe labour shortage are open to all comers. Labour market training is undergone by over 100,000 persons every year, which corresponds to the entire annual school intake or the total number of students at all universities and graduate schools in Sweden. Nowadays this training is provided to equal numbers of men and women. If the Riksdag passes a Bill which I presented recently, labour market training in future will be utilised by even more women and will help them to obtain permanent employment. Among other things, the Bill provides for a considerable increase in training grants and for the abolition of the existing means test applied to the earnings of the trainee's husband or wife.

All these reforms and measures have contributed to a rapid increase in the employment rate among women, especially married women with small children. This fact, together with the conviction that men should take a more active part in the care of their children, has stimulated a heated discussion in political organisations, trade unions and the mass media about the necessity of reducing the working day from eight to six hours.

The expansion of day care centres and other child care facilities is also of vital importance for equality between men and women. The Government stimulates the expansion of these facilities by substantial financial subsidies.

The Nordic countries and certain ILO Conventions

I hope that the foregoing outline of the situation in Sweden will make it a little easier for the reader when I now turn to discuss certain ILO Conventions and our attitude to them.

Although public opinion and the measures adopted in this field are not, as already mentioned, identical throughout the Nordic countries, we do to a great extent share the same basic principles and the same objectives. We share the view that everybody is entitled to work and that children are the joint responsibility of both parents. Our aim is to establish a more humane role for men and women alike and to enable both sexes to combine gainful employment with the care of their children.

The table will serve to illustrate the current situation regarding the ratification of certain ILO Conventions by the Nordic countries. As will be seen, the basic Conventions, Nos. 100 and 111, have been ratified by all of them. On the other hand the remaining Conventions, containing provisions concerning special safety precautions and allowances on behalf of women, have received far fewer ratifications.

MATERNITY (AND PATERNITY) PROTECTION

First I would like to consider the Conventions protecting women during and after pregnancy. With the exception of Convention No. 102

167

RATIFICATIONS BY THE NORDIC COUNTRIES OF ILO CONVENTIONS
PARTICULARLY CONCERNING WOMEN

Convention	Denmark	Finland	Iceland	Norway	Sweden
No. 111 (1958): Discrimination (Employment and Occupation)	×	×	×	×	×
No. 100 (1951): Equal Remuneration	×	×	×	×	×
Nos. 3 (1919) and 103 (1952): Maternity Protection					
No. 102 (1952): Social Security (Minimum Standards)					× (Part VIII)
Nos. 4 (1919) and 89 (1948): Night Work (Women)					
No. 45 (1935): Underground Work (Women)		×			Ratified 1936, denounced 1967
No. 127 (1967): Maximum Weight					
No. 13 (1921): White Lead (Painting)		×		×	×
No. 136 (1971): Benzene		Riksdag Bill for ratification, Jan. 1975			

concerning minimum standards of social security, Part VIII, which Sweden has ratified, these Conventions have not been ratified by any of the Nordic countries. This does not reflect any denial of the need for special security and protection for women in this situation. In many cases the decision not to ratify was prompted by the fact that at the time Nordic legislation did not satisfy the requirements of the Convention in question. Since then legislative reforms have been enacted in the Nordic countries to establish rules concerning protection and financial security during and after pregnancy which in many cases are more advanced than the provisions of the Conventions, although discrepancies still exist.

One of the major obstacles to Swedish ratification of Conventions Nos. 3 and 103 concerning maternity protection has been and still is the requirement of six weeks' compulsory leave after confinement (Article 3). The view held in Sweden is that protection in connection with childbirth should not prevent a woman from resuming work earlier if a medical examination shows her to be fit to do so. Also, as we want to implement the principle that the responsibility for children lies on *both* parents, we do not wish to provide special benefits for the mother other than in cases directly connected with her physical needs. It is in accordance with this principle that the Swedish Government last year changed maternity benefits insurance into *parenthood* benefits insurance. The parenthood benefits are paid for a total period of seven months. The parents can divide this period between them as they like and the benefits—amounting to 90 per cent of the income forgone—are paid to that parent who stays at home and has the major part of the care of the child. Working fathers and mothers also have the right to sickness benefits if they need to stay at home to take care of sick children.

A Bill containing similar provisions has been presented in Norway, and Finland too has begun to consider the transformation of maternity benefits into parental benefits.

While on the subject it may be of interest to note that it was not possible for the Swedish parental benefit reform to respect the complete equality of the sexes, owing to Sweden's ratification of Convention No. 102, Part VIII. Men in domestic work with gainfully employed wives are now a discriminated group. Admittedly the group is a very small one, but the persons affected do not receive the same benefit payments as housewives with gainfully employed husbands. I will refrain from going into further detail concerning the complex background to this state of affairs. Suffice it to say that even a Convention adopted with the best of intentions can have undesirable consequences.

Obviously we have to have special provisions protecting women as mothers. As is pointed out in the aforementioned ILO report, the important thing is to carry out

periodic reviews of the situation to ensure that the protective framework is up to date in the light of scientific and technological advances. If this test for grounds of protection and removal of protection is adopted and this approach to revision is accepted, there would seem to be little danger or possibility that such distinctions in the treatment of men and women as might persist would constitute any serious obstacle to equality of opportunity for women.[1]

OTHER CONVENTIONS

I now turn to other protective measures expressly concerning women. These are to be found in Conventions Nos. 4 and 89 concerning night work by women in industry and No. 127 concerning maximum weight, none of which has been ratified by any Nordic country, No. 13 concerning white lead, which has been ratified by Finland, Norway and Sweden, and No. 45 concerning underground work by women, which has been ratified by Finland. Then there is also Convention No. 136 concerning benzene, which Finland is proposing to ratify but which has not been adopted by any of the other countries.

---

[1] ILO, op. cit., p. 48.

Safety legislation for the benefit of women over and above the protection provided for pregnant women and nursing mothers has never been popular with the women's organisations in Sweden. For instance, the first Social Democratic Women's Conference, held in Stockholm in 1907, was opposed to a special ban on night work for women. A prohibition of this kind was introduced in 1909 in the teeth of powerful opposition and remained in force until 1962. Women's organisations in Denmark and Norway have also been opposed to special provisions of this kind, and no such legislation has been introduced by the Governments of those countries. The Finnish Working Hours Act, passed in 1946, is basically opposed to the employment of women on night work, but Finland has not ratified ILO Convention No. 89 either, owing to discrepancies between the content of the Convention and current Finnish legislation.

The Convention (No. 45) concerning underground work by women was ratified by Sweden in 1936, but the ratification was withdrawn in 1967. This somewhat unusual action of denouncing an ILO Convention was supported by a powerful body of public opinion, not least among women. No reasonable grounds could be seen for the exclusion of women from this part of the Swedish labour market. In presenting to Parliament an amendment to the Workers' Protection Act relaxing the prohibition on women's employment in underground work, the Swedish Minister of Health and Social Affairs said:

> The ILO Convention was drawn up in the interest of the workers. But if, because of social, technical and environmental progress, a Convention comes to be regarded as an obstacle to them, then the workers' interests must be decisive in determining whether or not the country still wishes to be bound by the Convention. In Sweden women workers would stand to gain by being allowed to enter mining work that is now restricted to men. I would remind you that in the mining districts there are few employment opportunities outside the mining industry.

Special protection for women?

Although there are still groups in the Nordic countries maintaining that women need the protection of special regulations, the main consensus of opinion appears to be that special provisions on behalf of women are contrary to the principle of equal treatment. Dangerous, heavy and dirty work is hazardous to women, but it is also hazardous to men. Workers of both sexes should be given the same protection. If night work and other inconvenient forms of work are necessary, they should be shared equally by men and women. In discussing these matters, one should also bear in mind the current course of developments in the labour market. In Sweden, as in other industrialised countries, matters concerning the working environment are today attracting an unprecedented degree of interest. We have every reason to expect that the concerted efforts of society and of the employers' and workers' organisations will result in major transformations of working conditions. We may expect changes causing matters of health and safety to be regarded to a greater extent than previously from the viewpoint of the individual *as* an individual rather than as a member of a particular sex or some other group. The aims of the demands we make concerning working conditions are being widened. We are trying to tackle these problems on the basis of a comprehensive appreciation of the circumstances of the individual, including both working conditions and conditions in the domestic and leisure environment.

The current view is that a person's suitability for a particular job must be decided on individual grounds and not according to sexual identity. There are still a number of jobs—though the number is declining—which require physical strength, and the physical work capacity of women is on average 30 per cent lower than that of men. Yet there are still greater differences of physical work capacity between individuals of the same sex than between the average man and the average woman.

Whenever new workplaces are built or existing ones rebuilt, care must be taken to ensure that they can provide employment for as large a proportion of the population as possible—not just less strong women, but also men who are not so strong, handicapped persons of both sexes, elderly persons, and so on.

Swedish industrial safety legislation is now in the process of being reviewed, and in the terms of reference of the review committee it is emphasised that the trend towards equality calls for the avoidance wherever possible of special provisions for the benefit of women. The principle should be for special provisions of this kind to exist only in cases where they are expressly justified by the biological functions of women. Apart from the special rules applying to women in connection with childbirth, there may be cases in which special rules are needed for the protection of women of childbearing age. The allusion here is to hazards of the working environment which may impair a woman's childbearing capacity or damage a foetus. But we are beginning to realise that similar risks may also be incurred by men. Extremely close attention must therefore be given to these problems.

For example, microwaves affecting the testicles can cause temporary sterility. Chromosome changes have been observed in workers exposed to lead and solvents. It is not clear what effects these changes can have on the procreative capacity of men and women. Precautions may therefore still have to be taken in future to safeguard the reproductive function.

Banning sexual discrimination

When discussing international Recommendations and Conventions, some consideration should also be given to the question of legislation against sexual discrimination. In Reykjavik last February the Nordic

Council adopted a recommendation calling on the various governments to investigate the possibility of co-ordinating their efforts to provide adequate legal guarantees of the equal rights of men and women. A Bill containing a general ban on sexual discrimination has now been presented in Norway. In Sweden the Advisory Council on Equality between Men and Women has undertaken a review of legislation of this kind in various countries, including the United States, Canada, Norway and the United Kingdom. The Advisory Council has not recommended general legislation against sexual discrimination. On the other hand we have recommended the continued use of legislation in specific areas (as has been practised, for instance, in the context of the regional development policy mentioned earlier). We have also called for a review of current Swedish legislation and a reduction of the number of rules according separate treatment to men and women. The main reason why we do not want to have a general law is that we are afraid it would preclude or impede positive measures aimed at strengthening the position of women.

Experience from the United States has in fact shown (as was made clear, for example, at a United Nations seminar held in Ottawa in September 1974) that results are obtained not by legislation against sexual discrimination as such but by positively discriminatory measures.[1] These measures can be taken without imposing any general ban on sexual discrimination. Indeed, such legislation can be an obstacle. Quotas, which we have tried out in Sweden with a certain measure of success (the 40 per cent recruitment requirement mentioned earlier) are thought to be at variance with the American law. The Norwegian Bill attempts to surmount this problem by the provision that positive special treatment of either sex on account of inferior status is not to be regarded as discrimination against the opposite sex.

Workers with family obligations

Recommendation No. 123 concerning the employment of women with family responsibilities can generally be said to have become outdated in view of developments in our countries and in view of the general conviction today that responsibility for children at home rests equally with men and women.

Our discussions nowadays are concerned with the parents of small children—not only mothers—and their ability to combine gainful employment with domestic responsibilities. Heavy investment in day nursery amenities, which is one of the most insistent demands now being made by the Swedish Confederation of Trade Unions (LO), is a fundamental precondition of the universal right to work. As things stand in Sweden, municipal day nursery facilities are only available for about one child in

---

[1] See also an article by Doris D. Wooten, Assistant Director of the Office of Federal Contract Compliance, US Department of Labor, in *Contact* (New York), 1972, No. 6.

six, and there are roughly the same number of places available in private nurseries. Our aim must of course be to cater for the full requirement.

One of the principal objectives of Norwegian family policy is to enable both parents to combine gainful employment with the proper care of their children. A number of proposals to this end are being discussed. They include a longer period of leave for the care of children, paid leave of absence for the father as well as the mother on the birth of a baby, reduced working hours for parents of infant children, the right to leave of absence from work when a child is ill, part-time employment and flexible working hours, and a wider range of social amenities.

The same ideas can be found in Sweden. In its report published in 1972 the Committee on Family Policy observes that the economy of the young family is based on the earned income of the parents. So the best form of financial support that can be given to a young family is for both parents to be enabled to work. As I mentioned earlier, Sweden has replaced the former system of maternity benefits with a parenthood benefits scheme, under which either parent can stay at home for up to ten days a year with sickness benefit to look after a sick child. Then there is the discussion that is now going on in Sweden concerning the introduction of a six-hour working day. We have clear evidence to show that the working hours we have at present are a burden to many families where both husband and wife are gainfully employed. In many cases the problem is " solved " by the woman working part time.

Part-time employment is very common among women in Sweden, while in Finland, to take another example, it is very uncommon indeed. Our attitude to part-time work in Sweden can be described as ambivalent.

The Advisory Council on Equality between Men and Women is at present engaged on a survey of the scope of part-time employment in Sweden, together with its effects and causes. As already mentioned, we now know that nearly 40 per cent of the women in Sweden work part time as against 2 per cent of the men. We know that many women do not put in enough hours to qualify for different benefits such as holidays, insurance, severance pay, and so on. Another thing we find is that part-time workers earn less per hour on average than full-time ones. Part-time workers tend less often than full-time workers to belong to trade unions. What is more, contrary to popular supposition, part-time employment does not seem to be a transitory stage between full-time employment in the home and full-time gainful employment outside the home. A large proportion of part-time workers have worked part time for many years.

Until the survey is complete we are not prepared to undertake any final evaluation of part-time employment, but even at this stage it can be stated quite categorically that for many women with homes and children to look after part-time employment represents the only possible way of entering the labour market. As a way into working life, then, part-time employment meets the bill perfectly, but at the same time it reinforces the idea of the home being the woman's principal responsibility, and it does not help to strengthen the position of women in the labour market.

I therefore agree with the ILO that part-time employment " should not be regarded as a substitute for action to strengthen the social infrastructure so as to permit full-time work wherever this is desired, or as a substitute for shorter working hours for all ".[1]

The view that all of us, men and women alike, have the same rights and obligations in working life, in society and to our children, does not seem to me to be stated strongly enough in the ILO report on equality of opportunity and treatment of women workers. Otherwise I think this report reflects a very modern approach to issues of equality.

The responsibilities of trade unions

Many of the reforms that have been made in the context of working life in Sweden during the past few years have been aimed at increasing the influence wielded by workers in their places of work. This is also true of the major reform we are now preparing which will abrogate the unilateral right of the employer to direct and allocate work. The aim is to enable workers to influence production, personnel policy and other matters.

In this way an alert trade union movement will acquire greater opportunities for orienting recruitment and personnel policies, which in turn will enable it to work for greater equality between men and women in working life. For this reason women must also strengthen their position within the trade union movement itself.

The value of work

Work is the foundation of the continued existence and development of any society. It is also fundamentally important to the individual members of society, because it enables them to provide for their material needs, it enables them to participate in the development of society, it involves them in a community where they can arrive at joint decisions aimed at the improvement of their circumstances, and in favourable conditions it is a source of vocational pride and self-respect. We regard work as fundamentally positive, but there is none the less a bitter element of truth in the dictum that we produce not only goods but human wrecks as well—people who at the end of their working day do not have the energy it takes to be a good parent or play an active part in the affairs of the community.

The struggle for equality between men and women must form part of the struggle for social and economic equality in society as a whole. Our

---

[1] ILO, op. cit., p. 65.

reforms in the context of working life must therefore have the following aims:

— Everyone must be entitled to work according to his or her ability.

— Everyone must be entitled to work that is meaningful.

— Everyone must be entitled to personal respect and to respect for his or her work.

— Everyone must be entitled to security of life and health at work.

— Everyone must be entitled to combine active parenthood with gainful employment.

— Work must form part of a social continuum in which the fruits of labour are used to build a society characterised by a sense of community and human dignity.

Handicrafts: a Source of Employment for Women in Developing Rural Economies

Jasleen DHAMIJA [1]

ALL OVER THE DEVELOPING WORLD it is being said that women should have a greater share in economic activity. Alarming figures are cited regarding the low level of participation and crash programmes are drawn up to deal with the problem. In fact, the question can only be raised meaningfully when the real position has been assessed. In most parts of the developing world, and especially in rural areas, women's time is so fully occupied that they are barely able to cope with their existing duties and responsibilities.

To draw up a realistic programme for increasing women's labour force participation, therefore, it is necessary first of all to examine the social structure in which they are placed. In rural society woman is seen as a home-maker and as the man's helpmate in the field. She grows food for the household, looks after the animals, preserves vegetables and fruit, repairs the walls of the house, draws water, cooks, and makes and mends the family's clothes. In her spare moments she spins wool. Furthermore, during most of her adult life she is either pregnant or has a nursing child at her breast, or both.

At an age when they can barely take care of themselves, young girls are saddled with the responsibility of looking after a still younger child and assisting their mothers with the domestic tasks. When there is any formal education to be had, it is usually the male child that gets it. In many societies a girl of 11 or 12 is considered ready for marriage.

Thus a close scrutiny of the way village women in developing countries spend their time shows that they can do nothing more unless some way is found of reducing their routine tasks. The women themselves are in no doubt about this. At a recent seminar in Africa [2] the female

---

[1] ILO expert in handicrafts organisation and marketing.

[2] See the report of the Regional Seminar for Africa on the Integration of Women in Development, with Special Reference to Population Factors, Addis Ababa, 3-7 June 1974 (New York, UN doc. ST/ESA/SER.B/6, 1975). See also David A. Mitchnik: *The role of women in rural development in the Zaire* (Oxford, Oxfam, 1972).

participants identified the following activities as being the most burdensome:

— carrying water
— performing agricultural tasks with traditional tools
— carrying wood and heavy loads
— pounding and grinding
— cooking with traditional equipment and fuels.

The lack of cheap transportation to markets and of organised outlets for surplus products was also cited as a major inconvenience. In enumerating these points the women indicated that the main problem is the lack of time- and labour-saving facilities in rural areas.

Even assuming some progress in these directions, it is obvious that, to have any hope of widespread acceptance, economic activity for women must be compatible with their role as home-makers. Hence the promise offered by handicrafts.

The case for handicrafts

In many countries women are already the custodians of crafts, which are part of the cultural life of the people and have been passed down from mother to daughter. Such crafts may be closely linked with folk rituals and festivities, and have thus been preserved over the centuries without loss of intrinsic quality.

In many parts of Central Asia and the Middle East, for example, carpet weaving is the mainstay of the family. The sheep are sheared by the men, after which the women wash the wool, sort it and comb it out. Both sexes spin it as they go about their daily routine. The women then colour it with dyes made from herbs, roots and tree-bark collected from the forest or from the kernels, skins and seeds saved from fruit and vegetables. After this the carpet can be started. Once it is on the loom, the household becomes creditworthy and the local shopkeeper, who often acts as the middleman, will provide the essentials of life such as wheat, salt, oil, tea and sugar, and even wool, on account. Formerly any surplus production was always sold at the local weekly markets or at fairs. Later, when the commercial value of the craft was recognised, the middleman appeared and organised production and marketing, not always with happy results.

It is essential that the importance of handicrafts and the role of women in artisanal production should be recognised in development planning. Perhaps they can best be appreciated by consideration of the following factors.

EMPLOYMENT

One of the major problems faced by any developing country is the provision of employment. Many such countries are primarily agricultural. Agriculture, however, does not provide year-round employment and during periods of drought a high proportion of the population may be out of work. Usually, large numbers of people living in rural areas are still engaged in subsistence farming. Though mechanisation increases output, it often renders still more people surplus and lengthens periods of unemployment. As is well known, this leads to mass migration from the rural to the already overcrowded urban areas, where the new arrivals anyway lack the necessary skills for finding employment. The education system, often colonial in origin, is usually not geared to producing technically qualified persons. This leads to a surplus of unskilled candidates for the available jobs with consequent exploitation of labour and the possibility of political instability as its corollary. The most exploited of all are the women, who are generally paid less for equal work.

An imbalance between rural and urban employment opportunities further exacerbates this problem. Anything that can be done to expand opportunities for remunerative employment in rural areas, drawing on traditional skills and using local raw materials, therefore deserves the closest attention in development planning.

TECHNOLOGY

In an emerging economy, the level of technology and available skills is fairly primitive. Even if it were possible, it is not desirable to effect too rapid a change from primitive to advanced technology. It is essential at first to improve the existing technology—which in practice often means the handicraft sector—and to set about introducing intermediate technology only when the base of the educational system has been built up and technical schools and vocational training institutions have been in operation for a while.

Another argument in favour of developing the handicraft sector is that the improvement of existing technology and the adoption where necessary of new tools and techniques require far less capital investment than the introduction of more sophisticated technologies, while the artisan, by contributing not only labour and time but also some of his or her savings or future earnings towards the purchase of better tools, acquires a greater sense of personal involvement.

INVESTMENT IN TRAINING AND EQUIPMENT

The question of investment in training and its returns to the economy is another important factor. The per capita investment for training craftsmen in traditional skills is far less than that required for modern industries. An annual investment of US $200 for a period of one to two years would enable a craftsman to earn $450 per annum even in countries like Nepal and Afghanistan, where per capita income is below $100 per annum. The investment in plant needed to promote handicrafts is also far less than for any intermediate-technology industry, which is significant

179

when resources are limited and employment opportunities must be provided at different skill levels. A self-contained unit for processing textiles (or a woodworking or garment-making unit, etc.) can be set up with an investment of from $500 to $50,000. The smaller of these figures would be for a workshop operated by a single family of three active members, while the larger one is for a workshop employing 80 to 120 persons. The capital would also not remain blocked for long, since the start-up period in this sector never exceeds two years.

Handicrafts have another advantage over modern industry in that workplaces and manufacturing processes can be improved without any lengthy interruption of production.

RAW MATERIALS

In many countries the products of agriculture, forestry and mining are exported in the raw state. If they were processed first—which it is within the power of a good many handicrafts to do—a great deal of employment would be generated and the added value would bring in far more foreign exchange. In addition, some products could be marketed locally instead of having to be reimported.

MARKETING

Marketing is another important factor. Large-scale modern industries in developing countries have to compete with those of industrialised countries which not only have a great deal of experience and high standards of manufacture, but also a reputation in the market and powerful publicity organisations to promote their products. It is thus no easy task to find a market for the new products. In the case of traditional handicrafts which are a national speciality, however, a market exists in developed countries, which have a surfeit of machine-made goods, surplus purchasing power and a fascination for " exotic " hand-made products.

The flexibility of production already referred to is another advantage here. Changes in consumer taste can be catered for rapidly and without great expense by traditional industries.

SOCIOLOGICAL FACTORS

The most important argument of all in favour of the development of handicrafts is sociological. As societies evolve over the centuries, they develop their own norms, their own set of values, which in non-industrialised societies assign a role to each individual as an integral part of the community. One must not suddenly destroy the basis and values of a way of life without putting some valid alternative in their place.

Contrast the concept of man promoted by the advocates of industrialisation in the past two centuries with that of traditional societies. The first sees man as motivated by self-interest, in a competitive society,

180

whereas in the second he is seen as an integral part of the tribe or community with defined rights and duties in a co-operative endeavour. Instead of trying to change these values we should build on them. Rapid industrialisation without any attention to traditional employment sectors would tear society from its moorings, bringing in its train the usual evils of juvenile delinquency, broken homes and a life lived under constant pressure. It may prove fruitful for the Third World countries to remember Mahatma Gandhi's message of self-reliance, of the need to develop village industry, to preserve national cultures, and to avoid imitating consumer-oriented societies. In India, for example, great importance is attached to the development of facilities for handicrafts in both urban and rural areas, and nowadays this sector is not only one of the biggest employers but also one of the most important sources of foreign currency.

The promotion of handicrafts [1]

In order to develop the handicraft sector on the right lines there needs to be an institutional framework which penetrates to the basic production units at village level, supplying the women with improved equipment and tools and training in the associated techniques.

Often minor adaptations of traditional equipment suffice to raise efficiency and improve the quality of the product. In the case of the primitive narrow loom, for instance, if the reeds are changed and a simple pulley system is introduced for the warp, the weaver can produce greater widths to suit modern market requirements. Longer warp threads can also be accommodated in the narrow space, thus reducing the labour of preparation and also keeping the warp threads under cover, making it possible to work the loom throughout the year. Again, in the case of pottery, the mounting of ball-bearings on the wheel allows output to be tripled. In the processing of fibres, primitive methods of extraction are not only tedious but wasteful. The use of even hand-operated Respador machines increases extraction by 100 per cent and reduces labour time by 75 per cent. In such ways the application of modern research and technology to traditional crafts and skills can yield excellent results.

Tools and equipment should be such that they can be used in the home. They could be supplied at subsidised rates and, as mentioned above, bought by the women over a period of time out of their earnings. In addition, there is a need for centres offering common facilities such as the provision of raw and semi-processed materials, designs, technical

---

[1] In this connection the reader is referred to the report on the ILO/ECA/YWCA/SIDA Workshop on Participation of Women in Handicrafts and Small Industries, Kitwe, Zambia, 9-20 December 1974 (Geneva, doc. ILO/TF/AFR/R.19, 1975). The recommendations adopted by the Workshop, concerned as they are with the development of both handicrafts and small-scale industry in urban as well as rural areas, are considerably more comprehensive than the proposals presented here.

guidance, finishing, quality control, packing and marketing of the products. These can also develop the ability to work together.

A programme of this sort does not disrupt the pattern of life. By tending to eliminate the middleman, moreover, it can help to secure a better return for the work put in. But it obviously calls for a considerable long-term educational effort at several different levels. Not only do certain elementary management skills need to be imparted, but a favourable climate of opinion has to be fostered by encouraging a greater spirit of enterprise among women and more comprehension on the part of men. Such conditioning can begin at a very early age.

Obviously, what has worked in one country will not necessarily be applicable to the very different conditions obtaining in another. The only absolutely common feature is the fact that both society and the women themselves benefit when the latter participate in economic activity, and that in rural societies handicrafts are the most suitable means of enabling them to do this while continuing to perform their vital role in the home. The details of organisation and production will and indeed should differ from continent to continent and from country to country. However, it may not be irrelevant to cite one successful example of promotion in this field.

Experience in India has shown that women tend to adopt improvements in techniques and designs more quickly when their effectiveness has first been demonstrated, and with a certain amount of assistance they have proved themselves fully capable of forming co-operative societies. Indeed, the co-operative spirit already exists among the women, since they are used to working together on the occasion of festivities or during times of crisis. The strange thing is that in many areas co-operative education and assistance in the formation of co-operatives are given only to men, even where the women do most of the work. In many countries of the Middle East, for instance, although the women do the actual weaving of carpets, it is the men who form the co-operatives and direct all their affairs. Clearly, the women will need assistance in forming co-operatives and also in managing them until they are able to cope with the organisation themselves.

Here again, the Indian co-operative promotion programme appears to be a good model. The Government offers a loan of up to ten times the share capital. In addition, managerial assistance is provided to the extent of 100 per cent during the first year, 75 per cent during the second, 50 per cent during the third, and 25 per cent during the fourth. By this time the women are either able to run the society themselves or to pay for a manager out of its earnings. They take great pride in looking after the affairs of the co-operative and in contributing to the prosperity of the community.

Co-operatives are of course an effective means of organising production in urban areas as well, but they have to be closely linked with marketing agencies that can place their products and provide guidance concerning market trends.

Thus promoted by governments or public agencies and combined with appropriate facilities and training, handicrafts and rural industries represent the best method of providing gainful employment for women without disturbing the existing pattern of society. Better economic returns must go together with a sense of greater fulfilment both for the individual and for the community.

———————————

Women Workers and the Trade Unions in Austria: an Interim Report

Edith KREBS [1]

THE EUROPEAN LABOUR MOVEMENT, and particularly the European trade union movement, owe their origin to the rapid expansion of industry in the second half of the nineteenth century. The struggle for women's rights really began at the same time. Initially promoted mainly by the middle classes, it could not at this level enjoy the broad popular support required to bring about fundamental changes in the position of working women. For women not only suffered from inferior status at work and from lack of political rights, but in their capacity as housewives and mothers were—and to some extent still are—the worst-paid and most overworked (though indispensable) members of society.

The small but steadily growing number of women who were prepared to fight for an improvement in their lot were gradually enrolled in the militant working-class movement, and protection of women against exploitation at work but above all in their maternal role figured ever more prominently among the workers' demands. To such effect that today, at least in the German-speaking world, the basic forms of protection of women and comprehensive maternity care are no longer objects of dispute but are generally recognised as essential features of a society that is increasingly preoccupied with the welfare of its children.

In the following pages I shall begin by considering the over-all trends in women's employment, the emergence of sexual stereotypes and consequent division of the labour market into men's and women's occupations, and the discrimination against women this entails as regards pay and employment opportunities. I shall then show that women are poorly represented at the higher levels of the Austrian trade union movement, and that although the unions have been extremely active in promoting the protection and equitable treatment of women workers, the progress made is largely due to the efforts of male trade unionists.

---

[1] Vienna Workers' Chamber.

Men's work and women's work—two worlds apart?

Society accepted the entry of women into the labour force as the inevitable but far from desirable consequence of the first major wave of industrialisation. Having had modesty and a sense of inferiority instilled into them from childhood, women perhaps found it normal that they were admitted to only a restricted range of jobs on the grounds that many others were too strenuous or demanding for them. In fact many of the so-called "women's jobs" were by no means so light and easy: laundresses and nurses undoubtedly performed heavy physical labour, while farm women had and to some extent still have to carry out tasks that would tax the strength of many men in the long run.

But the stigma of "light work" or "women's work" persisted and was reflected in the wages paid. Gradually, however, technological and economic progress, together with improved education and vocational training, enabled women to perform skilled work too, even managing to make some sort of white-collar career for themselves (though often at the cost of remaining single). Hesitatingly and unwillingly, the universities and technical colleges began to open their doors to them, although they were still excluded from careers in engineering. It was the two world wars that opened up the wide range of jobs in the metalworking industries to women. The emergency put an end to all discussion as to the suitability of women for such work; in fact they were pressed into it, and duly proved themselves. After both world wars there was an attempt to put the clock back, but this was only partly successful. If the memory of women's sterling service in all kinds of jobs during the crisis years gradually faded, a new factor began to weigh increasingly in the minds of certain influential, progressive people, namely the position achieved by Soviet women in a wide range of manual and professional occupations. Very slowly, the view began to gain ground that women's capacities were very much greater than had previously been thought.

The process of freeing themselves from the straitjacket of "suitable occupations" has of course only just begun, and women still have a long way to go before their choice of trade or profession is truly free, based on the individual's personal aptitudes rather than the preconceptions of society. In Austria, at least, educationists, parents and even to a large extent employers and trade unions have yet to rid themselves of a heavy load of centuries-old prejudice.

The participation of women in economic activity is still widely regarded as a twentieth-century phenomenon. Such a view ignores the fact that women have always been involved in the production process, even if mostly in the domestic sphere, and that the middle-class woman with nothing to do but mind the house and children is a product of the intellectual and economic climate of the nineteenth century. Today's economic forces are all working in the opposite direction, yet this is still the " ideal " that is held up to us by parents, the educational system, the mass media and the advertising industry, with the result that it appears to many members of both sexes as the outcome of a " natural " division of roles between man and woman in the family and in society.

According to the results of an OECD inquiry [1] based on reports from ten different countries, the expansion in women's employment is one of the most striking social developments to have taken place in almost all the industrialised countries since the end of the Second World War. Obviously, this is a trend that increasingly calls into question—and has done much to change—the existing structure of society, the organisation of work and the allocation of responsibilities within the family. The reaction which was discernible in the late 1940s and early 1950s could no longer stop the movement. Whereas prior to the Second World War women worked mainly in clerical and factory jobs as well as in other people's homes, from this time on there was an ever-increasing amount of employment open to them in the steadily expanding service industries. More recently the trend has been reinforced by the many women who return to work once their families are old enough to look after themselves, and by younger women who seek jobs in spite of having small children. In countries where female participation in the labour force is traditionally high, for example Austria, Denmark, Finland and Sweden, the rate has remained fairly stable.

In general the OECD report noted that the female participation rate was positively correlated with the level of women's education, that more highly educated women suffered less from unemployment, that turnover and absenteeism were highest among married women with small children, that women were far more often engaged in part-time work than men, and that opportunities for female employment were both more attractive and more numerous in the towns than in the country.

There is nothing surprising about these findings, but they should clearly incite us to draw some conclusions.

What most noticeably distinguishes " men's work " from " women's work " is first the difference in prestige, and second the difference in pay. This also applies when men and women are doing substantially the same work. Jobs habitually performed by women are not only much worse paid than those usually chosen by men but are also worth less in terms of social recognition. This is curious because in some instances women need substantially more knowledge and skills to advance in their profession than is the case in the more highly valued " male " occupations with which they might be compared. The higher we go up the occupational ladder the more flagrant this becomes. It is symptomatic of the whole situation that there is no feminine equivalent in the German language of many high-ranking posts, as there is for the lowlier positions more

---

[1] OECD: *The role of women in the economy* (Paris, doc. MS/5/73.3, 16 Nov. 1973).

" likely " to be occupied by women. The unfortunate thing about this is not so much the fact itself as that it strikes nobody as regrettable or even as a linguistic absurdity.

The Austrian trade unions have indeed recognised, but have not taken any very active steps to remedy, the fact that all this adds up to discrimination. Worse still, occupations which are on the decline as regards pay and prestige mysteriously become suitable for women even when they were previously considered too heavy, morally dangerous, etc. A typical example is men's bespoke tailoring. On the other hand, jobs that are regarded as having a future very quickly come to be considered " men's work ". Thus in the early days of computer technology many women became programmers, but as soon as this work started to be relatively well paid it was described as ill-suited to the feminine mind and thus made unattractive to girls.

The result of all this is that the demand for labour comes to reflect the model of an employment market split down the middle. On the one hand are the skilled jobs offering working conditions, promotion prospects and pay befitting the prestige of these occupations and often the higher qualifications demanded. On the other are essentially the less-skilled jobs, usually unpleasanter working conditions, few or no prospects and worse pay. Even when the qualifications demanded are the same for men and women, the fact is often irrelevant and in no way alters the above-mentioned advantages and disadvantages. Men and women simply have different possibilities of access to two separate, sex-typed labour markets, and it is virtually beyond the power of the individual to overcome the barriers between them. It seems highly probable that the findings of American research into the job opportunities of racial minority groups are also applicable to women's employment; these indicate that better general education and vocational training do not have the beneficial effect that one would expect in such cases because access to the labour market is governed by discriminatory practices. That this type of discrimination is hardly ever exercised against the male sex is demonstrated in Austria, for example, by the fact that campaigns to recruit men as social workers and nurses are being conducted with success, whereas there is virtually no recruiting among women for so-called " men's jobs ". Indeed, the few girls who seek to obtain suitable professional or vocational training to equip them for such work can count on no support from public opinion against the prejudices of their families, employers and fellow workers.

This lack of interest on the part of society as a whole is reflected in the trade unions' not very effective efforts to broaden the scope of vocational training for girls by opening up occupations hitherto reserved for men and through appropriate wage policy measures. For regardless of the fact that the ILO's Equal Remuneration Convention (No. 100) was ratified over 20 years ago, the provisions it contains are reflected neither in the practical application of collective agreements nor in employers' grading policies.

In the course of the past decade the expressions " men's wages " and " women's wages " have almost entirely disappeared from Austrian collective bargaining and wage agreements. Many industries have opted for the institution of several wage categories within which payment is made according to either qualifications or the type of work performed. In addition, numerous agreements contain the express proviso that age and sex shall not be taken into account in fixing piece rates, which theoretically implies recognition of the principle of equal pay for men and women. As always, however, there is a big difference between theory and practice. The principle is only applicable in cases of equal work, and whether work is " of equal value " is determined by criteria that emphasise the qualities usually attributed to men. Physical strength is rated above dexterity and perseverance in carrying out complicated or monotonous tasks. In evaluating different jobs no account is taken of modern discoveries regarding psychological and physiological stress. In occupations where women are traditionally employed in large numbers, they are placed in the lowest wage categories and this contractual financial disadvantage is then compounded by company personnel policy, which almost always treats male staff more favourably. Women are only admitted to the so-called " men's jobs " when no men are available, in which case they do nearly always receive equal pay.

The consequences of such procedures can easily be seen in the wage differentials between men and women. While it has to be remembered that women workers are often less qualified than their male counterparts and work shorter hours, this does not explain the fact that in Austria women's earnings average only about 68 per cent, or roughly two-thirds, of men's. In this respect it should be borne in mind that women in Austria do significantly more piece-rate working than men (40 per cent of total working time in 1971 against 17 per cent for men).

That the unfavourable position of women with regard to remuneration does not apply only to manual workers is shown by the fact that in July 1973 one male white-collar worker in three earned more than the national insurance contribution ceiling of 9,375 schillings a month, whereas only one female white-collar worker in 18 was in the same position.[1]

We may therefore conclude that, even though there is full recognition of the principle of women's right to equal pay for work of equal value, the unions have not been able to secure its implementation in practice; it may be added that not all unions have tried equally hard to do so. Even the very considerable efforts of the union officials responsible for the interests of women members have been ineffectual in reducing the

---

[1] As of August 1975, 100 Austrian schillings = $5.63 or £2.60.

incongruously wide gap between men's and women's earnings or in materially improving the promotion prospects of duly qualified women, which remain far inferior to those of their male colleagues.

In support of this statement let us consider a few more examples from Austria. There is not a single woman among the 65 heads of department in the various ministries, not even in the field of education where women unquestionably play a major part. In 1973 only 40 of the country's 265 general secondary schools had women heads (i.e. some 15 per cent), even though 40 per cent of secondary school teachers were women. Moreover, practically all the 40 schools in question were for girls, not co-educational. In 1974 only 21 out of a total of 920 established university professors were women, and only 12 of the 157 unestablished professors.

In 1974, again, out of 1,514 judges and candidate judges there were only 64 women, of whom 50 were attached to the Vienna District Court; in the same year only five of the 179 public prosecutors were women, and all of these worked for the Viennese Attorney-General's office. Not a single university clinic in the whole of Austria has a woman director, and in the hospitals and welfare centres of Vienna in 1973 there were 112 men and only six women chief physicians even though nearly 40 per cent of the doctors in the city are women.

The picture is the same in politics. Although there are two women ministers and one secretary of State in the Federal Government, the provincial governments of Vienna and Lower Austria have only one woman member each. While some 10 per cent of the deputies in the Vienna provincial parliament are women, that of Tyrol cannot boast even one woman deputy. Finally, there are only 12 women among the 184 members of the national Parliament, i.e. no more than 6.5 per cent even though women account for over 50 per cent of the electorate.

I shall revert to the trade unions' attitude to these questions in a moment.

Women in the Austrian trade union movement

A few figures on the size and distribution of the Austrian labour force will help to place the following comments in perspective. In round figures there were 2,655,000 wage and salary earners in Austria in 1974, of whom 1,018,000 were women. It was the first time that the number of female workers (averaged over the year) had exceeded the million mark. Since 1954 the proportion of female workers has been growing rapidly and in 1974 it reached 38.3 per cent. In 1973 wage and salary earners were distributed as shown in table 1 (average figures).

On 31 December 1973 the Austrian Federation of Trade Unions had 1,559,513 members, of whom 434,515 or 27.9 per cent were women. Their distribution among the individual unions was as shown in table 2. Nearly

TABLE 1. DISTRIBUTION OF WAGE AND SALARY EARNERS IN AUSTRIA BY CATEGORY AND SEX, 1973

Category	Male		Female	
	No.	%	No.	%
All workers	**1 629 819**	**61.5**	**1 019 814**	**38.5**
Manual workers	947 450	65.9	489 788	34.1
White-collar workers	430 179	49.2	443 992	50.8
Civil servants	241 712	81.4	55 185	18.6
Registered unemployed	10 478	25.4	30 849	74.6

TABLE 2. WOMEN MEMBERS OF AUSTRIAN TRADE UNIONS, 1973

Union	No. of women members	% of union membership
White-Collar Workers in Private Industry and Commerce	117 263	41.9
Municipal Workers	59 479	41.6
Public Service Workers	51 141	34.5
Metalworkers and Mineworkers	47 690	16.7
Textile, Clothing and Leatherworkers	46 580	65.8
Arts and Liberal Professions	4 575	31.1
Construction and Woodworkers	7 182	3.6
Chemical Industry Workers	16 931	23.7
Railway Workers	6 193	5.4
Printing and Paper Workers	6 459	25.7
Commerce, Transport and Communications Workers	8 928	31.1
Hotel and Catering Workers	10 171	58.4
Agricultural and Forestry Workers	4 662	17.6
Food, Drink and Tobacco Workers	15 992	32.9
Postal and Telegraph Workers	13 148	20.7
Personal Service Workers	18 121	91.7

three-quarters (74 per cent) of women trade unionists are concentrated in the first five unions listed here.

Anyone who is familiar with the European trade union scene will concede that both the over-all and the female unionisation rates are remarkably high in Austria and indicate a large degree of union consciousness on the part of both sexes. This is matched by the relatively high number of trade union posts held by women, which is none the less kept lower than it might be by the fact that most women have domestic and maternal obligations in addition to their jobs. The virtually unaltered distribution of household responsibilities has almost always encouraged husbands to engage in social and political activities while offering no incentive to their wives. Similarly women are welcome as trade union members and their assistance is particularly appreciated at the lower levels, yet they seldom attain positions of leadership. A few examples will serve to corroborate this assertion.

None of the presidents of the 16 unions affiliated to the Austrian Federation of Trade Unions is a woman, even though women make up over 90 per cent of the membership of the Personal Service Workers' Union, two-thirds of the Textile, Clothing and Leatherworkers' Union, and almost 60 per cent of the Hotel and Catering Workers' Union. In the first and the third of these, however, they have at least elected women vice-presidents. This year, for the first time, a woman has acceded to the post of General Secretary of a union—the White-Collar Workers' Union in Private Industry and Commerce. The new president of this union has shown that he is fully alive to the fact that there are now more female than male white-collar workers in Austria and that over 40 per cent of his membership is female. This figure carries all the more weight when one remembers how many women are employed in petty retailing, where trade union organisation is particularly difficult. The number of female trade union secretaries is extremely low: a mere 18 out of a total of 392 in 1974. In the Federation itself there was only one out of seven, and she was in charge of the Women's Department. In the Federation's regional secretariats only six out of 105 secretaries were women.

Of course, this picture would be misleading if, as they could perfectly well do, the Austrian trade unions appointed women to the leading posts in the various bodies in which they have the right to nominate representatives. Yet here too the situation is identical. The directorships of the social security institutions are held entirely by men, and there are very few women among the senior officials. In 1974 there were 176 men in the highest grade as against two women; in the second grade nine men and one woman; in the third 312 men and only 11 women. In the workers' chambers, which are the constitutional guardians of Austrian workers' interests, the 40 per cent of female employees are represented by a single woman vice-president in a western district and not so much as one president. The Vienna Chamber, in whose area 44 per cent of wage and salary earners are women, does not have a woman vice-president, the highest posts being occupied exclusively by men. Turning to the actual staffs of the chambers, there is no woman director or deputy director. Of the 16 secretaries in charge of major departments only one is a woman, while of the 39 who head smaller departments two are women, one of whom is in charge of the Women's Section of the Vienna Chamber, a post which could not very well be held by a man.

The protection of women as workers and mothers

This is a field in which the trade union movement has scored some of its greatest successes. The preceding section of this article was devoted to the negative side of the record, which any woman active in the trade unions must feel bound to point out. However, the very fact that she is in a position to do so herself, rather than through some male intermediary, and can be sure to obtain a hearing is due in large part to the educational and other activities of the unions. Let us consider a few examples of trade union achievements with regard to the protection of women workers, especially in their role as mothers.

The need for special protection of pregnant women was already recognised in Austria in the nineteenth century. Lack of antenatal care often led to women's health being severely undermined. Frequently they were obliged to stand by their machines right up to the onset of labour and had to start work again only a few days later. In 1885 the excessive number of premature births and miscarriages and the high infant mortality rate led to a reform of industrial legislation, whereby mothers were not allowed to work for four weeks after their confinement. Three years later the Sickness Insurance Act provided them with a daily benefit of 60-75 per cent of " normal local earnings ". These modest provisions remained unchanged until the First World War, in the course of which the period during which resumption of work was prohibited was extended, together with the payment of benefit. In addition, expectant mothers could now qualify for sickness benefit for up to four weeks prior to their confinement. After the war these provisions were further extended, but still without any guarantees as to security of employment, so that they often remained meaningless. Not until the Second World War was protection against notice of dismissal enacted, and then it remained largely irrelevant inasmuch as it was compulsory for women to go out to work anyway.

As soon as the Second World War was over the trade unions set to work to obtain a new Maternity Protection Act, and in 1957 they finally succeeded.[1] The numerous resolutions of women's conferences and the campaign carried on by the unions in Parliament—above all by women trade unionist MPs—bore fruit in the new Act, which covered the majority of female wage and salary earners in Austria, though with special provisions regarding women employed in certain branches of the public service, in private households and as homeworkers. In the first place, and as a complete novelty, the Act introduced the notion of maternity leave. Originally unpaid and limited to six months, three years later it became paid leave up to the child's first birthday.[2] The unions

---

[1] ILO: *Legislative Series*, 1957—Aus. 1A.

[2] Ibid., 1960—Aus. 2.

also succeeded in having it made unlawful to employ a woman for six weeks before and a minimum of six weeks after her confinement, the latter period being extended to eight weeks for a nursing mother and to 12 weeks for a nursing mother whose child was born prematurely. Furthermore, only in exceptional cases, and even then only with the prior permission of a conciliation board, could women be dismissed, with or without notice, during their pregnancy or until four months after their confinement. Finally, the entitlement to leave was backed up with protection against dismissal, with or without notice, until four weeks after resumption of work.

These provisions remained essentially unchanged until 1974, when they were further extended. On this occasion Maria Metzker, parliamentary representative for working women in Austria, addressed the Upper House. The extent to which the idea of comprehensive maternity care had taken root in Austria during the intervening 17 years was shown by the fact that not only were the new amendments adopted unanimously but none of Mrs. Metzker's arguments was even challenged. Seventeen years of educational work and propaganda on the part of the unions and the workers' chambers, of keeping women informed of their rights and of representing them in court, had created a social climate in which it had become impossible to oppose improvements in the protection afforded to working mothers.

Another and complementary example is the above-mentioned maternity leave and its practical implementation. Doctors and psychologists are overwhelmingly of the opinion that care of the child in its own home during its first year of life is of the greatest importance for its proper development. When the Maternity Protection Act of 1957 was being drawn up, therefore, leading women officials of the Austrian Federation of Trade Unions began to examine what could be done to enable working mothers to stop work during the first year of the child's life with a guarantee of subsequent re-employment. Thus the idea of maternity leave came into being. Since the beginning of 1961, as we have seen, the maximum period has been up to the child's first birthday, and in most cases the maternity leave benefit makes it possible for mothers to take advantage of it. The benefit at first normally amounted to half the level of unemployment pay (in fact, it took the form of an unemployment benefit), and might not fall below a certain sum. This sum was raised a number of times, but as there was a means test on the combined family income some working mothers were ineligible. Moreover, the amount was such that others, who were the sole support of their families, could hardly consider living on it.

The year 1974 brought substantial progress in this respect thanks to the efforts of the Minister for Social Affairs, himself a former trade unionist. The maternity leave benefit is now calculated on the same basis for all, married women receiving 2,000 schillings and women who are the sole support of their families 3,000, both sums being subject to annual revision. All women who have been employed for a certain period are now entitled to the benefit, with the result that it has come to be regarded more as a social service available to all than as some kind of charity. Its popularity is shown by the fact that, according to soundings by the workers' chambers, almost 90 per cent of working mothers now take advantage of the facility.

In some quarters efforts are being made to get maternity leave extended to three years, but this suggestion is being vigorously opposed by most trade unionists, particularly by women ones, on the grounds that such a measure would in all probability mean the end of suitable employment for skilled or highly qualified women. On the other hand the unions have finally succeeded in getting the period of maternity leave to count for pension purposes, so that women lose no entitlement on this account.

By their opposition to the proposed extension of maternity leave—which is impractical on economic grounds—and by their efforts to have such leave validated for pension purposes, the unions have clearly demonstrated their maturity and great sense of responsibility. On the one hand every effort must be made to obtain the best possible protection for mothers, women and every other category of worker, but on the other such measures should not frustrate employment in general or the demand for skilled workers in particular.

The restriction of night work for women is a story in itself. In 1950 Austria ratified the Night Work (Women) Convention (Revised), 1948 (No. 89). By the terms of the Night Work (Women) Act, 1969 [1], the provisions of the Convention were made directly applicable under Austrian law for the first time and the same protection was extended to women white-collar workers. Amended in 1972, the Act applies to all women workers aged 18 and over, the principal exceptions being women employed in transport, radio and telecommunication services, news agencies, the hotel trade, federal, provincial and local administrations, pharmaceutical staff in chemists' shops, doctors, nursing and similar personnel, and women holding responsible technical or managerial positions. The trade unions, which have hitherto always fought for further restrictions on night work for women, now find themselves in an awkward situation owing to the increasing number of women in skilled occupations. The vast majority of women workers are still in subordinate, underpaid positions and get little or no help in the home from their husbands. For them the restrictions on night work will continue to be of vital importance for a long time to come. The position of the skilled or highly qualified woman, who may find her career hindered by the prohibition on night work, is entirely different. To find some way of

---

[1] ILO: *Legislative Series*, 1969—Aus. 3.

reconciling the conflicting needs of the two groups is going to call for all the skill the unions can muster. It is really up to the ILO to point out a practicable course.

However, the unions have not only tried to solve the major problems facing women workers such as night work, maternity care and protection in respect of heavy or dangerous jobs. They have also begun to speak up increasingly for women workers weighed down by their double and treble work burdens, educating the community—which profits from their work—to understand that it must provide these women with certain facilities and assistance if their position within the family is to be fundamentally improved.

The unions have supported various moves to promote equality between wives and husbands in the home and have pressed tirelessly for the provision of adequate crèches and nurseries. They have also called for the introduction of all-day schools as an alternative to the customary Austrian half-day schools. Recently they have been campaigning for a statutory right to leave with pay for parents with sick children. The workers' chambers, which are headed by trade unionists, were the first to propose that alimony payments to women supporting their families should be advanced by the State and recovered subsequently from the ex-husband. This idea has quickly gained support and will probably be implemented in the near future.

It will be clear from what has been said above that the Austrian trade union movement has devoted an appreciable amount of time and energy to furthering the interests of women, but when we speak of " the movement " we mean the males who run it. Certainly they took advice from women and threw their weight behind the demands made on their behalf, but nevertheless in accordance with the apparently still valid principle of " all for women, nothing (or as little as possible) by them ". A great deal has in fact been achieved but, as already pointed out, the existing structure of male dominance has remained intact even in the trade unions, and there is no doubt that it will persist for a long time yet unless something fundamental is done about it.

A glance at the International Confederation of Free Trade Unions suggests that this is in no way a peculiarly Austrian phenomenon. In the issue of *Free Labour World* marking the 25th anniversary of the Confederation there was an article on its activities on behalf of working women.[1] In the short paragraph concerning women in the policy-making bodies of the ICFTU it was proudly reported that at the Ninth World Congress in 1969 the ICFTU Women's Committee had succeeded in getting a woman elected to the Executive Board in a consultative capacity, and that at the following Congress in 1972 no fewer than three women had been elected to the Board as substitute members. How modest we women still are! Or

---

[1] Nov.-Dec. 1974, pp. 34-36.

have we perhaps become modest on realising how difficult it is to obtain equal opportunities even within our own organisations? Anyone who reads *Free Labour World* regularly will notice that women are hardly ever mentioned in the text and that to judge from the pictures the ICFTU might be exclusively a male preserve. Perhaps this is just a coincidence, but it could also be symptomatic.

No doubt the material progress and enhanced occupational status already achieved by women give grounds for hoping that the efforts to obtain full recognition of their contribution will eventually be crowned with success, but the difficulties still to be overcome in what remains essentially a man's world lead one to fear that the road will be a long and hard one.

*   *   *

It has of course not been possible in this brief outline of the position of working women and of trade union action on their behalf, in this enumeration of achieved and unachieved goals, to attempt an answer to a question which is frequently heard nowadays: namely whether the full integration of women into economic life, so often demanded by women trade unionists in every country, is really the best of all possible roads to self-fulfilment. The fact is that while such goals as self-fulfilment are conceded to be important, the more practical concept of material " achievement " is now accepted in both East and West as the proper yardstick and driving force of continued development in this field; and any discussion of self-fulfilment is likely to be mere theorising about possible future roles for both sexes rather than an attempt to chart a practicable course for the generation now at work.

In our present social and economic situation the attempt to obtain wider and fuller acceptance of the working woman represents the only way for women to break out of the ghetto of " womanhood " and its associated roles of mother, housewife and faithful but subordinate companion of man. Not until women's right to a trade or a profession is generally recognised will it be possible to give them fuller access to occupations offering better pay and career prospects. To achieve this, however, fundamental changes are needed in the education of boys and girls, and as school is the place where society can most directly influence their upbringing this is where the attempt must begin. So long as women are brought up to think of giving up work as a way of evading its difficulties, and so long as they are only too ready to stop working if their husbands prefer them to stay at home, the efforts to secure full equality with men in all aspects of working life will continue to interest only a small if growing percentage of women. Moreover, so long as it is regarded as socially quite acceptable for women to stop work, not because of compelling family obligations but simply in order to withdraw into a supposedly less harassing, more comfortable way of life, the

197

woman who really cares about her job will continue to be the object of suspicion if not indeed discrimination at work.

Not until the less desirable jobs no longer go automatically to women or immigrant workers, not until there are no more " men's " or " women's " jobs but simply jobs, can we achieve that solidarity of all workers which is needed if the trade unions' efforts to humanise working conditions, that most vital of contributions to the attainment of a truly human world, are to be crowned with success. Only then will there be no more meaning in August Bebel's dictum: " oppression is the common lot of women and workers ".

Appendix: Texts concerning Women Workers Adopted by the 60th Session of the International Labour Conference, 4-25 June 1975

A. Declaration on Equality of Opportunity and Treatment for Women Workers

The General Conference of the International Labour Organisation,

On the basis of the Universal Declaration of Human Rights, reaffirming the principle of non-discrimination and proclaiming that all human beings are born free and equal in dignity and before the law, and declaring that all efforts must be made to provide every worker, without distinction on grounds of sex, with equality of opportunity and treatment in all social, cultural, economic, civic and political fields,

Conscious of the resolutions, declarations, covenants, Conventions and Recommendations of the United Nations and the specialised agencies, particularly the instruments adopted by the International Labour Organisation designed to eliminate discrimination against women and to promote equality of opportunity and treatment for them,

Convinced of the special importance of the guarantee of equal rights and opportunities for men and women in their economic and social life and in social development,

Aware of the great economic, social and cultural differences existing among the various regions and countries of the world and among areas within countries and which condition the rate of progress towards greater equality of opportunity and treatment,

Considering that the establishment of a new international economic and social order in accordance with United Nations Resolutions will contribute towards ensuring better employment, conditions of work and life for women, especially in developing countries,

Aware of the need to devote particular attention to the situation of women in countries under foreign domination or subject to the practices of apartheid,

Aware of the invaluable role of women workers in every national economy and of the need to enable women to exercise their right to gainful employment, regardless of family situation, on a footing of equality with men and to maximise their contribution to development,

Aware that the position of women cannot be changed without changing also the role of men in society and in the family,

Concerned that considerable discrimination against women workers persists and is incompatible with the interests of the economy, the development of social progress,

199

social justice, the fundamental rights of men and women, and the welfare of th
family and society,

Convinced that women's lack of vocational qualifications is one of the causes c
such discrimination,

Convinced that all efforts must be made to promote and ensure equality c
opportunity and treatment for women workers in law and practice,

Conscious of the important responsibility and contribution of the ILO in stimula
ing efforts to this end,

Aware also of the needs of developing countries and the need to achieve fu
employment as a basis for more balanced and equitable economic and social d
velopment,

Conscious that women's problems in the world of work can be approached ar
solved only within the same general framework of economic and social developme
as those of men,

Believing that a long-term programme of practical international action w
improve the situation of women and increase their effective participation in ;
sectors,

Desirous therefore of setting forth certain principles as targets to be achiev
progressively in relation to the integration of women in economic life, understandi
that such integration presupposes deliberate planning of different social functior

Solemnly proclaims this Declaration on the occasion of International Womer
Year:

Article 1

(1) There shall be equality of opportunity and treatment for all workers. /
forms of discrimination on grounds of sex which deny or restrict such equality ;
unacceptable and must be eliminated.

(2) Positive special treatment during a transitional period aimed at effect
equality between the sexes shall not be regarded as discriminatory.

Article 2

In the promotion of equality of opportunity and treatment between women ?
men in economic and social life, full account shall be taken of the principles contair
in international resolutions, declarations, covenants, Conventions and Recommen
tions adopted by the United Nations and by the specialised agencies relating to
prevention of discrimination against women.

Article 3

All measures shall be taken to guarantee women's right to work as the inaliens
right of every human being and to revise, as necessary, existing laws, collec
agreements, practices or customs which limit the integration of women in the wc
force on a footing of equality with men.

Article 4

All measures shall be taken to educate public opinion and to foster social attitudes and behaviour which encourage and ensure equality between women and men in working, family and social life.

Article 5

(1) Measures shall be taken to ensure that boys and girls receive the same basic education and have access to the same forms of vocational orientation and guidance and to all forms and levels of basic vocational training for all occupations and professions in accordance with the principles laid down in the Recommendation concerning human resources development adopted by the Conference at its 60th session.

(2) Measures shall be taken to urge institutes of vocational guidance and training to help and to encourage girls and women to make full use of available orientation, guidance and training facilities and to choose and enter all occupations freely, including those hitherto reserved in practice for men.

(3) Measures shall be taken to ensure the placement of girls and women who have completed training programmes on an equal footing with similarly qualified boys and men. For this purpose, maximum encouragement should be given to co-operation between training instructors and the official placement services.

(4) Measures shall be taken to prohibit stipulations regarding the sex of applicants public employment notices.

(5) Special measures shall be taken to facilitate the continuing education and training of women on the same basis as men and to provide retraining facilities for them, especially during and after periods of absence from the labour force.

Article 6

(1) With a view to stimulating women's integration in the workforce on a footing of equality with men, all measures shall be taken to encourage a more equitable balance in their distribution in the various sectors of the economy, in the various branches, professions and occupations and the various levels of skill and responsibility.

(2) In accordance with the provisions of the Discrimination (Employment and Occupation) Convention, 1958 (No. 111), and of the Discrimination (Employment and Occupation) Recommendation, 1958 (No. 111), there shall be no discrimination the grounds of sex in employment or occupation.

(3) There shall be no discrimination against women workers on the grounds of marital status, age or family responsibilities.

(4) Special measures shall be taken to ensure that the potentialities, aptitudes, aspirations and needs of women, including those living in rural areas, as well as those of men are taken fully into account in employment promotion programmes and strategies.

(5) Positive measures shall be taken to stimulate the equal access of women to positions in both the public and the private sectors.

(6) So far as possible, jobs and workplaces shall be so designed as to be suitabl for all workers, women as well as men.

Article 7

(1) Women workers shall be guaranteed the right to equal remuneration for wor of equal value in accordance with the provisions of the Equal Remuneratic Convention, 1951 (No. 100), and the Equal Remuneration Recommendation, 19: (No. 90).

(2) Special measures shall be taken to ensure equal remuneration for work equal value for women also in occupations in which women predominate and measure the relative value of their work with full regard to the qualities essential performing the job.

(3) Special measures shall be taken to raise the level of women's wages as co pared with that of men's and to eradicate the causes of lower average earnings f women possessing the same or similar qualifications or doing the same work work of equal value.

(4) Special measures shall be taken, as necessary and appropriate, to ensu equality of treatment for workers employed regularly on a part-time basis, t majority of whom are women, particularly with respect to pro rata fringe benefi

Article 8

(1) There shall be no discrimination against women workers on the groun of pregnancy and childbirth and women bearing a child shall be protected fr dismissal on such grounds during the entire period of pregnancy and matern leave. They shall have the right to resume their employment without loss of acqui rights.

(2) Adoptive parents shall also be entitled to time off to care for a child with losing the right to resume their employment or their acquired rights.

(3) Because maternity is a social function, all women workers shall be entit to full maternity protection in line with the minimum standards set forth in ' Maternity Protection Convention (Revised), 1952 (No. 103), and the Materr Protection Recommendation, 1952 (No. 95), the costs of which should be borne social security or other public funds or by means of collective arrangements.

(4) All couples and individuals have the basic right to decide freely and responsi on the number and spacing of their children and to receive the necessary informati education and means to exercise this right.

Article 9

(1) Protection of women at work shall be an integral part of the efforts aime continuous promotion and improvement of living and working conditions of employees.

(2) Women shall be protected from risks inherent in their employment occupation on the same basis and with the same standards of protection as men the light of advances in scientific and technological knowledge.

202

(3) Studies and research shall be undertaken into processes which might have a harmful effect on women and men from the standpoint of their social function of reproduction.

(4) Measures shall be taken to extend special protection to women for types of work proved to be harmful for them from the standpoint of their social function of reproduction and such measures shall be reviewed and brought up to date period-ically in the light of advances in scientific and technological knowledge.

Article 10

In order to ensure practical equality of opportunity and treatment between men and women workers, all appropriate measures shall be taken to strengthen the social infrastructure and to provide the necessary supporting services and equipment in the community, in particular child-care and education services; such services and facilities shall be designed to meet the needs of children of all ages and the needs of their parents and shall be subsidised, run or supervised by the competent public authority.

Article 11

There shall be no discrimination against women in respect of social security and provisions concerning retirement and pensions, and differences in the treatment of men and women under such schemes shall be reviewed and revised.

Article 12

Review of the taxation system shall be considered wherever such system consti-tutes an obstacle to women's employment.

Article 13

In order to improve the status of women together with that of men in developing countries, special efforts shall be made to ensure that women, particularly in rural areas, are accorded an equitable share of all resources—national and international—available for development and that they are closely associated with development planning and implementation at the international, national and community levels.

Article 14

Equality of opportunity and treatment for women and men in working life shall be guaranteed by means of legislation, collective agreements or contractual arrange-ments of binding character. Measures shall be taken to enforce application of this principle, including procedures for complaints, conciliation, appeal and recourse to the courts.

Article 15

Members shall strengthen their national administrative machinery in order to give, together with employers' and workers' organisations, full effect to all measures aimed at preventing all forms of discrimination against women workers and at promoting and ensuring equality of opportunity and treatment for them.

203

B. Resolution concerning a Plan of Action with a View to Promoting Equality of Opportunity and Treatment for Women Workers

The General Conference of the International Labour Organisation,

Noting the obstacles still opposing the achievement of equality of opportunity and treatment for women workers,

Considering that sustained efforts must be made at the national, regional and international levels to overcome these obstacles and to enable women to enjoy full equality with men, without any discrimination with regard to employment and occupation, vocational training and conditions of life and work,

Having adopted a Declaration on Equality of Opportunity and Treatment for Women Workers;

Adopts the following Plan of Action with a view to ensuring the implementation of the principles set forth in the Declaration on Equality of Opportunity and Treatment for Women Workers.

FUNDAMENTAL PRINCIPLE

Any action aimed at establishing equality of opportunity and treatment of women workers must be determined on the basis of the fundamental principle that all human beings (men and women) have the undeniable right to work.

I. NATIONAL ACTION

1. *General Policy*

Member States should undertake to take specific action within the framework of national development planning to promote equality of opportunity and treatment for women workers in education, training, employment and occupation and to set up effective machinery, on a tripartite basis, and with the participation of women, for planning, stimulating and evaluating such action and for applying the policy of equal opportunity and treatment at all levels.

2. *Women's Participation in the Workforce*

Measures should be taken to guarantee the right to work and to free choice of profession and occupation, and fully to integrate women on an equal basis and without discrimination in working life, including, specifically, measures appropriate in the national circumstances:

(a) to carry on a policy of economic and social development that will ensure full employment for women and men; and to open all employment opportunities for women by breaking down any barriers to women's employment in particular areas of work based on a sex-type division of labour or on the grounds of their marital status or age;

(b) to develop counselling, training and employment policies which take account of individual aptitudes, capacities and interests, irrespective of sex;

(c) to stimulate and create real opportunity for access of women to higher levels of skill and responsibility in the occupational structures;

d) to analyse internal regional differences both in women's rate of activity and in the character of their participation in the workforce and take positive measures to provide equal work opportunities for both men and women in all regional development planning and action;

e) to ensure adequate and appropriate attention to women's integration in work life in all national economic and social development planning and action;

f) to ensure adequate and appropriate attention to all special categories of women who may encounter particular difficulties, such as migrant women who are frequently the victims of discrimination and exploitation and who also run social risks;

g) to apply the same criteria to all workers in cases of redundancy or dismissal;

h) to promote changes of attitudes towards the employment of women, irrespective of marital status or age (taking into account the provisions of Conventions and Recommendations dealing with minimum age of admission to employment), including the promotion of positive attitudes towards women's employment by employers and workers and their respective organisations, by men and women themselves and by society as a whole;

i) to devote greater attention to women workers in the rural sector in order to promote fuller participation by such workers in the workforce and in national development.

3. *Vocational Guidance and Training*

Equality of opportunity and treatment for girls and women in respect of vocational guidance and training should be promoted to conform to the principles set forth in the relevant section of the Human Resources Development Recommendation, 1975, which reads as follows:

VIII. PROMOTION OF EQUALITY OF OPPORTUNITY OF WOMEN AND MEN IN TRAINING AND EMPLOYMENT

54. (1) Measures should be taken to promote equality of opportunity of women and men in employment and in society as a whole.

(2) These measures should form an integral part of all economic, social and cultural measures taken by governments for improving the employment situation of women and should include, as far as possible—

a) educating the general public and in particular parents, teachers, vocational guidance and vocational training staff, the staff of employment and other social services, employers and workers, on the need for encouraging women and men to play an equal part in society and in the economy and for changing traditional attitudes regarding the work of women and men in the home and in working life;

b) providing girls and women with vocational guidance on the same broad range of educational, vocational training and employment opportunities as boys and men, encouraging them to take full advantage of such opportunities and creating the conditions required for them to do so;

c) promoting equality of access for girls and women to all streams of education and to vocational training for all types of occupations, including those which have been traditionally accessible only to boys and men, subject to the provisions of international labour Conventions and Recommendations;

d) promoting further training for girls and women to ensure their personal development and advancement to skilled employment and posts of responsibility, and urging employers to provide them with the same opportunities of extending their work experience as offered to male workers with the same education and qualifications;

(e) providing day-care facilities and other services for children of different ages, in so far as possible, so that girls and women with family responsibilities have access to normal vocational training, as well as making special arrangements, for instance in the form of part-time or correspondence courses, vocational training programmes following a recurrent pattern or programmes using mass media;

(f) providing vocational training programmes for women above the normal age of entry into employment who wish to take up work for the first time or re-enter it after a period of absence.

55. Special vocational training arrangements and programmes, similar to those envisaged in clauses *(e)* and *(f)* of subparagraph (2) of Paragraph 54 of this Recommendation, should be available to men having analogous problems.

56. Account should be taken of the Employment Policy Convention and Recommendation, 1964, in the implementation of measures for the promotion of equality of opportunity of women and men in training and employment.

4. *Promotion of Equality of Opportunity and Treatment in Employment and Occupation*

All necessary measures should be taken:

(a) to ratify, as necessary, the Equal Remuneration Convention, 1951 (No. 100), the Discrimination (Employment and Occupation) Convention, 1958 (No. 111) and all other relevant Conventions of the ILO, in so far as they are concerned with sex discrimination. Workers' and employers' organisations should, through collective agreements or in other ways, assist in realising full implementation of the provisions of these instruments;

(b) to eliminate all forms of discrimination against women in all sectors of social and economic activity and at all levels of skill and responsibility;

(c) to ensure women's access to qualified employment in all sectors of economic and social activity and their in-service training;

(d) to promote, in particular, through government action, equal opportunities for women, such action to include legislation relating to equality of opportunity for women workers, and effective machinery under public control, for its enforcement; and to ensure strict application of the principle of non-discrimination in all sectors and especially those under public control;

(e) to create inter alia through educational and promotional activities, conducted in particular through the mass media and schools, social attitudes that are favourable to the employment of women including, especially, married women and women with family responsibilities;

(f) to ensure that the right to work for women does not depend on the existing economic situation or on any other consideration and, therefore, that social measures for families are applied at all times without discrimination so that women are not discouraged from participation in economic life.

5. *Social Security*

Measures should be taken to eliminate all discriminatory treatment in social security schemes, in particular as concerns the payment of benefits, and to review the position of heads of families and single persons with regard to entitlement social security benefits.

6. *Review of Protective Legislation*

Measures should be taken to review all protective legislation applying to women in the light of up-to-date scientific knowledge and technological advances and to revise, supplement, extend to all workers, retain, or repeal such legislation according to national circumstances, these measures being aimed at the improvement of the quality of life.

7. *Right to Maternity Protection*

All necessary measures should be adopted:

(a) in the light of scientific knowledge and technological advances, to extend the scope and to raise the standards of maternity protection, it being understood that the costs would be borne by social security or other public funds or by means of collective arrangements;

(b) to ensure that all couples and individuals have access to the necessary information, education and means to exercise their basic right to decide freely and responsibly on the number and spacing of their children;

(c) to make it possible for women workers to take leave for a reasonable time after the period of maternity leave without relinquishing their employment and all rights resulting from their employment being fully safeguarded.

8. *Strengthening the Social Infrastructure*

(1) In order to make women's right to work outside the home without discrimination fully effective in practice, measures should be taken along the lines laid down in the Employment (Women with Family Responsibilities) Recommendation, 1965 (No. 123), in particular:

(a) to adapt, as far as possible, working life to the needs of workers;

(b) to develop services and facilities meeting the needs of children of all ages and other dependants of workers, taking particular account of the migrant mother's need not to be separated from her children, regardless of her place of origin;

(c) to provide to all workers (men and women) information, assistance, community services and social amenities, to facilitate the harmonious combination of home and work responsibilities;

(d) to reduce household drudgery.

(2) Educational and promotional measures should be taken as necessary and appropriate to encourage a more equitable sharing among family members of household tasks, including child-rearing.

(3) Special attention should be given to the question of flexible working hours and of shorter working days for all workers where national circumstances permit, with a view to facilitating the harmonious accomplishment of family and work tasks and to promoting practical equality of opportunity and treatment for women workers.

9. *Administrative Arrangements to Promote Equality of Opportunity and Treatment for Women Workers*

Measures should be taken as necessary and appropriate:

(a) to establish a national tripartite commission on the status of women workers

to direct action aimed at promoting equality of opportunity and treatment for women in economic and social life;

(b) to set up a central unit or appropriate administrative machinery which might serve as the secretariat of the national commission on the status of women workers. Such unit or machinery should develop and co-ordinate research and statistics, planning, programming and action on equality of opportunity and treatment for women workers, and disseminate knowledge and information pertaining to women's preparation for work life and their integration in the workforce, and provide a mechanism for systematic consultation with employers' and workers' organisations.

10. *Women's Effective Participation in National, Regional and International Bodies*

(1) The effective participation of women should be ensured in all national decision-making bodies, government commissions, advisory boards, councils, conferences and in all appropriate national and internal regional and community bodies.

(2) Measures should be taken to ensure that women are considered for and appointed to delegations on the same basis and by the same standards as men, whether to the International Labour Conference, to regional conferences of the ILO or to other national, regional and international meetings convened under the auspices of the ILO and other intergovernmental organisations.

11. *General Measures*

In order to ensure full equality of opportunity and treatment for women workers, measures should be taken to:

(a) achieve equality of opportunity and treatment for all workers in education, training, employment and occupation;

(b) change the still widely prevailing traditional attitudes of men and women to their role at work, in the family and in society.

III. ILO ACTION

1. *Regional Action*

Measures should be taken or envisaged to strengthen ILO action at the regional level with a view to promoting equality of opportunity and treatment for women workers, in particular:

(a) by placing the question of equality of opportunity and treatment for women workers on the agenda of future sessions of regional advisory committees and regional conferences;

(b) by studying the possibility of creating regional commissions on the status of women workers which will initiate regional and national programmes of action for the advancement of women in economic, social and cultural life and the promotion of equality of opportunity and treatment for them and by strengthening the ILO's regional field structure so that these programmes can be imple-

mented effectively and so that the ILO can co-operate closely on questions of importance to women at the regional level with other organisations of the United Nations system and with non-governmental organisations, especially employers' and workers' organisations;

c) by promoting, in co-ordination with other bodies, in-depth studies on constraints on women's employment within different cultural and economic patterns and on possible means of relaxing or abolishing these constraints;

d) by ensuring that ILO activities undertaken in the various regions, or its activities in co-operation with other United Nations agencies in connection with the World Employment Programme, or through technical co-operation projects, will promote the effective participation of women in development. Care should be taken to ensure that these activities do not lead to the perpetuation, maintenance or furthering of discrimination against women and to ensure the implementation of international labour standards, in particular Conventions Nos. 100, 103 and 111.

2. *International Action*

(1) The necessary measures should be taken with a view to furthering:

a) the review and revision, if necessary, of ILO standards relating to the employment of women and other relevant instruments, including Conventions Nos. 100 and 111 and all protective instruments, in order to determine whether their provisions are still adequate in the light of experience acquired since their adoption and to keep them up to date in the light of scientific and technical knowledge and social progress;

b) the development of new standards concerning discrimination on the basis of sex in areas not covered by existing standards and active promotion of equality *de facto* and *de jure.*

(2) Steps should be taken to initiate or strengthen research activities on problems of special interest to women, including those relating to the impact of technological progress on women's employment and conditions and to family care and planning and other aspects of the social infrastructure. As concerns the rural sector of developing countries, research activities should be initiated on the problems of poverty, illiteracy and lack of technical skill that have a direct bearing on women's employability and conditions of life and problems relating to family care and planning and other aspects of social infrastructure.

(3) Industrial Committees and analogous bodies should be invited to utilise a greater number of women experts, to give greater consideration to the position and problems of women within the industries concerned, and to promote further participation by more women's representatives, particularly from economic sectors where women are employed in the majority.

(4) Measures should be taken to review the contribution and status of women workers in a changing world at the end of the Second Development Decade and the beginning of the Third Decade, for example, by providing for a Conference discussion in 1980 to evaluate progress made towards greater equality of opportunity and treatment for women workers in practice and to plan further action to this end.

(5) Measures should be taken by the International Labour Office to set an example in its own organisation so that any discrimination against women may be avoided and women may have equal opportunity of access to all posts. In addition, a unit of the International Labour Office should have the responsibility to study more closely the problems of women workers, to promote equality of opportunity and treatment for them, and to ensure that the needs of working women receive due attention in all aspects and all areas of the work of the Office, including employment training, industrial relations, labour legislation and administration, social security and other related problems. The International Labour Organisation should also restructure and activate its existing tripartite body to promote equality of opportunity and treatment for women workers in the above-mentioned and other fields.

(6) The ILO, in conjunction with other bodies and experts of the countries concerned, should collect and analyse statistical and other data on women and men pertaining both to developed and developing countries, such as are necessary for reviewing the status of women workers and measuring their total contribution to economic and social life.

C. Resolution concerning Equal Status and Equal Opportunity for Women and Men in Occupation and Employment

The General Conference of the International Labour Organisation,

Considering the need for continued ILO action after the expiry of International Women's Year with a view to achieving progress in the direction of equal status and equal opportunities for women and men in occupation and employment, and a better working environment both for women and men;

1. Invites the Governing Body of the International Labour Office to instruct the Director-General—

(a) to study the need for new international instruments concerning equal opportunities and equal treatment for women and men in occupation and employment with a view to supplementing the provisions of the Equal Remuneration Convention, 1951 (No. 100), and the Discrimination (Employment and Occupation) Convention, 1958 (No. 111);

(b) to carry out thorough and sufficiently extensive studies on matters relating to special protection for women and men as the case may be.

2. Invites the Governing Body—

(a) to call upon member States to supply reports under article 19 of the Constitution on the Maternity Protection Convention, 1919 (No. 3), the Maternity Protection Convention (Revised), 1952 (No. 103), and Part VIII (Maternity Benefits) of the Social Security (Minimum Standards) Convention, 1952 (No. 102), with a view to evaluating whether the provisions of these Conventions are adequate in the light of today's concept of the right to maternity protection;

(b) on the basis of the reports under article 19 of the Constitution to be supplied by member States in 1977 on the Employment (Women with Family Respon-

sibilities) Recommendation, 1965 (No. 123), to place on the agenda of the earliest possible session of the International Labour Conference the question of workers with family responsibilities, with a view to the adoption of a new instrument.